Abraham Lincoln
His Life in Print

Abraham Lincoln

His Life in Print

Books and Ephemera from the David M. Rubenstein Americana Collection

PREFACE BY
David M. Rubenstein

ESSAYS BY
Robert Bray, Joshua Claybourn, Jonathan Earle, Martha Hodes, Harold Holzer, Glenn W. LaFantasie, Chandra Manning, Edna Greene Medford, Lucas E. Morel, David S. Reynolds, Edward Steers Jr., Ted Widmer

EDITED BY
Mazy Boroujerdi

THE GROLIER CLUB, NEW YORK

Preface

DAVID M. RUBENSTEIN

WHEN PEOPLE LEARN that I, like so many others, consider Abraham Lincoln to be the most important president in U.S. history, two questions usually arise: Exactly why do I think Lincoln was such a great leader? And what can leaders of today learn from Lincoln? My answers are generally rooted in what I have read in biographies about Lincoln and seen in original historical printings from Lincoln's life.

One can understand why I get asked these questions. Over the years, I have interviewed many leaders and historians, including principal leaders of governments and businesses and prominent historians, whose subjects are often the government and business leaders of the past. Many of these interviews appear in my recent books—for example, *How to Lead* (2020) and *The American Experiment* (2021). And around the time when this present catalogue is sold, I will have published *The Highest Calling*, a collection of my conversations about the presidency, with both presidents and presidential scholars. *Abraham Lincoln: His Life in Print*, while different in its structure from my other books, continues the same exploration of history and leadership, but it does so by examining original printings from America's past rather than through interviews.

Before I discuss Lincoln, let me spend a few words to explain how this catalogue and exhibition came to be. The materials featured here are from my personal collection, which I have been building for more than a decade. My interests are in American print history, from the country's origins to the nineteenth century. I began by acquiring singularly important pieces, which I immediately put on display—for example, the Magna Carta (1297), which was the precedent for the Declaration of Independence, is now on display at the National Archives Museum; and the Abel Buell map (1784), the first map printed in America, is now on display at the Library of Congress. I collect for many reasons, but chiefly I want to present original printings in a manner that satisfies those who are historically curious and makes curious those who are historically unconcerned. Original printings focus the human brain in ways that replicas cannot; humans feel a greater

Page 6: Alexander Gardner, Abraham Lincoln, head-and-shoulders portrait, 1865 (printed later). Gelatin silver print

sense of the past conveyed by an original, and thus they learn more and understand history better.

Because a subject such as Lincoln cannot be conveyed in a single document or map, I have focused a part of my rare book collection on the story of his remarkable life. As with all printed works, the story is best told in an organized sequence. Presented as a whole, the story of Lincoln truly delights those who love books, history, learning, America, and the presidency.

As you will see in the following pages, Lincoln's greatness was his ability to master his circumstances and, in so doing, overcome the disadvantages he was given. When he assumed the presidency, he had to preside over a country that was breaking in two. To the country's good fortune, Lincoln's lifetime of countering disadvantages prepared him for the moment. He had overcome the poverty of his youth when he taught himself how to be a lawyer, and he had compensated for a mostly nonexistent formal education by becoming a lifelong reader. He turned his relative obscurity into an advantage at the 1860 Republican Convention and made his rural western origins an asset in that year's general election. Of course, those born with the greatest, incomparable disadvantage in the nineteenth century were enslaved people, and I do believe that Lincoln's upbringing gave him the perspective to condemn slavery early in his career and the clarity (moral and pragmatic) to end slavery while in office. I would like *Abraham Lincoln: His Life in Print* to show the print evidence of how Lincoln was clearly shaped by, but then in turn shaped, his turbulent times.

Lincoln became a great leader by clearly recognizing that the supreme objective of his administration was to save the Union, and by recognizing as well that saving the Union required the tireless pursuit of victory in the Civil War. I say "recognize" because all leaders soon realize that their plans must change; only those who identify this early enough and can nimbly adjust their plans have a chance at eventual success. Lincoln ran on a platform of containing slavery, keeping the territories free, and opposing the Kansas-Nebraska Act as a clear violation of the Missouri Compromise and the Northwest Ordinance. The South's response to his winning the presidency was secession from the Union. This all began before his predecessor had left the White House, but unlike President James Buchanan, President Lincoln could not avoid the problem of secession. From this predicament, we received Lincoln's First Inaugural Speech, his most eloquent statement about the importance of the country remaining undivided.

To fully understand the Civil War that followed, it is helpful to look at the original printings from the era. *Abraham Lincoln: His Life in Print* shows the arc of the conflict. Few expected, when Lincoln was sworn in, that the war would, in time, last more than five years or would kill over 600,000 men. Union victory ultimately resulted from the sacrifices and heroism of all those who fought for the country. Victory required Lincoln to become two things he had not been: a military strategist and a late-blooming abolitionist. Schoolchildren learn that these two are connected in that the Emancipation Proclamation was a "war measure" to turn the

South's forced labor into the North's armed forces. If we look at the printings of the Proclamation shown here, we see that its purpose ultimately became moral in nature. This catalogue has two chapters each on the Civil War and the abolition of slavery. We hope even those of you who have already read about these subjects will learn new things here. One aspect that I have come to appreciate in recent years is Lincoln's handling of his generals—it is as fascinating as his more well-documented relationships with his cabinet.

Our clearest path to learning what Lincoln actually thought is by looking at his speeches and executive orders. Of course, Lincoln's shrewdness as a politician means we will never fully understand every dimension of his mind. Still, his speeches and orders tell us what he thought would have a practical effect, politically and administratively. Ask yourself what it means to "look" at a president's speeches or orders. Is it only to read their texts? One can also learn how, where, when, and by whom the texts were conveyed. To me, one of the benefits of looking at original printings of any type—whether from the Civil War, Revolutionary War, or Second World War—is learning the contexts of historical events. You could say that collecting speeches by Lincoln has its limitations; because there was no TV or radio then, speeches existed only as sounds from a rostrum. But by looking at the Lincoln speeches in this book, you learn that there were in fact various transcribed versions of them, that the speeches were put in the service of political parties, that printings of them appeared across the American West, and that speeches issued as pamphlets literally "spoke" to other pamphlet speeches.

Lincoln is an ideal subject for an exhibition about American print history because he was the ultimate interpreter of America's founding documents. His speeches and executive orders are full of thorough readings of and reflections on the original printed works that give us our liberties and protections, our form of government and sense of citizenship. This understanding is evident in his debates with Stephen A. Douglas, in his Cooper Union address, in the Emancipation Proclamation, in the Gettysburg Address, and in his two inaugural addresses. It follows that for us today, being in the presence of important printings from U.S. history, seeing them in the context of exhibitions, and learning what historians say about them help sustain our democracy. Lincoln's greatness as a leader came from seeing America's potential in the intentions of the founding generation. His changing the course of history was made possible by his being a student of history. He is a model statesman worth remembering during this and every election year. My hope is that *Abraham Lincoln: His Life in Print* will be useful to you as you reflect on America's unique, distinctive, and extraordinary qualities.

WASHINGTON, DC
2024

Introduction

MAZY BOROUJERDI

THE IDEA GUIDING the making of *Abraham Lincoln: His Life in Print* is best expressed with the phrase *through books, the man, through the man, the country*. The objective was to create a picture of Lincoln made of books and ephemera and, in doing so, tell a story about the United States. Creating a verisimilar picture of Lincoln is complicated by the superabundance of works relating to him, and innovation is perforce required to make sense of the quantities. We like to think we have furthered the appreciation, if not the study, of Lincoln by applying a set of theses to American print history, thus creating a hybrid kind of Lincoln vade mecum. The result is a book about books—but this is not a bibliography. This is a visual biography that uses the model of an artist monograph, where the "retrospective" is of original, historical printings organized into themed chapters, each given thrust by a thesis. By relying on original historical printings, we have created a somewhat noninterpretive picture of Lincoln's political life, antislavery views, military successes, and legacy beyond death. We believe that this is an essential Lincoln product.

All roads lead to and from Abraham Lincoln. This is the conclusion one reaches when reading nineteenth-century American history. Two circumstances define the period: the conquering of the West and the course of the Civil War. Lincoln stands where the two intersect. Were it not for the West, there would have been no war. The magnifying impact of new states, the disputes over the territories, and the contest of rivaling populations represented in Congress meant that all-out conflict between free and slave powers was inevitable. Likewise, owing to the Civil War, the West was fundamentally altered: the Homestead Act, the Pacific Railroad Act, and Lincoln's patronage appointments in federally managed lands were all bulwarks against slavery but with lasting social effects. Lincoln's 1850s statements on a West without slavery sparked secession; Lincoln's administration of the Civil War defined the qualities of fifteen eventual new states. It is not a coincidence that the first president born in the West is the

Page 10: Alexander Hesler, Portrait of Lincoln, 1860. Platinum print

same president who led in the Civil War. Lincoln could not have become president were it not for his origins in the West.

Lincoln's centrality to the nineteenth century means that within American print history, he can be understood on both rudimentary and innovatory levels. He is a prism that refracts American history into a broad spectrum of books and ephemera. If a collector or an institutional entrant wished to begin amassing Lincoln materials, it would take barely a fiscal quarter to assemble an interesting maiden shelf of history-indicating titles. A catch-all approach, I imagine, is what most people use. *Abraham Lincoln: His Life in Print* provides an example of how collecting with a thesis yields a more serious shelf. Today one can still buy accessible works that tell the tale of slavery's drawn-out, incremental demise, with Lincoln as a pivotal presence. With Lincoln as the cynosure, one can collect the rise of the Republican Party, the tactics of the Civil War, the Golden Age of American Oratory, antebellum or postbellum constitutional thought, Whig philosophies, political journalism, the national banking system (i.e., U.S. currency), and universal suffrage, to give a few tips. Wherever one looks in the nineteenth century, one discerns Lincoln's doings.

Abraham Lincoln is the most self-made man in American history, and he made himself through books. Where Lincoln was not willing himself into existence through books—becoming literate, an attorney, a politician—books irrespectively built him. This explains the dichotomies of the man. If he were the least formally educated president, he would seem by his speeches to have been the most erudite. If he were the least well-known presidential candidate in 1860, the preponderance of Lincoln campaign biographies made him the most knowable. If he was initially surpassed in military contrivance by his generals, he learned his way to military supremacy. If in the 1850s he gave only qualified statements about restricting slavery's growth, the amplifying effect of print made him the South's abolitionist bogeyman. If at fifty-six he was the fourth youngest president at death, in the 160 years that followed, more books have been written about him than any other human. His story is the story of books—autodidacticism, propagandism, filiopietism, etc. *Abraham Lincoln: His Life in Print* celebrates the vitalizing power of books and ephemera.

To tell Lincoln's story, from rural poverty to the White House to canonization, we have enlisted the help of some of our favorite writers, each of whom has contributed a short explanatory essay on an aspect of Lincoln's life or a phase in his improbable upward, eastward, heavenward journey. Each chapter has both an essay and descriptions of books and ephemera, which collectively form the corresponding facet of Lincoln. One can read the essays first, but when reading the descriptions, it is best to do so in sequence, as they link into a narrative. The identity of each chapter comes from the voice of the essayist, the material composition of the historical printings, and the primary argument we put forth. For Lincoln novices, we provide an immersive introduction. For Lincoln enthusiasts, we provide a contemporaneous bibliocosm of his life that corresponds to the standard biographies. In our era, when most biographies devote their attention to narrow portions of Lincoln's life, we intend this publication to deliver a welcome overall story of how possibly Lincoln was made.

In producing *Abraham Lincoln: His Life in Print*, the metaphor of creating a "picture" of the man extended into abstraction before it became clear again. It is too precious to say the picture is a portrait, Lincoln's countenance appearing from each brushstroke of an old book or ephemeron. It becomes a landscape, curving from the woods of Kentucky to Pennsylvania Avenue in the capital. It is a genre painting of a barnstormer in an Illinois town hall. It is a heroizing mural of a farmhand becoming president. The events and emotions of Lincoln's story make any simple picture of him difficult to hold still in one's mind. We are assisted in this by the indispensable element of our project: the featured writers and their essays. Their patent expertise and the concision of their treatment of Lincoln helped form the picture. Each could expatiate at length about any part of Lincoln's life and legacy, but we are grateful they agreed to clarify discrete but important phases. We learn from reading their essays that any picture of Lincoln is really a conceptual one that reflects only the era looking back at him. This book reflects our era.

Abraham Lincoln: His Life in Print would not be possible without David M. Rubenstein, the person behind the collection and the mission to present it to the public. Every generation has its great collectors, but only rarely is there a great collector whose acquisitions are part of a larger program of historical preservation. It is rarer still that preservation is part of David's even larger vision of philanthropy, one that is civically minded, factually committed, and intentionally patriotic. The notion for a Lincoln catalogue and exhibition was born of talks with David and our shared opinion that the sixteenth president can serve as an organizing principle as much as any cause or event can. That this catalogue plays a small role alongside David's undertakings to restore the Washington Monument, Monticello, or Arlington House (to name three of maybe two dozen or so of his major charitable causes) is especially gratifying because it puts books on the continuum of historical splendor that surrounds all Americans. The books and ephemera in this catalogue are the result of David's fondness for history and his perspicacity as a collector.

NEW YORK CITY
2024

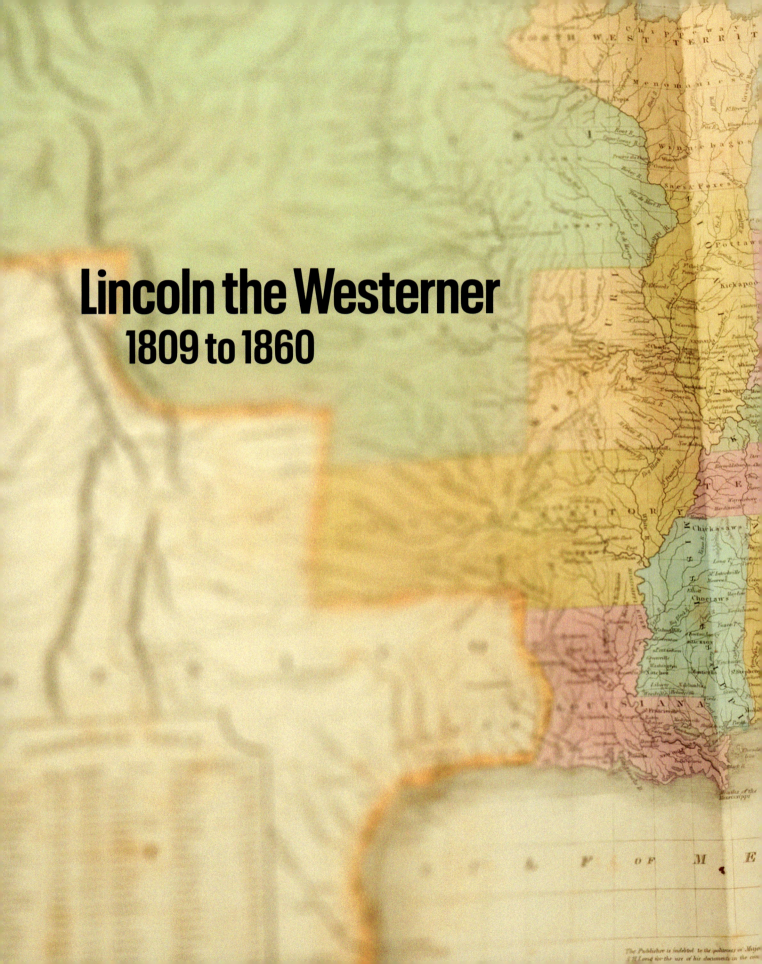

Lincoln the Westerner
1809 to 1860

"The Fairest Portion of the Earth"

JOSHUA CLAYBOURN

OF HIS FIFTY-SIX LIVING YEARS, Abraham Lincoln spent fifty of them in what was then considered the American West and another two years as a countrified congressman from a western district elected to the House of Representatives. Only for the four years of his presidency did he both live in Washington, DC, and preside over the entirety of the Union—in that his leadership held the country together during the Civil War. His not being a creature of the capital is not unique; all presidents come from their constituencies, and of the fifteen men who previously had been head of state, only five had been vice president, with another five having mostly been in the military, where they became acquainted with lands in every direction away from the Eastern Seaboard. What is unique about Lincoln is how much his presidency and the Civil War have eclipsed our appreciation of this very determining facet of his life: that he is America's first western-born president, the first raised outside the original thirteen colonies, and the first from beyond the Appalachian Mountains, which, since Britain's Royal Proclamation of 1763, had served as the starting point of the frontier, European territories, and Native lands. His life embodies much that we associate with the mythology of the early West: agriculture, Indian Wars, rough-hewn work, settlement towns, river navigation, and slave-free self-sufficiency.

Lincoln was born in 1809 in a humble, one-room log cabin in Sinking Spring Farm, Kentucky, about three-fifths of the way to the state's present western edge (about fifty miles due south of Louisville), near where the distinctive "knobs," or cone-shaped hills, end and where the cave-pocked limestone of the plateau yields to the shale of the Western Coal Fields. His grandfather, also named Abraham, brought his family, including Lincoln's then two-year-old father, to the area in the early 1780s, following the expeditions and business exploits of the frontiersman Daniel Boone.[1] The Boones and Lincolns knew each other; Abraham Sr. and Boone shared Pennsylvania origins, militia experience in the Revolutionary War, and a yearning to own larger tracts of land.[2] They found this land in the rugged terrain of what was called Kentucke County, a possession of Virginia. The

Pages 14–15: Detail from Anthony Finley, *New American Atlas* (Philadelphia: Finley, 1826) (see page 27)

Page 16: Detail from Cecil B. Hartley, *Life and Times of Colonel Daniel Boone* (Philadelphia: Evans, 1860)

Lincolns, along with thousands of other war veterans and mostly Scotch Irish families from the South-Atlantic States, were the original pioneers of Kentucky—but were not the original inhabitants, a privilege held by the Native peoples from the Shawnee, Chickasaw, Cherokee, and about a dozen other tribes. Despite this indigenous presence, in the second half of the eighteenth century, dominion claims to the territory were successively made by France, then Britain, then Virginia, and then finally the United States, when Kentucky became a state in 1792.

Of the region's many bloody battles, skirmishes, and encounters that ensued between white settlers and Native peoples, the one that factors most in the Abraham Lincoln story is the telling of how his grandfather is murdered and almost scalped but avenged immediately by his uncle Mordecai, who shoots the tribesperson, thus also saving the life of his father, Thomas, then age eight, who witnesses the attack but is immobilized by fear.[3] Years later Lincoln would describe the story in a letter as "the legend more strongly than all others imprinted upon my mind and memory."[4] Understandably so: he no doubt heard it from his father, who was burdened by the economic consequences of the event for the rest of his life. Thomas's mother resettled more centrally in Kentucky, but as he matured and built his own family, Thomas would move many times throughout Kentucky, initially searching for manual employment but eventually for more arable land. Lincoln's father was good-humored but greatly uneducated, and in 1806 he married Nancy Hanks, whose family origins remain debated, but who in her orphanhood learned how to read.[5] Abraham Lincoln was their second child; the first was a daughter named Sarah. Nancy taught Lincoln how to read and perhaps much more: Lincoln would later tell a law partner, "All that I am or hope ever to be I get from my mother."[6]

Historically, the expression "West" has meant both the regions beyond earlier established states and, naturally, the newer states formed from these once distant regions. The importance of the West in the Abraham Lincoln story is twofold, as it was the land that shaped the sixteenth president but also shaped the United States. The terms of the 1783 Treaty of Paris that ended the Revolutionary War required from Britain both its recognition of the sovereignty of the colonies and its relinquishing of all lands east of the Mississippi River, which crucially became the Northwest Territory. After the United States Constitution was ratified, from this vast tract came, in whole or part, the new states of Ohio, Indiana, Illinois, Michigan, Wisconsin, and Minnesota. Playing out at the same time was the process of "state cessions," where century-old colonial claims to Trans-Appalachian lands were surrendered for interstate harmony and parity, giving us the states of Kentucky, Tennessee, Alabama, and Mississippi. All this could happen only by the federalizing of the thirteen colonies and their recognizing themselves as part of a greater country. In essence, the birth of the United States is equivalent to its expansion. And, with the promise that the size of the country will rightfully double or triple, the West meant, for early-nineteenth-century Americans, the promise of extending Americanness.

In 1816 Lincoln's family moved to Indiana, the year it became a state, and entered a landscape that was challenging and transforming. Their reasons for moving, by Lincoln's telling, "was partly on account of slavery; but chiefly on account of the difficulty of land titles in K[entuck]y."[7] Thomas had relocated three times after acquiring farms with defective titles, meaning they were not his to own, a common problem in Kentucky, which inherited Virginia's primitive system of unsurveyed land grants. The other legacy of Virginia was that Kentucky was a slave state. The Lincolns were Baptist, and there is some record showing their congregation was opposed to bondage.[8] We can assume that Thomas's opposition was economic too, perhaps primarily so, for in his work as a hired hand, he could not compete with slave labor. Indiana had the boon of both properly surveyed land sold by the federal government and status as a free state. What it also had, in abundance, was dense forests and untamed wilderness. Lincoln described it as "a wild region, with many bears and other wild animals still in the woods."[9] Here began years of arduous labor for Lincoln, of "clearing away surplus wood" of an "unbroken forest," so that they could farm, split rails for fences, and build their log cabin home. "Though very young," Lincoln said of himself, "[he] was large of his age, and had an axe put into his hands at once."[10]

The benefit to the national interest of pioneer families such as the Lincolns was that they were creating the state of Indiana, where Lincoln lived from ages seven to twenty-one, truly by hand: roads for wagons, stores for

Scene from Humphrey Marshall, *History of Kentucky* (Frankfort, KY: Henry Gore, 1812) (see page 24)

Scene from Patrick Campbell, *Travels in the Interior* (Edinburgh: John Guthrie, 1793) (see page 24)

commerce, etc. The town of Pigeon Creek was founded the year the Lincolns arrived; within a few years, enough trees were felled to create multi-acre farms for the forty or so families living there, along with a church, mill, and post office.[11] Lincoln's mother died in 1818 of milk sickness—drinking milk from a cow that ate poisonous white snakeroot. Thomas remarried Sarah Bush Johnston, whom he knew from Kentucky and who brought her three children into their Indiana household. (Lincoln's sister died in 1828 during childbirth.) At the time, as the United States grew and melded, what connected its many distant parts was the enormous inland waterway system, the Rivers Ohio, Missouri, Arkansas, and their tributaries, all feeding into the Mississippi, which together served as a sort of national highway system for the transport of people and goods. The teenage Lincoln worked on the water for earnings, primarily ferrying people across the local Anderson River and, in time, paddling them out to steamships in the Ohio River. In 1828, as the forward oarsman on a flatboat, he transported goods for trade to New Orleans, where he witnessed for the first time slavery as it happened in the Deep South.[12]

✳   ✳   ✳

The West shaped Lincoln's first two decades with its formidable naturalness and accompanying hardship. From his third decade on, Lincoln became the embodiment of the West by shaping himself around the opportunities it afforded him, eventually achieving a preeminence that entitled him to improve the region. It happened in Illinois, a place that, in Lincoln's words, "surpasses every other spot of equal extent upon the face of the globe."[13] Within a year of his family's 1830 move there, the last stop of their decades-long western journey, Lincoln left their Coles County home for the hamlet of New Salem, 120 miles west. He was twenty-one, poor, unschooled, and without benefactors. He worked odd jobs at a store and a mill, attended a local debating club, and began reading zealously to compensate for his absent education.[14] Within a year, he volunteered for his county's militia in the Black Hawk War, a seventeen-month series of bloody engagements against Sauk, Fox, and Kickapoo Tribes over land, its possession, treaties, and cultivation. His unit did not fight, but did elect him its captain, an honor Lincoln later said was the "success which gave me more pleasure than any I have had since."[15] While serving, he met John Todd Stuart, a lawyer who would encourage Lincoln to study law. Upon his return to New Salem in 1832, he ran for the state legislature but fell short in votes.

When Lincoln again ran for state office in 1834, he won as a member of the Whig Party, but he did so without any overt declaration of his stance on national politics.[16] His interest in the party at the time may have been pragmatic and personal. Whig economics was built around the "American System," an ideology involving centralized banking and government spending on "internal improvements" such as roads and canals, which greatly benefited the new West. The leader of the Whigs and chief formulator of its vision was Henry Clay, the august senator from Kentucky, whom Lincoln revered and later called "my beau ideal of a statesman."[17] In 1832 Clay, in a key speech, extolled "self-made men, who have acquired whatever wealth they possess by patient and diligent labor."[18] This oration introduced a phrase into America's folk vocabulary, which Lincoln, the most self-made man in American history, likely took as gospel. We should note that the Whigs also regularly emerged, from the 1830s to the 1850s, as the keepers of the Union, such as during the South Carolina nullification (i.e., state supremacy) crisis and the many compromises around granting California statehood—a fact that foreshadows Lincoln's eventual presidential doctrine of unity. Another powerful Whig senator, Daniel Webster of Massachusetts, uttered the famous pro-Constitution words, "Liberty and union, now and forever, one and inseparable."[19]

Lincoln won reelection three times and, while doing so, studied law on his own by borrowing books from others. He passed the Illinois bar in 1836 and moved to nearby Springfield to join Stuart's law practice while the two served together in the Illinois House.[20] In his eight years in office, he rose high in Whig leadership, labored to secure funds to build canals, and successfully steered a bloc that voted to move the state capital to Springfield from Vandalia. In 1838, at the Young Men's Lyceum, a lecture venue in

A comparative view of the population of the Valley of the Mississippi, showing the proportional increase of the several states, parts of states, and territories, from 1790 to 1830. A period of 40 years.					
States, parts of States, and Territories.	1790.	1800.	1810.	1820.	1830.
Western Pennsylvania, and a fraction of New York,	75,000	130,000	240,000	290,000	330,000
Western Virginia,	90,000	110,000	132,000	147,540	204,175
Ohio,		a 45,000	230,760	581,434	937,000
Indiana,			24,520	147,178	341,582
Illinois,			12,282	55,211	161,055
Kentucky,	73,677	220,959	406,511	564,517	700,000
Tennessee,	35,691	105,602	261,727	422,813	550,000
Mississippi,		b 8,850	40,352	75,448	120,000
Louisiana,			76,556	153,407	214,693
Arkansas Territory,				14,273	30,608
Missouri,			c 20,845	66,586	140,000
Huron Territory, d					3,688
Total,	274,368	620,411	1,445,653	2,518,407	3,732,801

a. Including Indiana, Illinois, and Michigan.
b. Including Alabama.   c. Including Arkansas.
d. Included within Michigan, but will soon form a separate territory.

Population table from John Mason Peck, *A Guide for Emigrants* (Boston: Lincoln and Edmands, 1831). This was a popular handbook for early 19th-century settlers.

Springfield, he made a curious but revealing early speech warning against mob rule in western lands after several racist disturbances in Illinois, Missouri, and Mississippi. Its subject was "reverence for the constitution and laws," but its language held that the strength of the country emanated from the West: "We find ourselves in the peaceful possession, of the fairest portion of the earth[.] All the armies of Europe, Asia and Africa combined . . . could not by force, take a drink from the Ohio, or make a track on the Blue Ridge, in a trial of a thousand years."[21] His central idea was that, as the country grows, so too do the stakes of the Constitution and the American legal system: they can be strengthened by the vigilance of citizens or weakened by an "increasing disregard for law."[22] The sentiment reveals the primacy of the law in Lincoln's mind—his being a lawyer does not seem like an accident.

What would Lincoln do if the West and the law were at odds? A chapter in his life tells us the answer. In 1842, Lincoln left state office but continued campaigning for the Whigs. Also that year, he married Mary Todd (a cousin of Stuart's), whom he had met in 1840. He contrived with two other Whig functionaries to take turns running for United States Congress to avoid splitting the vote. Lincoln's moment to win the seat came in 1846; the following year the couple and their two sons left for Washington, DC. The country and Mexico were at war following the United States' annexation of Texas and the western territory Texas laid claim to, which exceeded what was in place in extant treaties and maps. The presidency of James K. Polk had created a pretext for the war by marching troops, without congressional approval, deep into the disputed land, resulting in a Mexican attack. America's reflexive declaration of war was very popular both in Congress and broadly with the public.[23] Lincoln, a lone voice in the Illinois delegation, was against it, stating that "war with Mexico was unnecessarily and unconstitutionally commenced by the President."[24] Lincoln's stance against the war put the rule of law before an unconstrained expansion of the West. For this, he would pay a political price. Back home, his political enemies, the press, and his constituency castigated him.[25] He did not attempt to run for reelection.

NOTES

1. Louis A. Warren, "Three Generations of Kentucky Lincolns," *The Filson Club History Quarterly* 12, no. 2 (Apr. 1938): 68–70.

2. David Herbert Donald, *Lincoln* (New York: Simon & Schuster, 1995), 70–115; J. Henry Lea and J. R. Hutchinson, *The Ancestry of Abraham Lincoln* (Boston: Houghton Mifflin, 1909), 63–64; Marion Dexter Learned, *Abraham Lincoln: An American Migration* (Philadelphia: William J. Campbell, 1909), 112–13 and 140–41.

3. Lea and Hutchinson, *The Ancestry of Abraham Lincoln*, 82; Ida Tarbell, *The Early Life of Abraham Lincoln* (New York: S. S. McClure, 1896), 24, 27.

4. Abraham Lincoln, John G. Nicolay, and John Hay, eds., *Complete Works of Abraham Lincoln* (Biographical Edition) (New York: Francis D. Tandy, 1905), 180.

5. Jesse W. Weik, *The Real Lincoln* (Boston: Houghton Mifflin, 1992), 43–44; Doug Wead, *The Raising of a President* (New York: Atria Books, 2005), 111.

6. Emanuel Hertz, *The Hidden Lincoln* (New York: Blue Ribbon Books, 1940), 73–74.

7. Roy P. Basler, ed., *The Collected Works of Abraham Lincoln*, 8 vols. (hereafter *Collected Works*) (New Brunswick, NJ: Rutgers University Press, 1953), 4:61; Olivier Fraysse and Sylvia Neely, trans., *Lincoln, Land, and Labor, 1809–60* (Urbana: University of Illinois Press, 1994), 8–12.

8. Donald, *Lincoln*, 23–24; Noah Brooks, *Abraham Lincoln and the Downfall of American Slavery* (New York: G. P. Putnam's Sons, 1899), 8–9.

9. *Collected Works*, 3:511.

10. *Collected Works*, 4:63.

11. Fraysse and Neely, *Lincoln, Land, and Labor*, 36–37; Francis Marion Van Natter, *Lincoln's Boyhood* (Washington: Public Affairs Press, 1963), 11–13; David Herbert Donald, *We Are Lincoln Men* (New York: Simon & Schuster, 2003), 3–6.

12. *Collected Works*, 2:320; Richard Campanella, *Lincoln in New Orleans* (Lafayette: University of Louisiana at Lafayette Press, 2010), 35–142.

13. *Collected Works*, 1:135.

14. Stephen B. Oates, *With Malice toward None*, repr. (New York: HarperCollins, 2011), 20.

15. *Collected Works*, 3:512.

16. Michael Burlingame, "Abraham Lincoln: Life before the Presidency," University of Virginia, Miller Center, https://millercenter.org/president/lincoln/life-before-the-presidency (accessed Dec. 1, 2023).

17. *Collected Works*, 3:29.

18. Henry Clay, "Speech…in Defence of the American System" (Washington: Gales and Seaton, 1832), 20.

19. Daniel Webster, "Speech…Relative to the Public Lands" (Washington: Gales and Seaton, 1830), 68.

20. Oates, *With Malice toward None*, 45.

21. *Collected Works*, 1:109.

22. *Collected Works*, 1:109.

23. Oates, *With Malice toward None*, 83–85; Weik, *The Real Lincoln*, 96, 172–73.

24. *Collected Works*, 1:432.

25. Donald, *Lincoln*, 124–26.

THE DAVID M. RUBENSTEIN AMERICANA COLLECTION

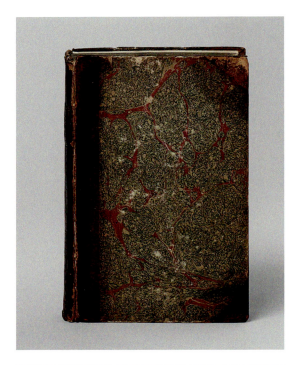

Patrick Campbell, *Travels in the Interior Inhabited Parts of North America*
EDINBURGH: GUTHRIE, 1793

The book shown here and on page 20 is a rare Americanum referred to as Campbell's *Travels*. It describes neither the places Lincoln knew nor the Jacksonian Period when Lincoln came of age, depicting instead the 1790s American Northeast. But its folded engraved plate provides the truest depiction of the centrality of trees in the lives of pioneers. Encountering thick, old-growth, virgin forest, European descendants obtained timber for shelter, transportation, energy, and barriers. From a field of stumps, a farm could be cultivated. Lincoln's youth in the early West resembled the scene shown on this plate. His later fame as a "railsplitter" meant he had chopped wood for fences.

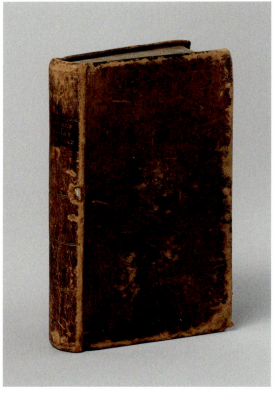

Humphrey Marshall, *The History of Kentucky*
FRANKFORT [KY]: GORE, 1812

Lincoln's life began in Kentucky, a state whose first standard history, shown here and on page 19, is by Marshall. Its main plate shows an ambush killing of a white settler by members of a woodland tribe. The author tells us the victim is John Stewart, brother-in-law to Daniel Boone, the celebrated frontiersman; Boone and his brother Squire are the two men retreating into the thicket. Lincoln's grandfather followed Boone to Kentucky in 1782. Four years later, he too was shot and killed by a tribesperson and almost scalped, were it not for Lincoln's uncle Mordecai, fourteen years old at the time, who shot the attacker as Lincoln's young father watched. The plate is one of the undeniable rarities in Americana, existing in as few as three known copies.

John Filson, *The Discovery, Settlement and Present State of Kentucke*
WILMINGTON [DE]: ADAMS, 1784

Filson's *Present State of Kentucke* is the first published work on what became Kentucky but was still a part of Virginia at the time. It is chiefly a promotional tract, rich in descriptions about the region's geography and resources, much of it overstated, but written in a flowing style befitting an author who was a schoolteacher, not an explorer. The appendix provides the first published biography of Daniel Boone and his riveting exploits, creating the legend of the indomitable backwoods pioneer. Filson originated the fiction of Kentucky as a "Dark and Bloody Ground," absent of Native residents, who he incorrectly stated used the land only for hunting and war.

G. A. Imlay, *Topographical Description of the Western Territory of North America*; [with] John Filson, *The Discovery, Settlement and Present State of Kentucke*
NEW YORK: CAMPBELL, 1793

Gilbert Imlay, the Revolutionary War veteran, Kentucky land speculator, novelist, and deserting lover of the English proto-feminist thinker Mary Wollstonecraft, wrote the most widely distributed account of Kentucky, which, in its first American edition, is paired with a new edition of Filson. From Imlay we learn of the absurdities of acquiring land in Kentucky due to "surveys made out in the most artful manner" and policies that opened "the dangerous avenue [of] fraudulent practices." The difficulty of obtaining clear title to land resulted in Lincoln's father losing a farm three separate times and was the reason the family ultimately left Kentucky for Indiana.

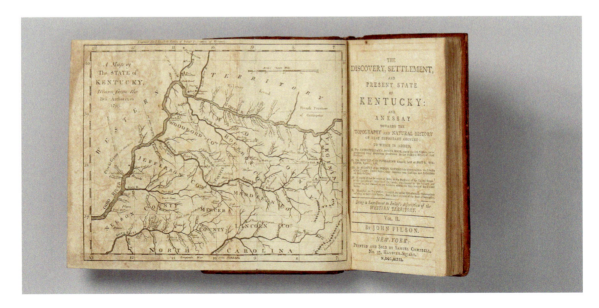

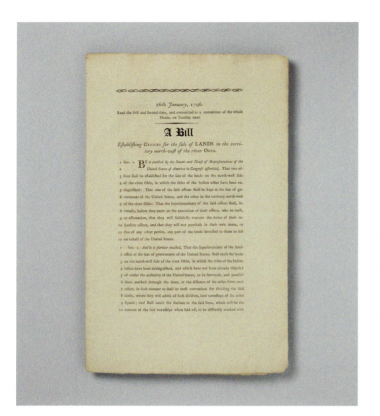

[U.S. Congress], *A Bill Establishing Offices for the Sale of Lands*

[PHILADELPHIA]: N.P., 1796

In Lincoln's words, the move of his family to Indiana in 1816 was "chiefly on account of the difficulty in land titles in K[entuck]y." Obtaining land in Indiana was a more orderly affair, one organized by Congress in the Public Land Act of 1796, seen here in an unrecorded draft. Among the priorities of the early Congresses was the dispensation of land, to generate revenue, compensate war veterans, build an American population presence in the outermost territories, and, in the words of Thomas Jefferson, "to employ an infinite number of people in their cultivation." The land in Indiana was scientifically surveyed and sold in square-shaped townships and lots.

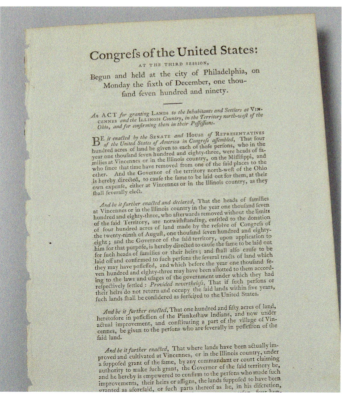

[U.S. Congress], *Act for Granting Lands…at Vincennes and the Illinois County*

[PHILADELPHIA: CHILDS & SWAINE, 1791]

When the Lincolns moved to Illinois in 1830, it had been a state for twelve years, a status it achieved after satisfying the settler population requirement prescribed by the 1787 Northwest Ordinance. The Land Act of 1791, seen here, helped by clarifying eligibility for obtaining acreage in the area where Lincoln settled. As their spelling suggests, Illinois and Vincennes were French; the region was ceded to the British after the French and Indian War. After the Revolutionary War, three colonies claimed it, but ultimately Virginia administered it. It then became part of the Northwest Territory, then St. Clair County, then Indiana Territory, then Illinois Territory.

Anthony Finley,
New American Atlas

PHILADELPHIA: FINLEY, 1826

The significance of Lincoln's Western origins can be understood through contemporary maps, such as in Finley's *New American Atlas*. The first three territories to join the Union from the Old Northwest, where slavery was prohibited, were Ohio, Indiana, and Illinois. This was accomplished by 1818, and thus gave the slave-free North an 11-to-10 edge in number of states. Finley, publishing at the prewar acme of popularized cartography, brought the territorial news to the Eastern Seaboard. In 1830 the Lincolns moved from Spencer County, Indiana, near Kentucky, to Macon County, Illinois, which does not yet exist on this map (about sixty miles north of Vandalia).

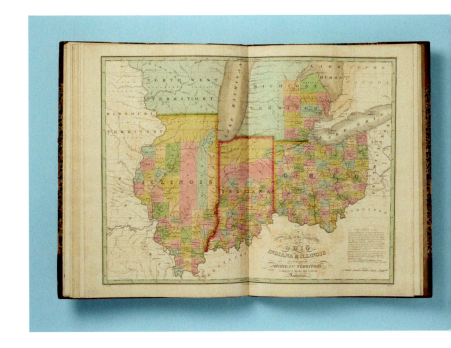

Anthony Finley,
New American Atlas

PHILADELPHIA: FINLEY, 1826

Both the North and South had eleven states in 1819 after Mississippi joined the Union. In 1820 a crisis began when Missouri wanted admission as a slave state. This map shows how northerly Missouri's location is, which was the reason for the crisis, and how coextensive its section of the Mississippi River is with Illinois's, which affected Lincoln's thinking on the subject. The Missouri Compromise gave statehood to Missouri only after such was granted to Maine, thus maintaining the balance between free and slave states. It also prohibited slavery north of Missouri's southern border, here highlighted. The violation of this compromise in 1854 reawakened Lincoln's political ambitions.

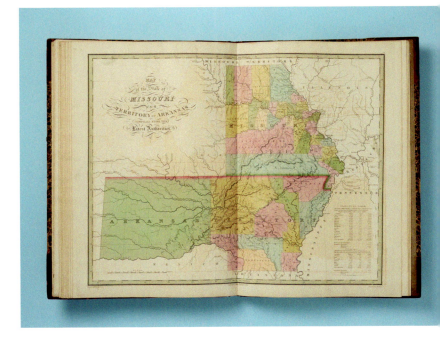

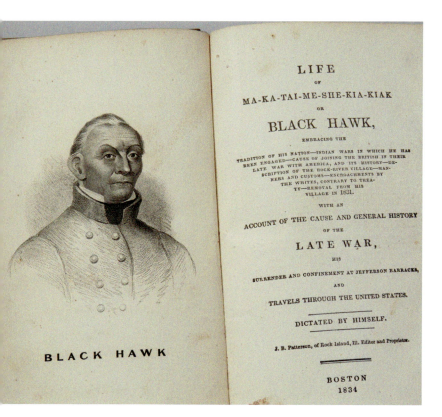

Black Hawk, *Life of Ma-Ka-Tai-Me-She-Kia-Kiak*

BOSTON: N.P., 1834

Just over a year after Lincoln's family moved to Illinois, he left home; then, just under a year after he next settled in New Salem, 120 miles west, he joined a local militia for the Black Hawk War. Named after the sixty-three-year-old Sauk warrior who resettled 1,500 of his tribespeople on lands from which they were forced off a few years previous, it was a series of savage battles across Illinois and the Michigan Territory conducted by the U.S. to expel them. Lincoln's battalion never saw action, but his being elected as their captain was a proud moment for him—and his first taste of leadership. Black Hawk's autobiography was the first by a non-naturalized Native American.

[George Armroyd], *A Connected View of the Whole Internal Navigation of the United States*

PHILADELPHIA: CAREY & LEA, 1826

Only twice in his youth did Lincoln travel outside of the West, both times on the Mississippi River to the Deep South by flatboats, which he helped construct. "He was a hired hand merely," wrote Lincoln about himself, tasked in 1828 and 1831 with bringing goods to sell in the lucrative markets of New Orleans. This period was at the peak of America's Canal Age—best represented in Armroyd's *Internal Navigation*—when man-made waterways linked cities and settlements to natural fluvial transportation routes. On these two trips, Lincoln observed the horrors of the institutional-scale slavery demanded by the South's plantation economy.

Report of the Committee on Internal Improvement
VANDALIA [IL]: SAWYER, 1837

In 1834 Lincoln entered public office as a member of the Illinois House of Representatives. He was elected by the people of New Salem, Illinois, on a platform advocating for the "internal improvement" of the state's infrastructure, primarily its waterways, a subject he knew well, given his past employment. Lincoln sat on the improvement committee, which released this 1837 report; here he would first meet his eventual political nemesis, Stephen A. Douglas, who also sat on the committee and who signed this copy of the report. In 1837 Lincoln also was successful in leading legislative efforts to move the state capital from Vandalia to Springfield.

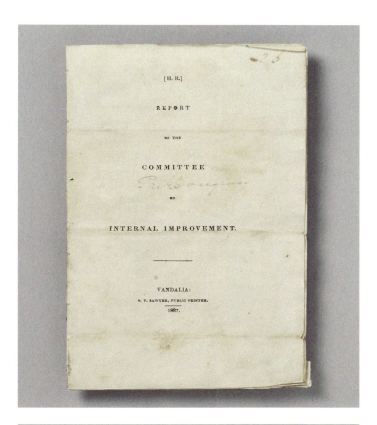

Abraham Lincoln, *Public Lands in Illinois*
VANDALIA [IL]: N.P., 1839

This rare printing has the prestige of being the first occurrence of Lincoln's name as the sole author of a work. As a Whig lawmaker, he was devoted to his party's program of public works through government financing. After the Panic of 1837, the spending he had advocated for had resulted in massive state debts. To relieve the budgetary burden, Lincoln proposed that Illinois acquire land within its borders, which the federal government still possessed, and then sell the land at a fourfold profit to settlers and speculators, resulting in both increased revenues and self-determined land ownership. The measure was never taken up by the U.S. Congress.

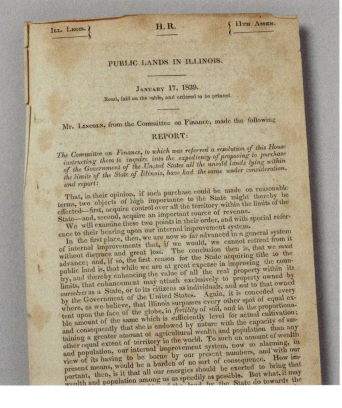

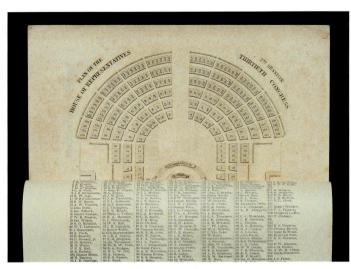

Congressional Directory, for the Second Session of the Thirtieth Congress

WASHINGTON: GIDEON, 1849

After eight years in the Illinois General Assembly, Lincoln spent four years as a Whig political operative, biding his time until he could successfully run for the 7th Congressional District in the U.S. House of Representatives. He won the 1846 election in August, left for Washington, DC, in the following October, and attended the convening of the Thirtieth Congress on December 6, 1847. Joining him on his travels were his wife, Mary, and boys Robert and Eddie. Lincoln's House seat was number 191 (last row). His committee assignments were Post Offices and Post Roads and Expenditures of the War Department. By April of 1848, Mary and the boys left Washington for her family home in Lexington, Kentucky.

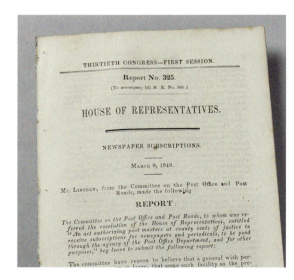

Abraham Lincoln, "H.R.301–30th Congress, Report No. 325: Newspaper Subscriptions"

WASHINGTON: N.P., 1848

Lincoln's suitability for the Committee on Post Offices and Post Roads can be traced to his time as postmaster in New Salem, Illinois. His former appointment was seemingly non-political: President Andrew Jackson, a Democrat, made it despite Lincoln being a Whig. Here in Congress, everything was political. New territories and states meant new postal routes, but to provide postal service to these lands meant that the federal government would legitimize them. Lincoln was ensnared in the political fracas related to Texas's admission to the Union, as a western tract that the state claimed was land possessed by Mexico. The disputed area would not receive its mail.

John Calvin Adams, *General Taylor and the Wilmot Proviso*

[BOSTON: WILSON & DAMRELL, 1848]

The Mexican-American War caused Lincoln's undoing in Congress. He opposed it and so was on the wrong side of administrative policy and public sentiment. Four months after annexing Texas, President James K. Polk sent federal troops across the disputed border in 1845, thus hastening the war. The Wilmot Proviso was a bill proposed in 1846 to prohibit slavery in states formed out of Mexican lands. It never passed but remained a political litmus test in Whig and Democratic campaigns for the next decade. Lincoln claimed to have voted for the measure forty-two times. His opposition to the war was so unpopular at home that he did not seek reelection.

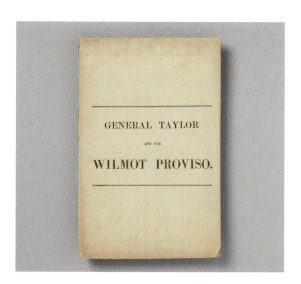

"Improved Method of Lifting Vessels over Shoals," *Report of the Commissioner of Patents*

WASHINGTON: OFFICE OF PRINTERS TO HOUSE OF REPS., 1850

"The President Elect's Mode of Buoying Vessels," *The Scientific American*

DEC. 1, 1860

Lincoln is the only American president to hold a patent for an invention: number 6469, granted by the U.S. Patent Office in May of 1849. Informed by his youthful experience on inland waters and his occasionally hindered boat travels as a congressman, Lincoln's invention was designed to provide additional buoyancy to watercraft to more easily clear shoals or freshwater sandbars made of sediment. Shown here is the original 1850 report, which prints Lincoln's invention summary, and an 1860 article in *Scientific American*, which wishes Lincoln "better success in presiding as Chief Magistrate over... the entire Union than he has had as an inventor."

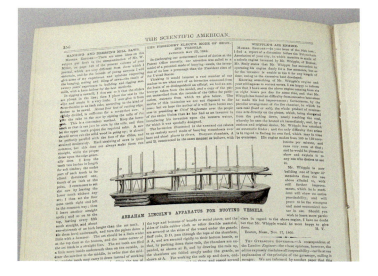

Lincoln the Reader
1810s to 1865

LINCOLN'S BOOKCASE.
(LINCOLN MEMORIAL COLLECTION, CHICAGO.)

"Go to Reading for Yourself"

ROBERT BRAY

NOT LONG AFTER he won his party's nomination for president at the May 1860 Republican National Convention in Chicago, Abraham Lincoln began a correspondence with John Locke Scripps, the chief editor of the *Chicago Daily Press and Tribune*. The objective was to assemble material for a campaign biography of the nominee, and this required Scripps to visit Springfield, Illinois, perhaps in early June, to interview Lincoln in person. At one point in the questions, Lincoln, reluctant to discuss his humble origins in detail, made a casual remark to Scripps that has resounded for decades and found its place in the better part of the thousands of biographies written about him:

> Why Scripps, [it] is a great piece of folly to attempt to make anything out of my early life. It can all be condensed into a single sentence, and that sentence you will find in Gray's "Elegy": "The short and simple annals of the poor."[1]

He had known that line, and indeed the entire poem, since encountering it in a schoolbook called the *Kentucky Preceptor*, which Lincoln likely read in Indiana during the 1820s as he began his coming-of-age years. (The book first appeared in print in 1806 and had editions through 1812. The time of Lincoln's birth in 1809 saw a democratizing increase in the number of educational primers, readers, and spellers printed in the newly incorporated western states.) As his confidant, law partner, and biographer William Henry Herndon later observed, when Lincoln found literature to his liking, long or short, he "assimilated [it] into his own being."[2] We can assume that Thomas Gray's "Elegy Written in a Country Churchyard" (1751), at a medium length of 128 lines, was among Lincoln's first literary assimilations. The process was a kind of mental screenshot, and once Lincoln's brain contained a thing, it stayed there.

Herndon also said, trying to both compliment but humanize the president, that he had never known anyone who "read less and thought more" than Lincoln.[3] A remark such as this might reveal Herndon's mixed views

Pages 34–35: Detail from John G. Nicolay and John Hay, "Abraham Lincoln: A History," *Century Illustrated Monthly Magazine* (New York), Nov. 1886 to Apr. 1890 (see page 257)

Page 36: Anthony Berger and Mathew B. Brady, *President A. Lincoln Reading the Bible to His Son*, ca. 1865. Albumen print

William Doughty, frontispiece portrait of Thomas Gray, *The Poems of Mr. Gray* (York: Ward, 1788), William Mason (editor)

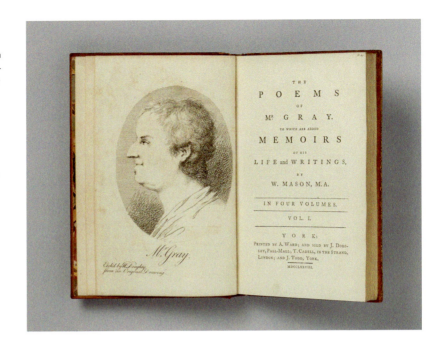

about, if not mixed motivations regarding, the nature of his subject (something that Herndon freely admitted and has complicated his use as a primary source for biography). Herndon was insinuating that Lincoln's narrow range of reading harmed his overall education, literary and political. But the more favorable, albeit backhanded, implication is that it enhanced it by permitting Lincoln to retain, reflect on, and realize his convictions about important literary and political texts unobscured by broader reading. For example, in 1854, Lincoln called the first of America's founding documents, the Declaration of Independence, "my ancient faith," signaling the unassailability that the phrase "all men are created equal" had in his worldview.[4] This suggests that the act of reading for Lincoln was cause for thought and action predicated on philosophically deep reflection.

In Lincoln's mention of Gray's "Elegy," we see a politician ironically using an example from literature to explain the deprivations of his youth, literary or otherwise. If the twin qualities of Lincoln's early life were the drudgery of poverty and the spirit to achieve more, primarily through reading, then to cite Gray meant that these attributes remained with him into adulthood and that he believed sharing the truth made political sense. His journey to this level of literacy began modestly in Kentucky, where, through age seven, he learned the English alphabet and basic vocabulary from his mother, Nancy Hanks Lincoln, and sporadically from two teachers at vocal schools, where instruction came through strict (and loud) recitation. In 1816 the family moved to Indiana, and by 1818 Lincoln had gained a stepmother, Sarah Bush Johnston Lincoln, who gifted him his first books: the Bible, *Aesop's Fables*, and John Bunyan's *The Pilgrim's Progress*. From this early exposure came an immense appetite for reading that only increased as he grew up but which would be done entirely outside of a formal setting. A farmer recalled, "Abe was awful lazy...[He] was always reading and thinking."[5] By his own assessment, Lincoln had "went to A.B.C. schools by littles" (i.e., patchily) and that "the aggregate of all his schooling did not amount to one year."[6] From the American canon, Lincoln eventually got his hands on Benjamin Franklin's *Autobiography* and perhaps two different biographies of George Washington. But a frontier community like his could not offer much standard fare. So by age eighteen, reading whatever was available, he absorbed himself in a ponderous tome called *The Laws of Indiana*. This, I believe, lit the spark for what would be Lincoln's greatest feat in autodidacticism.

To a born reader, the advantages of becoming a lawyer are equally the financial promise of the profession and the requirement to do what one loves: be immersed in books. Thankfully, for the unschooled but well-read, becoming a lawyer in 1836 required not that one go to university but only pass the bar, which amounted to an oral examination before the state's Supreme Court. When he was twenty-one, Lincoln's family moved to Illinois; a year later he left home, and by 1834 he won his first election to public office in the Illinois state legislature (he had lost once previously two years earlier). During his second term, Lincoln achieved his law license through a self-study program he later advocated as: "Get books, sit down anywhere, and go to reading for yourself."[7] Specifically, he later wrote in a letter, the task is to "begin with Blackstone's *Commentaries*, and [read] it carefully through, say twice."[8] This is not uncommon; all attorneys must know that William Blackstone's *Commentaries on the Laws of England* (1765–69) most successfully explains the system of common law, developed in Britain and adopted in the United States, that is based contingently on legal precedent. What was exceptional is that Lincoln opted to purely read his way to becoming a lawyer, from Blackstone onwards, and not take the more customary, direct path of apprenticing at a firm. Without a law school or a law office from which to help oneself to books, Lincoln had to borrow them from friends. So, for what usually would take three years to study, Lincoln learned in four, no doubt "reading less and thinking more" throughout the process. Anecdotally, we know that eventually, after he set up his law practice, the desks and shelves were laden with books, legal and literary, American and English.[9]

Lincoln's personal reading habits were wide-ranging enough that we cannot exactly say where ideologically or temperamentally he stood. He knew passages from scripture by heart, and yet he enjoyed the pre-Christian, pantheistic mythology of Homer. He read the Romantics, particularly the shifting genres of Lord Byron, but he seemed equally enchanted by the formal verse of Alexander Pope. No great writer from history is more often associated with Lincoln than Shakespeare: eyewitness accounts say the president often read and quoted the bard, and no word might adequately sum up Lincoln's extraordinary and tragic life

The Early Home of Abraham Lincoln, ca. 1865. Albumen card

THE DAVID M. RUBENSTEIN AMERICANA COLLECTION

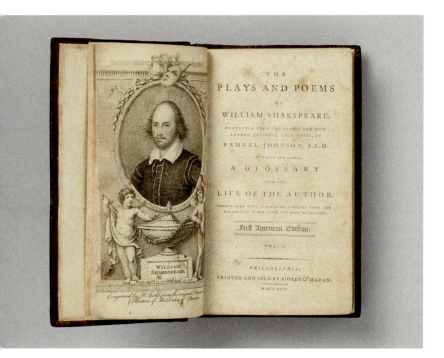

William Shakespeare, *The Plays and Poems of William Shakspeare*

PHILADELPHIA: BIOREN AND MADAN, 1795–96

President Abraham Lincoln was known to attend performances of William Shakespeare's plays, quote passages by him in conversation, and even study his works, especially the histories and tragedies, in part to find comfort and meaning during the Civil War. Shown here is the first American edition of the works of Shakespeare, printed in eight volumes in Philadelphia during the later years of George Washington's presidency. The publisher is Joseph Hopkinson, son of Francis Hopkinson, a signer of the Declaration of Independence. His preface goes to lengths to justify printing so decidedly an English writer as Shakespeare in newly independent America.

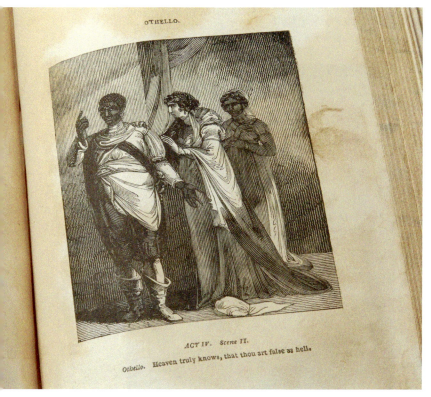

William Shakespeare, *The Works of William Shakspeare*

BOSTON: MUNROE [ET AL.], 1810–12

The young Lincoln likely first encountered Shakespeare in reading primers or elocution textbooks. As a young man, he heard Shakespeare recited by traveling lecturers passing through Springfield, Illinois, at the Young Men's Lyceum, a debating society. By the time he was a practicing attorney, Shakespearean pronouncements were a mainstay of his conversational repertoire. This book is the first illustrated American edition of Shakespeare, printed around the time of Lincoln's birth. Each play received a woodcut illustration by Alexander Anderson, America's first professional wood engraver. We highlight *Othello* because we believe that Lincoln's use of "better angels" in his First Inaugural Address comes from Gratiano's grief-stricken words about Desdemona.

Aesop, H. Clarke (translator), *Fabulae Aesopi Selectae, or Select Fables of Aesop*

WALPOLE [NH]: THOMAS & THOMAS, 1802

William H. Herndon, in his biography, wrote of Lincoln that he "kept the Bible and 'Aesop's Fables' always within reach, and read them over and over again." We might trace the origin of Lincoln's penchant and flair for parabolic language to the presence of these two books in his early life. A popular version of Aesop in late eighteenth- and early nineteenth-century America was the Clarke translation, which used the simplicity of the fables for the teaching of Latin. Originally printed in London, the first American edition of Clarke appeared in Boston in 1787, followed by editions in Philadelphia, Baltimore, and Exeter and Walpole, New Hampshire.

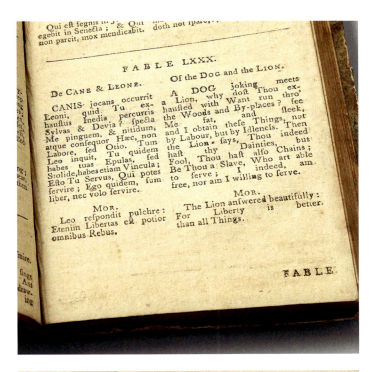

John Bunyan, *The Pilgrim's Progress*

HARTFORD [CT]: ANDRUS, 1832

No fewer than four relatives and acquaintances of Lincoln recalled to biographers his childhood fondness for the Christian allegorical work *Pilgrim's Progress*, written by the seventeenth-century Puritan writer John Bunyan. Their testimonies are available to researchers. What lacks attribution is the anecdote circulated in the late nineteenth century that his father gave him a copy of Bunyan, causing a young Lincoln to neither eat nor sleep over his excitement for receiving the book. The engraved edition shown here, which first appeared in 1824 when Lincoln was fifteen, is by a Connecticut publisher known for printing religious works.

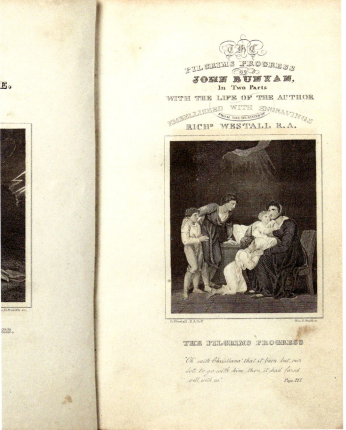

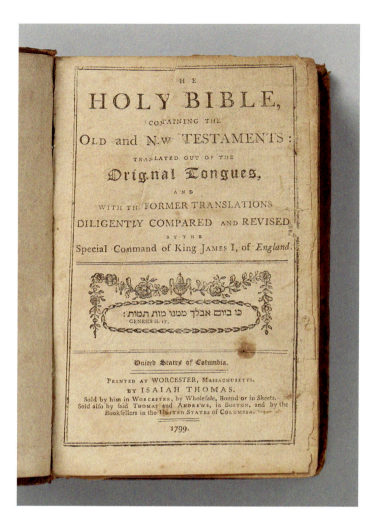

The Holy Bible, Containing the Old and New Testaments
WORCESTER [MA]: THOMAS, 1799

"A house divided against itself." "The judgments of the Lord are true and righteous altogether." "He from whom all blessings flow." "Four score and seven years." These and other instances of language borrowed from Scripture appearing in the speeches of Lincoln reveal the importance that the Bible had in Lincoln's lifelong reading. In a Republican barnstorming speech given in Cincinnati in 1859, he said, "The good old maxims of the Bible are applicable, and truly applicable to human affairs"—after thoroughly dismantling Stephen A. Douglas's appeal to faith fallacy that the Good Book justifies slavery. Shown here is an example of famed colonial printer Isaiah Thomas's first "standing" type (i.e., ready for press) twelvemo edition of the Bible.

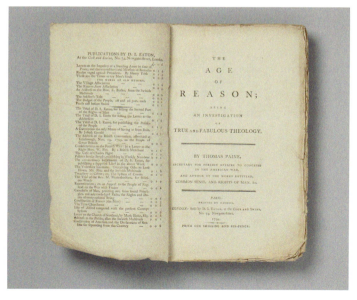

Thomas Paine, *The Age of Reason*
PARIS: BARROIS [LONDON: EATON], 1794

Lincoln's dalliance with Thomas Paine's deistic manifesto *The Age of Reason* occurred in his mid-twenties, soon after he left home and, we assume, stopped regularly attending church services. His stepmother said of him, "Abe had no particular religion"—i.e., he did not belong to a particular denomination. Deism asserts that there is a Creator but that the world is best explained by the laws of nature. Paine extended this line of thought to attack organized religion, particularly the Christian church. A book with a complicated printing history, it was a rampant, if scandalous, success when it first appeared, and it saw multiple editions made in both France and England for export.

Plutarch, *Plutarch's Lives*
WORCESTER [MA]: THOMAS [ET AL.], 1804

Plutarch is an example of when Lincoln did not read a book. John Locke Scripps was not able to send Lincoln a draft of his 1860 campaign biography of him before its printing. He was sure, he wrote in a letter, that all its facts were correct, except one: he assumed Lincoln had read Plutarch's *Lives* in his youth. In a later biography by Ida Tarbell, the muckraking journalist known for her frequent publishing detours into Lincoln's early life, we learn of Lincoln's response: "That paragraph...was not true when you wrote it...but I want your book [to] be faithful to the facts[.] I secured the book a few days ago, and have sent for you to tell you I have just read it."

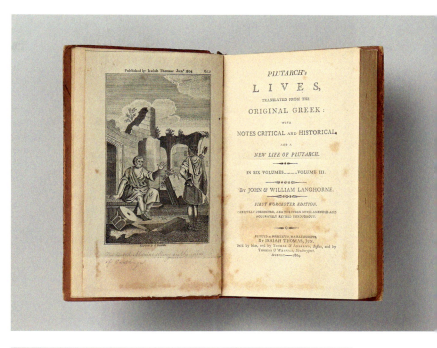

Homer, *The Iliad of Homer*
PHILADELPHIA: CRUKSHANK [ET AL.], 1795

In 1920 Talcott Williams, the first director of the Columbia Journalism School, shared this anecdote from 1860 about Lincoln in Illinois: "Julius Heath Royce, my father-in-law...was in the same hotel as Lincoln[.] Day by day [he] saw Lincoln reach across the table for the hotel castor and set it before his plate and lose himself in a volume, bound in dark cloth. Breakfast, dinner and supper brought the same absorption. He asked Lincoln what he was reading. He looked up with alert attention. 'I am reading Homer, the Iliad and Odyssey. You ought to read him. He has a grip and he knows how to tell a story.'" Shown here is the first American edition of the *Iliad*.

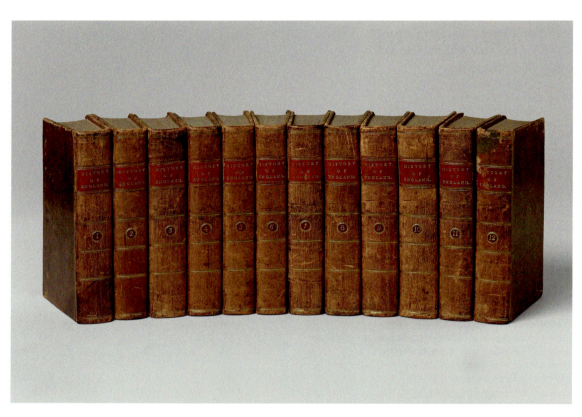

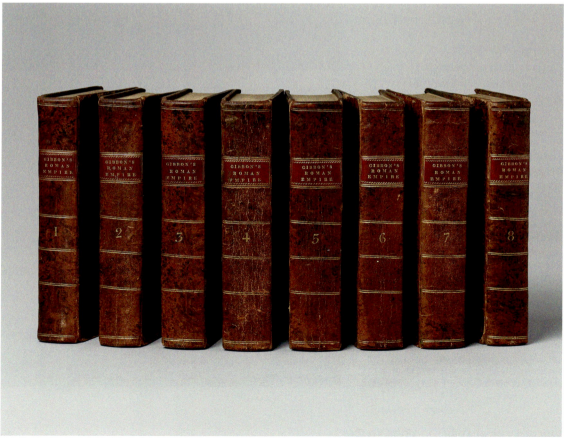

LEFT

David Hume, Tobias Smollett, *The History of England*
PHILADELPHIA: CAMPBELL, 1795–98

Edward Gibbon, *History of the Decline and Fall of the Roman Empire*
PHILADELPHIA: BIRCH AND SMALL, 1804–5

RIGHT

Francis Bacon, *Essays Moral, Economical, and Political*
BOSTON: GREENLEAF, 1807

Adam Smith, *An Inquiry into the Nature and Causes of the Wealth of Nations*
PHILADELPHIA: DOBSON, 1796

The selection shown here is of first or early American editions of classic books from the canon of Western thought that we are reasonably to very confident Lincoln read. The lifetime list of books that Lincoln read is not so extensive as to be unknowable, but it is varied in its many genres and themes. Which books are included on this list—and which may have influenced his writings—is a subject of continued debate among biographers and scholars. We know that from Illinois to his White House years, he had an enduring interest in political economy and history.

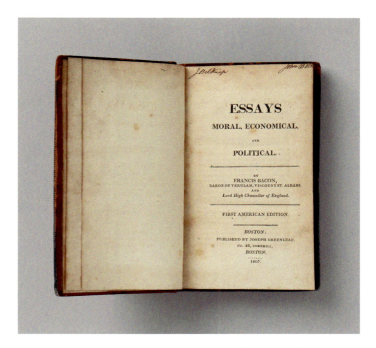

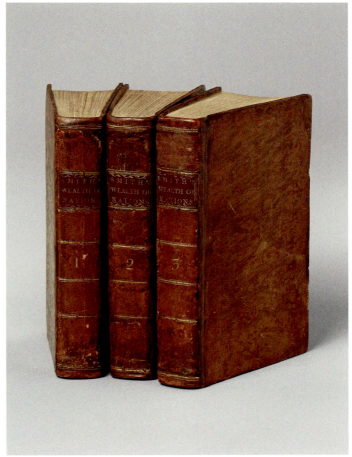

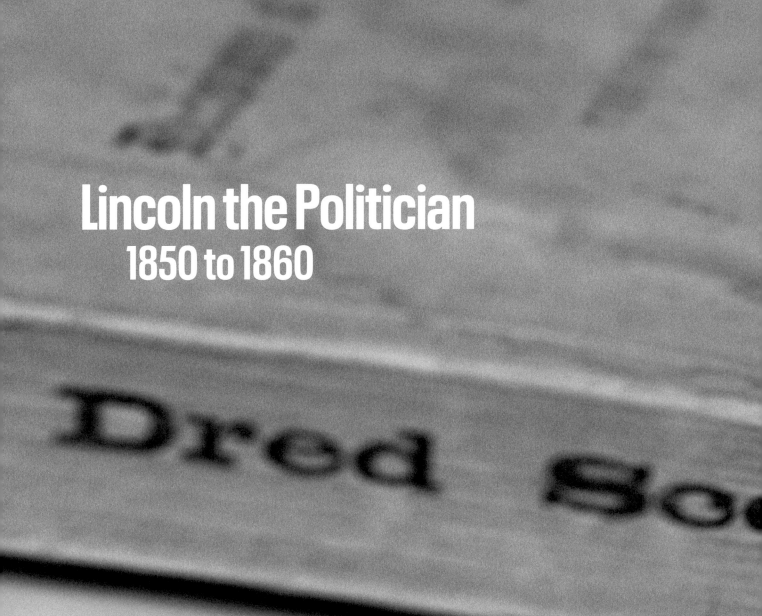

Lincoln the Politician
1850 to 1860

tt Case.

"The Vanquished This Year May Be Victor the Next"

TED WIDMER

THE DECADE OF Abraham Lincoln's life before he became president offers one of the most exemplary ascensions to political power in American history. To contemplate the sequence of events that propelled an Illinois country lawyer and political novice to the highest office in the land provides an instructive case for how unlikely players taking advantage of tumultuous events have shaped the destiny of the United States.

When the 1850s began, Lincoln appeared to be finished with public service. He had returned to Springfield in 1849, disappointed, after a single term in the House of Representatives that could be viewed as a failure. He later claimed, "I was losing interest in politics," although it would be more accurate to say politics was losing interest in him after he criticized a popular, expansionist war the country was waging against Mexico, angering many of his backers.[1] Illinois senator Stephen A. Douglas, his political nemesis for the decade, would recall Lincoln's unpopularity during this period, when "the indignation of the people followed him everywhere" and he was "forgotten by his former friends."[2] This is not a Lincoln we easily recognize today. The darkness undoubtedly deepened when his second son, Eddie, died on February 1, 1850. From this low point, Lincoln's ten-year journey to becoming America's sixteenth president necessitated an agile point-to-point navigation similar to that of the riverboat pilots whom Lincoln admired in his youth for "setting the course of the boat no farther than they can see."[3]

Clearly there was a logic at work, which stemmed from the superior qualities Lincoln was only beginning to discover about himself. Indeed, *logicalness* was one of them. As he later purportedly said to an inquiring minister, when he was studying the law, he developed a strong desire to learn how to demonstrate conclusive lines of reasoning. As an example of the extent he went to learn reasoning, he immersed himself deeply in Euclid's *Elements of Geometry* to improve his ability to work out a problem logically and then offer an unassailable proof.

Well-reasoned thought helped Lincoln's legal career, which dominated his attention in the years following his return to Illinois. He practiced the

Pages 52–53: Spine and front wrapper for *A Report of the Decision … in the Case of Dred Scott* (New York: Appleton, 1857) (see page 66)

Page 54: Samuel Montague Fassett, Abraham Lincoln, half-length portrait, facing right, 1859 (printed later). Gelatin silver print

Oliver Byrne's *Elements of Euclid* (London: Pickering, 1847), 224–25

Russell Lee, "The Posey Building of Shawneetown, Illinois, in which Abraham Lincoln and Robert Ingersoll had law offices," 1937. Gelatin silver print

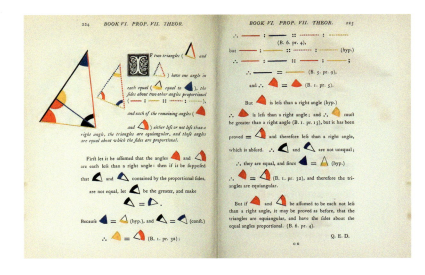

law "assiduously,"⁴ he later wrote, arguing cases large and small before judges and juries around the state. In these humble settings, he honed the skill of breaking down complex problems in ways ordinary citizens could understand. His enormous storehouse of homespun anecdotes helped, as did his capacities for deep research into judicial precedent and meticulously crafted legal arguments. As a result, Lincoln's law practice grew, keeping pace with the rising number of legal and regulatory issues emanating from the spread of locomotive travel throughout the Midwest. When the Illinois Central Railroad completed its 705-mile network between 1851 and 1856, it became the largest rail system in the world. The region grew exponentially in these years: Illinois's population doubled between 1850 and 1860, from 851,470 to 1,711,951, and Chicago swelled into one of the Midwest's largest cities.⁵ In this burgeoning western milieu, Lincoln remained a quick learner and a skilled counselor, capable of finding common ground between competing interests.

Population-minded political observers saw that if the non-slaveholding Midwest continued to develop at this pace, the South would be weakened in Congress and so lose the stranglehold it historically had had on the federal government (there is a reason why eight of the first ten presidents were born in the South). Jefferson Davis, the pro-slavery secretary of war from the Franklin Pierce administration who became a senator from Mississippi, was keenly aware of these demographics and did all he could during the 1850s to pursue his unrealized dream of a southern train route

56   CHAPTER THREE

across the continent. In this sense, Lincoln and Davis were already adversaries before they eventually led opposing sides of the Civil War. Realization grew among advocates and accommodationists of slavery that, for the South to accept any form of state-by-state American expansion, slavery must be permitted in the West, even if this meant breaking earlier agreements—or specifically, repealing the Missouri Compromise of 1820, which had outlawed slavery north of that state's southern border. Accordingly, Senator Douglas introduced what became in 1854 the Kansas-Nebraska Act. As a concession to allow for a transcontinental rail system originating out of Chicago, the act certified that any Western territory could be admitted to the Union as a slave state if its voting population chose it to be.

Northerners were outraged (Douglas joked that he could travel at night by the light of his own burning effigy). Lincoln's response was visceral. Before 1854, his practicing the law "had almost superseded the thought of politics in his mind," he wrote of himself in the third person.[6] But afterward, with uncharacteristic emotion, he wrote that the repeal of the Compromise "aroused him as he had never been before." Something was reborn in him—it was a political reawakening arising from a lifelong aversion to slavery, a lawyer's keen sense that the law was contravened, and a westerner's resentment that new states might enhance the South's numbers game.

The South would later describe the Civil War as an act of Northern "aggression," but throughout the 1850s, it was Southern leaders who were assertively trying to create new slave states from nearby lands, including Cuba, which they had hoped to seize, and broad swaths of Central America. The actions of the South betrayed that old agreements could be rendered worthless—including founding compacts like the Declaration of Independence, which promised a new kind of country where "all men are created equal." Even if this phrase was aspirational when written, it held the power of unassailable law for Lincoln. A fragment of paper from 1854 showed his mind deeply at work, contemplating the injustice of slavery. As any reader of Euclid could argue, the math was quite simple. Equal means equal.

> If A. can prove, however conclusively, that he may, of right, enslave B.—why may not B. snatch the same argument, and prove equally, that he may enslave A.?[7]

The years immediately following the Kansas-Nebraska Act saw Lincoln's return to politics. He began running for state office again but in a renewed manner that combined the courtroom flourish of a seasoned lawyer with the political immediacy of a true agent of history. Consider his October 1854 "Peoria Speech," in which he orated at length (over three hours) about the nation's future with a suasive force he had never shown before. Gone were the insecurities and jokes at his own expense; instead, Lincoln spoke with moral grandeur about slavery's existential limitations, going back to America's founding. Repeatedly, he turned to the words of Thomas

Jefferson, beginning with those that bore the country, of the "inalienable rights...of all men: life, liberty and the pursuit of happiness." The extension to this, Lincoln argued, was the 1787 Northwest Ordinance, also conceived by Jefferson, which explicitly forbade slavery beyond the Ohio River. Thereafter, the Missouri Compromise, in "excluding slavery North of the line, [used] the same language...as in the Ordinance of '87," Lincoln said. "It directly applied to Iowa, Minnesota, and to the present bone of contention, Kansas and Nebraska."[8] Lincoln's law partner, William Herndon, once described the way he looked, arms extended, his gray eyes flashing fire, when he invoked the Declaration and how it spoke to all of humanity. According to Herndon, "it was at such moments that he seemed inspired, fresh from the hands of his Creator."[9]

As Lincoln emerged as a leader of this great counterforce to the political status quo, it became clear that he was in the right place and time. His return from Washington in 1849, far from being a banishment to a distant backwater, was, in reality, an opportune move to an ideal environment in which to grow. As Washington sank more deeply into dysfunction (commentators were already calling it a swamp because of its poor drainage), Springfield was emerging as a kind of ground zero for the country's future. It adjoined the West, was connected to the East, and was the capital of a huge state with both Southern and Northern constituencies. In short, it was the political exemplification of mid-nineteenth-century America and a natural training ground for a national leader.

Lincoln found a political home in the fallout of the Kansas-Nebraska Act, which swept away some of the cobwebs of the past, including a Whig Party that had lost its way. Initially a Whig when emulating his ideological hero Henry Clay, Lincoln now helped to shape the newly formed Republican Party. It was a movement comprised mostly of slavery's enemies, and Lincoln's position within it seemed to grow with each new societally consequential insult from proslavery forces. The 1857 Supreme Court decision *Dred Scott vs. Sandford* declared that African Americans could never be citizens and thus could never receive federal protection. Lincoln's heated response in a June speech was praised as far away as New York.[10] He used the occasion to make clear he was speaking for a bloc that held firm political convictions: "We think the Dred Scott decision is erroneous. We know the court that made it, has often over-ruled its own decisions, and we shall do what we can to have it to over-rule this."

A year later, the Republicans signaled their growing political strength by nominating Lincoln to run against Douglas for his Senate seat. At the party convention, Lincoln opened his campaign with a widely noted address that used the words of the King James Bible to forewarn of the future of the country; the "House Divided" speech, as it became known, presented the uncomfortable but incontrovertible logic that a country so "divided against itself cannot stand," cannot be "permanently half slave and half free." Douglas's response

Matthew A. Brady, Stephen Arnold Douglas, head-and-shoulders portrait, between 1844 and 1896. Whole plate daguerreotype

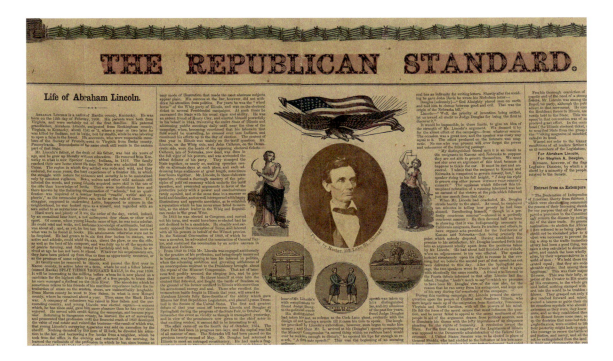

Detail from "Life of Abraham Lincoln," *Republican Standard* (Chicago: Rufus Blanchard, 1860). Colored broadside

was to label Lincoln an abolitionist, but in doing so, he was baited into participating in seven staged election debates with his adversary in different locations around the state. Huge crowds would follow and amass to hear the Lincoln-Douglas Debates, whose words, printed immediately in newspapers, still provide the single greatest explication of the opposing sides on the issue of slavery's expansion. At the time, Douglas was a well-known figure; thus, by debating him, Lincoln became at least his political equal. And although Lincoln would lose the election, his words were published across the country. As he put it in a speech in 1859, "The vanquished this year may be the victor the next."[11] This would be prophetic.

As the political stirrings began ahead of the 1860 presidential election, Lincoln was still less well-known than many other leading Republicans, especially those from the East. But in small, strategic ways, he and his friends continued to improve his chances as a recognized, viable candidate. In late 1859 Lincoln began to travel and stump more widely, visiting Wisconsin, Kansas, Indiana, and Ohio. In October a fateful invitation came for him to give a lecture in New York in February (this would become his famed Cooper Union Address). That December he penned a 600-word autobiography meekly describing his origins, which appeared in a small Pennsylvania newspaper (he added, in a note to a friend, "There is not much of it, for the reason, I suppose, that there is not much of me."). Lincoln also compiled and edited the book-form version of his debates with Douglas for distribution the following year. With each of these barnstorming and media advances, Lincoln sharpened the Republican arguments against slavery, but the odds remained long for him as a national candidate. Besides losing every election since his return from Washington, he had few friends outside

"NO HIGHER LAW."

PRICE $3 A HUNDR[ED]

of Illinois, and he freely admitted that his education was "defective." In a conversation with a German journalist, he laughed at the idea of achieving higher political office, exclaiming, "Just think of such a sucker as me as President!"[12] ("Sucker" was a nickname for an Illinoisan.)

But there was one political maneuver left for the Lincoln camp to do that would benefit the candidate more than anything. By advocating it in their party's planning committees, they managed to bring the 1860 Republican National Convention, where the presidential nominee would be picked, to Chicago. Lincoln's weakness had become his advantage: his lack of political prominence made Chicago a palatable, neutral city to the other, likelier front-runner candidates. The decision offered Lincoln a native edge in the nominating process—but even more, it gave a sense of political destiny to the ten years he had spent in Illinois.

Detail from *No Higher Law* (New York: Harned, 1850). Political cartoon condemning the Fugitive Slave Act of 1850

NOTES

1. James Mellon, ed., *The Face of Lincoln* (New York: Viking Press, 1979), 18.

2. Abraham Lincoln and Stephen A. Douglas, *Political Debates* (Columbus, OH: Follett et al., 1860), 69 (first debate, August 21, 1858); Mellon, *The Face of Lincoln*, 41.

3. David Herbert Donald, *Lincoln* (New York: Simon & Schuster, 1995), 15.

4. "Collected Works of Abraham Lincoln. Volume 3 [Aug. 21, 1858–Mar. 4, 1860]." In the digital collection *Collected Works of Abraham Lincoln*, https://name.umdl.umich.edu/lincoln3. University of Michigan Library Digital Collections (accessed June 28, 2024).

5. Michael Burlingame, *Abraham Lincoln: A Life*, vol. 1 (Baltimore: Johns Hopkins University Press, 2008), 310.

6. "Collected Works of Abraham Lincoln."

7. Ronald C. White, *Lincoln in Private: What His Most Personal Reflections Tell Us About Our Greatest President* (New York: Random House, 2021), 47.

8. "Collected Works of Abraham Lincoln."

9. Letter from William H. Herndon to Truman H. Bartlett, July 19, 1887, quoted in Emanuel Hertz, ed., *The Hidden Lincoln* (New York: The Viking Press, 1938), 192; Mellon, *The Face of Lincoln*, 30.

10. Burlingame, *Abraham Lincoln: A Life*, 442.

11. Abraham Lincoln, Address before Wisconsin State Agricultural Society, Milwaukee, Sept. 30, 1859, quoted in "Collected Works of Abraham Lincoln."

12. Henry Villard, "Recollections of Lincoln," *Atlantic Monthly* (Feb. 1904): 165–73.

THE DAVID M. RUBENSTEIN AMERICANA COLLECTION

"The Fugitive Slave Law," *A Document for the People*
WASHINGTON: BUELL & BLANCHARD, 1853

The first incendiary development in the political cauldron of the 1850s was the Fugitive Slave Act, which became law as part of the greater Compromise of 1850. It required citizens and governments of free states to be participants in the return of captured slaves. Lincoln later explained his deference to this law, viewing it as an extension of the Constitution's original fugitive slave clause: "I do not now, nor ever did, stand in favor of [its] unconditional repeal."

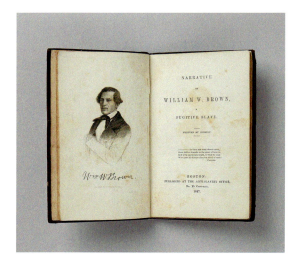

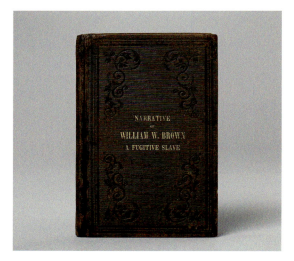

William Wells Brown, *Narrative of...a Fugitive Slave*
BOSTON: ANTI-SLAVERY OFFICE, 1847

The implications of the Fugitive Slave Law were profound. While the burden of capturing slaves fell to the U.S. Marshals, slavers were essentially granted permission to enter free states and replenish their supply of human chattel. The response in the North was intense: the abolitionist cause strengthened, and various "personal liberty laws" were passed to protect the legal rights of Blacks. For William Wells Brown, the esteemed abolitionist writer who had escaped slavery as a teenager, the protections were not enough: he remained with his family in England.

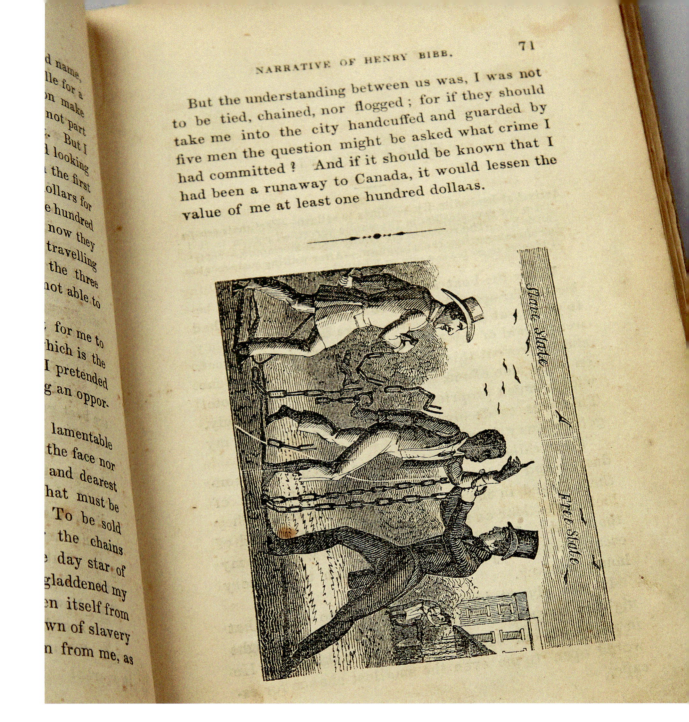

Henry Walton Bibb, *Narrative of the Life and Adventures*
NEW YORK: THE AUTHOR, 1849

From the canon of American slave narratives, no runaway escaped and was caught more times than Henry Bibb. Even after successfully escaping, he was caught trying to rescue his wife and young daughter (twice). The audaciousness of his adventures captured the public imagination and served as a model for Harriet Beecher Stowe when she wrote *Uncle Tom's Cabin*. After the Fugitive Slave Act passed, Bibb left for Canada, eventually establishing its first Black newspaper.

Stephen A. Douglas, "Kansas, Utah, and the Dred Scott Decision"

CHICAGO: N.P., 1857

In 1854 the Kansas-Nebraska Act passed, which repealed the Missouri Compromise of 1820 and thus supplanted the ban on slavery north of Missouri's southern border with the concept of "popular sovereignty." Now citizens in these northerly territories could decide for themselves whether they entered the Union as free or slave states. Stephen A. Douglas, the senator from Illinois, drafted the new law's language. Lincoln spoke forcefully against it; condemning the act reignited his public career and began his yearslong political collision with Douglas (see page 67, top).

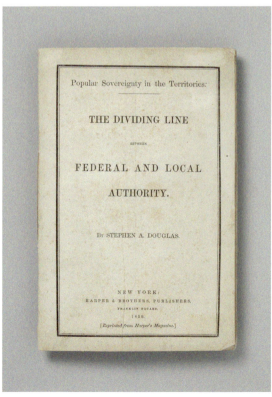

Stephen A. Douglas, *Popular Sovereignty in the Territories: The Dividing Line between Federal and Local Authority*

BOSTON: HARPER & BROTHERS, 1859

Popular sovereignty brought the specter of bondage to the West. Settlers from the North and South moved into Kansas to tip the scales of the constitutional referenda that would decide its fate. Resulting hostilities gave the name "Bloody Kansas" to the territory. In the end it was admitted as a free state. In Illinois and New York, Lincoln began making very learned, detailed speeches on the Founders' original intentions to keep the West free (see page 103, bottom). "With the author of the Declaration of Independence," said Lincoln, "the policy of prohibiting slavery in new territory originated."

Charles Sumner, "The Crime against Kansas"
WASHINGTON: BUELL & BLANCHARD, 1856

As career orators, both Lincoln and Charles Sumner, the senator from Massachusetts, were voices of moral clarity and defenders of the Declaration of Independence. But they differed in style: Lincoln sought consensus; Sumner would ridicule his opponents. In this Senate speech, Sumner said Douglas was Sancho Panza to South Carolina senator Andrew Butler's Don Quixote. Butler, he said, had "chosen a mistress…who, though ugly to others, is always lovely to him.…I mean the harlot Slavery." Butler was not present when Sumner spoke, but his relative, Preston Brooks, was. Brooks viciously beat Sumner with a cane, bringing bloody Kansas to the Congress.

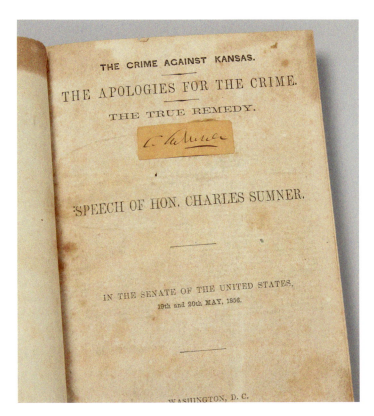

Republican Campaign Edition for the Million. Containing the Republican Platform
BOSTON: JEWETT, 1856

In this charged political atmosphere, the Republican Party was born. The Whig Party failed to remain coalesced after its northern and southern factions took opposing sides in the Kansas-Nebraska and Texas Annexation disputes. Antislavery Whigs joined forces with Free Soil Party elements, who did not want to see slavery expanded. Between 1854 and 1856, the Republican Party went from being a stopgap political syndicate born in the Midwest to a burgeoning national political party with an antislavery, "free labor" platform and a candidate for president.

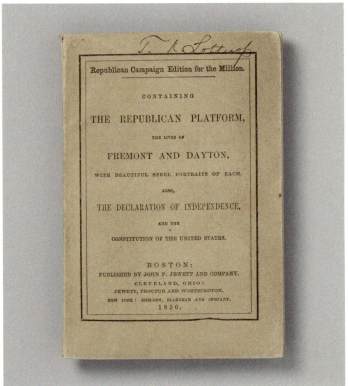

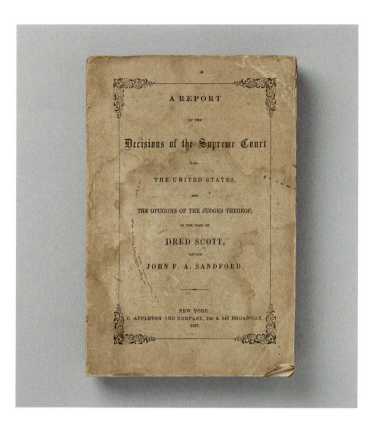

[Supreme Court], *A Report of the Decisions…in the Case of Dred Scott versus John F. A. Sandford*

NEW YORK: APPLETON, 1857

The third slavery-related cataclysm of the 1850s was the Supreme Court's tortuously reasoned and juridically repugnant decision in *Dred Scott v. John Sandford* (1857). The court validated slavery where it was presently practiced and stated that Congress lacked the right to prevent slavery in any territory or state acquired as a territory. In addition it asserted that any Black American, or "free negro of the African race, whose ancestors were brought to this country and sold as slaves, is not a 'citizen' within the meaning of the Constitution of the United States."

Abraham Lincoln, "Speech…in Reply to Judge Douglas"

[SPRINGFIELD, IL: N.P., 1857]

This is Lincoln's Dred Scott speech, a response to Stephen A. Douglas's defense two weeks earlier (see page 64, top) of the court's decision. Of Lincoln's many points, two are worth noting. First, America's founding protections of life, liberty, and happiness must extend to Black Americans: "In those days, our Declaration of Independence was held sacred by all, and thought to include all." Second, the unalienable rights cherished by Americans should be shared by those then enslaved. He said, "In [a slave's] natural right to eat the bread she earns with her own hands without asking leave of any one else, she is my equal, and the equal of all others."

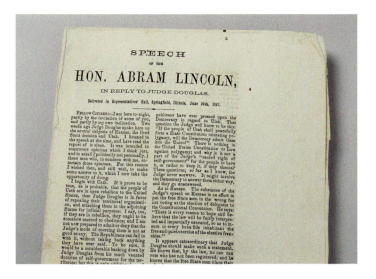

Abraham Lincoln, "Speech…Delivered in Springfield"

[SPRINGFIELD, IL: N.P., 1858]

By targeting Douglas, a strategy that resurrected Lincoln's political career, he made his fellow Illinoisan out to be the embodiment of the wicked forces safeguarding slavery's expansion. In contrast he portrayed himself as "the standard-bearer in behalf of the Republicans," the heir of Jefferson and the "Old Whigs" (Clay and Webster), who must "fight this battle upon principle, and upon principle alone." This speech is Lincoln's opening salvo against Douglas for the 1858 senate campaign: "Free men of Illinois—free men everywhere—judge ye between him and me."

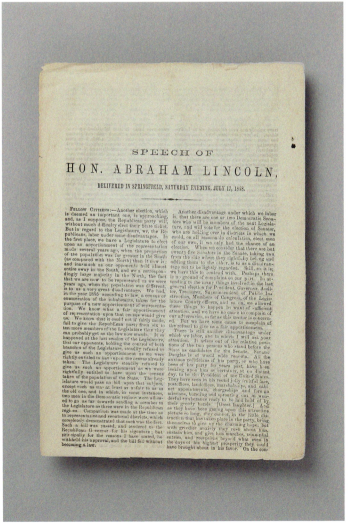

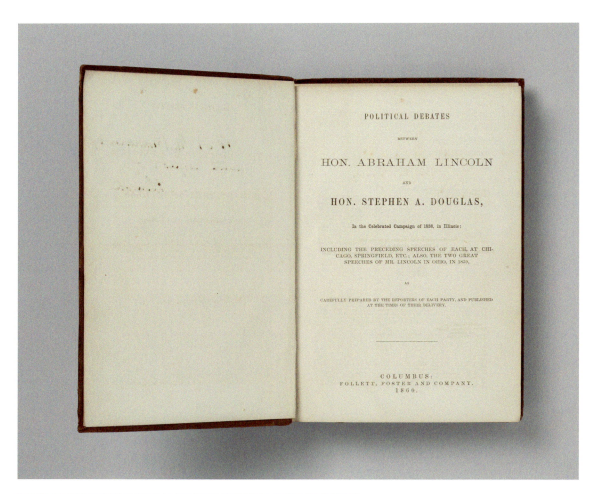

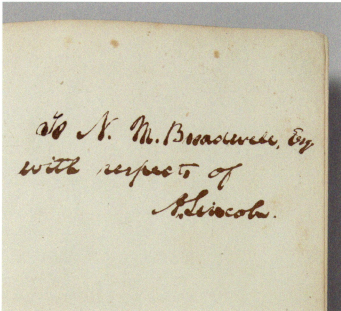

Abraham Lincoln and Stephen A. Douglas, *Political Debates*

COLUMBUS [OH]: FOLLETT [ET AL.], 1860

The most famous in-person political debates in American history were the seven held between Abraham Lincoln and Stephen A. Douglas in seven different Illinois districts across fifty-five days in the summer and fall of 1858. Now called the Lincoln-Douglas Debates, they were ostensibly election events for a U.S. Senate seat. However, because of their national subject matter, they quickly became widespread news, vaulting both men as spokespersons for the opposing sides of the controversy over slavery and its expansion. First printed in newspapers, Lincoln compiled them into what became a book-form version. This copy is one of only a few that he inscribed in ink.

Abraham Lincoln and Stephen A. Douglas, *Political Debates*

COLUMBUS [OH]: FOLLETT [ET AL.], 1860

The original book-form version of the debates was a scrapbook that Lincoln kept of newspaper clippings of the events, including transcriptions of the speeches. He was principled in selecting the texts, using a Republican source to obtain his words and a Democratic one for Douglas's. In the edition here, a rare paper-wrapper variant, we see that Lincoln also made the editorial decision to include his June 1858 "House Divided" speech, which asserted that a country cannot be both half free and half slave—"till a crisis shall have been reached and passed."

Stephen A. Douglas and Abraham Lincoln, *The Campaign in Illinois. The Last Joint Debate*

WASHINGTON: TOWERS, 1858

Lincoln did not ask for Douglas's permission to print the debates, although he offered Douglas a chance to make corrections. Douglas declined to be involved, but his supporters did distribute this pamphlet regarding the final debate. A more propagandistic treatment, it added commentary such as, "Lincoln's conduct...was most improper and ungentlemanly." The Senate seat election was decided by the Illinois General Assembly on a party-line vote: Douglas won. But the printings of their debates placed both men high in the national political firmament.

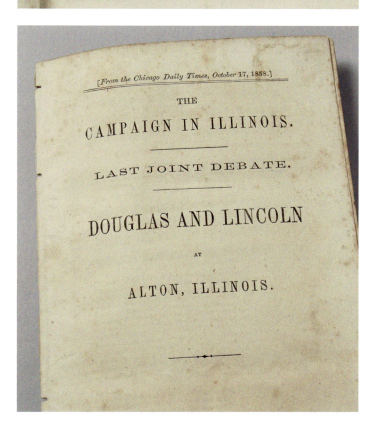

LINCOLN THE POLITICIAN · 1850 TO 1860

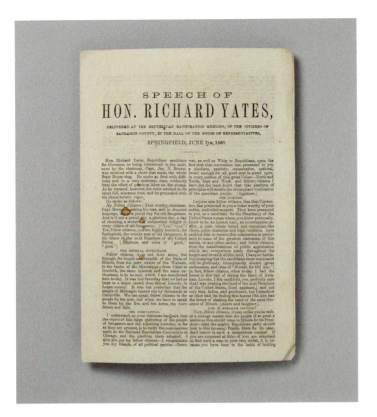

Richard Yates, "Speech…Delivered at the Republican Ratification Committee"

SPRINGFIELD [IL]: N.P., 1860

Despite losing the Senate race to Douglas in 1858, Lincoln maneuvered in 1860 to capture the Republican nomination for president. His many years as a player in Illinois politics served him well when his Republican allies secured the state to host the party's next ratifying convention. There his home-field advantage was evident from the boisterous support of the local flank. By shrewdly seeking to be the delegates' second choice, he emerged as the consensus candidate. This pamphlet is by one of Lincoln's insider allies, Richard Yates, who became governor in 1860.

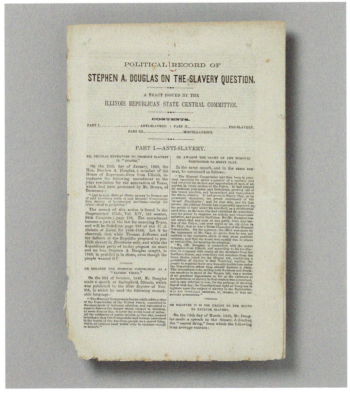

Political Record of Stephen A. Douglas

[SPRINGFIELD, IL]: ILLINOIS REPUBLICAN STATE CENTRAL COMMITTEE, 1860

Lincoln and Douglas remained political rivals in the 1860 campaign season, when each clinched their party's presidential nomination. Lincoln's Republicans viewed themselves as upstarts with a new platform to promote, which they did under the coalescing impact of Lincoln's ascendance. Douglas, on the other hand, had a lengthy record of stated views, many of which, between the 1840s and 1850s, contradicted each other, as this piercing Lincoln attack piece clearly lays out.

Salient Points of the Campaign

[SPRINGFIELD, IL]: ILLINOIS REPUBLICAN STATE CENTRAL COMMITTEE, 1860

This document links two storylines of Lincoln's run for the highest office: that he was the least experienced of the four leading contenders for the Republican nomination and that, later, when he won the presidency, he appointed these once adversaries to his cabinet. Judge Edward Bates was less well-known than the two frontrunners, William H. Seward, senator from New York, and Salmon P. Chase, governor of Ohio. But he arrived with newspaper endorsements. Here, Bates endorsed Lincoln within a month of the convention. He then served as Lincoln's attorney general.

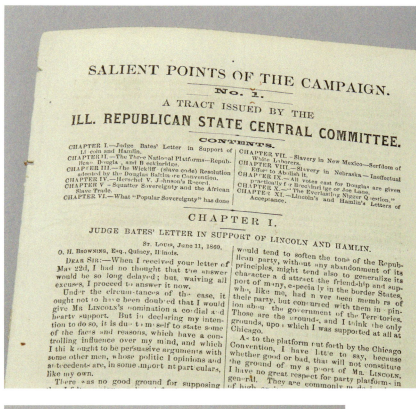

Republican Meeting

[WORCESTER, MA]: SPY CALORIC PRINTING HOUSE, 1860

By 1860 the Republican Party had ascended to a position of prominence, if not dominance, in the Northeast and what is now the Midwest (but which was then the westernmost edge of the contiguous states). This was true ideologically and politically. Ideologically, their program of free (i.e., self-determining) labor, settlement of western lands, and economic modernization found adherents. Politically, the party had electoral successes in Congress and became an organizing force at the local level, as this Massachusetts broadside demonstrates. After 1858 they were the majority in the House of Representatives and had 26 out of 66 Senate seats.

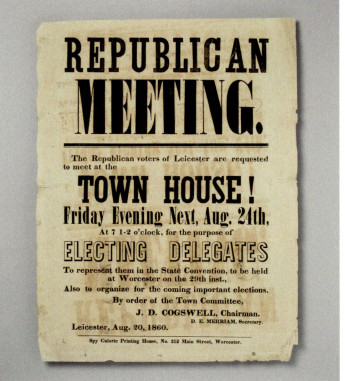

LINCOLN THE POLITICIAN · 1850 TO 1860

Lincoln the Candidate
1859 to 1860

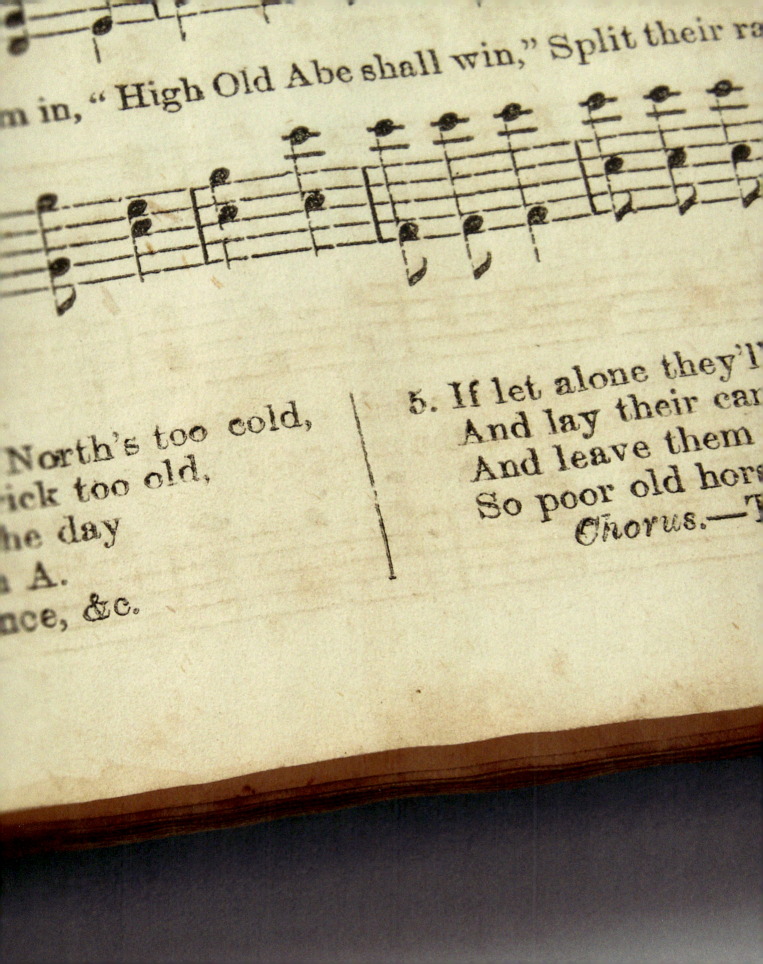

BUY THE CORRECT EDITION.

THE LIFE AND PUBLIC SERVICES

OF THE

Hon. ABRAHAM LINCOLN,

OF ILLINOIS,

REPUBLICAN CANDIDATE FOR THE PRESIDENCY.

BY D. W. BARTLETT,

Washington Correspondent of the "N. Y. Evening Post" and "Independent."

12MO. CLOTH. PRICE, $1 00.

WITH A FINE STEEL PORTRAIT.

ALSO,

A Cheap Edition of the Same, in Paper Covers,

PRICE, TWENTY-FIVE CENTS.

A GREAT CHANCE FOR AGENTS.

We want a good Agent in every county in the free States, to engage in the sale of the above work. Send us One Dollar, and we will mail you a sample copy of the book by mail, postage paid, and also a copy of our circular, giving terms to Agents by the quantity.

For Twenty-five cents, in stamps, a copy of the cheap edition will be sent, with terms, &c.

"Honest Abe, the Railsplitter"

JONATHAN EARLE

ABRAHAM LINCOLN WAS not planning to cast a ballot on November 6, 1860, the most consequential Election Day in U.S. history. To do so, he reasoned, would mean voting for himself, and the exceedingly modest candidate did not want to appear arrogant or haughty. So the lanky lawyer spent the day as he had most others during the campaign: receiving visitors in the office he kept at the Illinois State House of Representatives in Springfield, answering correspondence, and chatting with a close-knit circle of political allies and friends.

Lincoln's law partner, William Herndon, could hardly believe that the Republican nominee for the highest office in the land might not cast a ballot in the election. "Lincoln, you ought to go and vote," Herndon urged his friend, reminding him that his was not the only name on the Republican ticket and that every vote counted in what was expected to be a tight election in the state. The prodding worked, and partisans of all stripes cheered the candidate as he slowly made his way up the courthouse steps, with one Democrat going so far as to suggest casting a vote for Lincoln's opponent, Stephen A. Douglas, who, he reasoned, "has done all he could for you."

Lincoln's private secretary, John Nicolay, recalled the boisterous scene inside the polling place: "From the time he entered the room until he cast his vote and left it, wild hazzahing, the waving of hats, and all sorts of demonstrations of applause rendered all other noises insignificant and futile." In an era when political parties printed in advance partisan ballots that included the names of every candidate for office, Lincoln came up with a clever strategy for supporting other Republicans while remaining humble: the not-quite-yet-president-elect snipped off the top portion of the ballot containing his name and dropped the truncated card into the box.[1]

So was cast a single vote in this most pivotal of American elections. At the top of the ballot, the choice essentially asked voters to determine the nation's future: Should slavery's expansion be halted or allowed to continue unfettered?[2] The stakes produced a unique canvass featuring presidential nominees from four political parties instead of the typical two. But because

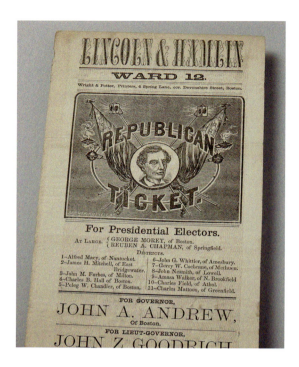

Detail from *Lincoln & Hamlin / Ward 12* (Boston: Wright & Potter, 1860). This Republican election ballot for Massachusetts shows presidential candidates at the "top of the ballot," as well as various "down ballot" office-seekers.

Pages 72–73: Detail from *The Wide-Awake Vocalist* (New York: Daggett, 1860) (see page 87)

Page 74: Rear wrapper for William H. Burleigh (editor), *The Republican Pocket Pistol* (New York: Dayton, 1860) (see page 81)

of the "winner-take-all" general ticket system used in most states, Lincoln captured a majority of the votes in the Electoral College while earning the support of slightly fewer than two in five voters nationwide.

Lincoln's election was an outcome no seasoned observer in any political party would have anticipated. D. W. Bartlett's 1859 compendium of biographical sketches of the twenty-one likeliest presidential candidates did not even include Abraham Lincoln.[3] After all, his national résumé was thin: one lackluster term in Congress, from 1847 to 1849, and then a series of headline-grabbing debates with Stephen A. Douglas, an old political rival from Illinois, as both men vied for a United States Senate seat in 1858 (Lincoln lost). But politics as usual became scrambled when, in October 1859, the abolitionist crusader John Brown invaded the slave state of Virginia and occupied the federal armory at Harpers Ferry, repository of 100,000 weapons, in a failed attempt to instigate a slave rebellion. It was an act viewed completely differently in the North and South. Many Northerners, impressed by Brown's eloquence at his trial, shocked the South with their sympathies (Ralph Waldo Emerson said Brown "has made the gallows as glorious as the cross"), while in the South, newspapers declared that violent insurrections like Brown's were the logical and inevitable outcome of Republican agitation to restrict slavery. The *Baltimore Sun*, heretofore the voice of border state moderation, resentfully announced that the South could not afford to "live under a Government, the majority of whose subjects or citizens regard John Brown as a martyr and a Christian hero, rather than a murderer and a robber."[4]

In the Republican Party, Brown's raid and the sectional crisis it provoked weakened the candidacies of prominent leaders like William H. Seward of New York and Salmon P. Chase of Ohio, who were considered to be more radical opponents of slavery, clearing the way for antislavery "moderates" like Lincoln and Edward Bates of Missouri. By the time the Republican National Convention met in 1860 to choose a nominee, Lincoln had sent a brief autobiographical sketch to his close friend Jesse Fell, who had it printed in newspapers on the East Coast. Lincoln was burnishing his reputation as a rising "man of the West," who had begun his life farming and splitting rails for fences in Indiana and Illinois, both recently admitted states from the Old Northwest. A concerted campaign by Lincoln's allies had already ensured that he was at least the second choice of many delegates. He captured the party's nomination on the third ballot after amassing enough votes switched from his opponents to far exceed the 234 needed,

CHAPTER FOUR

ending with 350 out of 466 delegates in the final round. The Democratic Party, one of the last surviving bi-sectional institutions during the deepening sectional crisis, suffered a cataclysmic split at the party's nominating convention in Charleston, South Carolina. Southern delegates were unwilling to back the candidacy of Douglas—the presumptive front-runner and only Democrat with a hope of attracting nationwide support. They instead chose to follow the radical "Fire-Eaters" out of the convention and endorse sitting Vice President John C. Breckinridge of Kentucky on the defiantly proslavery platform of the Southern Democrats. What remained of the once-mighty Democratic Party was left to nominate Douglas, while what remained of the old Whig Party formed the Constitutional Union Party and nominated John Bell of Tennessee on a platform of preserving the Union at all costs.

The centerpiece of the Republican Party's electoral appeal in the North was its unequivocal opposition to the expansion of slavery: "No new slave states" was a constant refrain on the campaign trail. Slavery, for most Republicans, was an immoral institution, a relic of "barbarism"; party members believed that confining the institution within its present boundaries condemned bondage to eventual extinction. This is not to say that Republicans were abolitionists; indeed, party candidates and opinion makers labored incessantly to separate themselves from the radicals agitating for an immediate, uncompensated end to slavery. Many Southerners, however, believed a Lincoln victory would mean an inevitable end to their "peculiar institution" because so many Republicans made this very point, repeatedly and unceasingly, in campaign literature and on the trail. After Lincoln clinched the nomination and, citing custom, withdrew from the hustings, his surrogates suggested such a plan explicitly.

Within this uncertain and evolving political landscape, Lincoln preternaturally understood the power of new media—especially photography

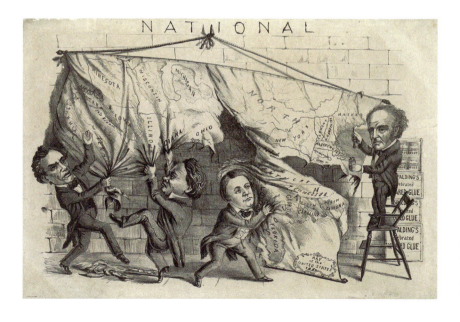

[Dividing the] National [Map] (n.p., 1860). Broadside political cartoon satirizing the 1860 election

Reynolds's Political Map of the United States (New York: Reynolds & Jones et al., ca. 1850s)

and national newspapers—to affect a political campaign. He also exploited the explosion in print culture to flood the market with a formidable series of presidential biographies. As Thomas A. Horrocks has written, these biographies successfully "packaged and promoted" evocative stories and images of the relatively unknown candidate as a compelling character who possessed essential qualities of leadership. The railroad lawyer and failed Senate hopeful was thus transformed into "Honest Abe, the Railsplitter," a homespun yet trustworthy candidate who appealed to rural Americans, new immigrants (especially German Protestants), and entrepreneurial Yankees alike.[5]

The campaign of 1860 is best understood as two separate presidential elections, one conducted in the North and one in the South. In the North, Lincoln and Douglas faced off against each other; in the South, the contest was primarily between Bell and Breckinridge. These sectionally segregated elections were almost entirely insulated from each other. In fact, the Republicans did not even appear on ballots across most of the South, and Breckinridge Democrats garnered little support north of the Mason-Dixon line. Lincoln won the election with just 39 percent of the popular vote, carrying 17 free states and their 180 electoral votes. Breckinridge won 11 slave states and their 72 electoral votes. Neither leading candidate captured a single state in the opposite section. Bell and Douglas—the only two candidates who had remotely possessed national appeal—trailed far behind, with 39 and 12 electoral votes, respectively. The majority of Americans voted for candidates who promised less, not more, compromise over the future of slavery.

Abraham Lincoln as "Railsplitter," masthead image from the *Railsplitter* newspaper, 1860

Because Lincoln's electoral victory proved that Southerners no longer controlled the levers of government necessary to preserve slavery permanently, South Carolina seceded from the Union just six weeks after the ballots were cast. Before the president-elect was able to take the oath of office, seven states had joined to form the Confederate States of America on February 8, 1861. The new president and Republican congressional majorities had been elected by Northern voters on a platform explicitly dedicated to halting the expansion of slavery. It was their coordinated exercise of the ballot that set in motion the dire crisis of the Union during the winter of 1860–61. And, as Lincoln himself would memorably say four years later, "the war came": a direct result of the choices made by the nation's voters.

NOTES

1. David Donald, *Lincoln* (New York: Simon & Schuster, 1995), 255; Donald, *Lincoln's Herndon: A Biography* (New York: Alfred A. Knopf, 1948), 143.

2. See, for example, Don E. Fehrenbacher, "The Election of 1860," in *Crucial American Elections* (Philadelphia: American Philosophical Society, 1973).

3. D. W. Bartlett, *Presidential Candidates…in 1860.* (New York: A. B. Burdick, 1859).

4. Oswald Garrison Villard, *John Brown, 1800–1859: A Biography Fifty Years After* (New York: Houghton, Mifflin and Company, 1911), 568.

5. Thomas A. Horrocks, *Lincoln's Campaign Biographies* (Carbondale: Southern Illinois University Press, 2014), 73.

THE DAVID M. RUBENSTEIN AMERICANA COLLECTION

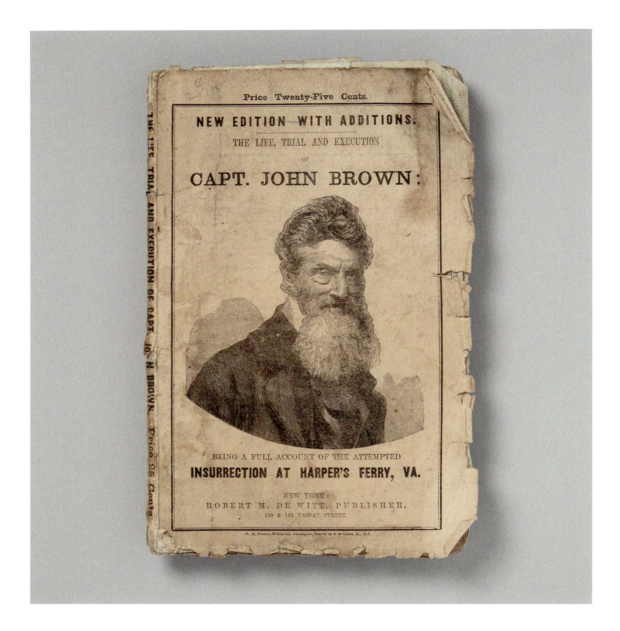

The Life, Trial and Execution of Captain John Brown
NEW YORK: DE WITT, [1859]

At the start of the 1860 presidential race, the figure who loomed the largest in American politics was not a candidate but a messianic abolitionist, who was executed by hanging in the previous December. John Brown's raid on Harper's Ferry catalyzed the country's sectional divisions. If this leader of twenty-one men could seize a government armory and try to start a slave revolt, what would stop others from attempting it? The South began viewing abolitionists as mortal foes—and viewing Republicans as abolitionists. Commentators in the North saw Brown as a martyr.

Political Text-Book for 1860

NEW YORK: TRIBUNE ASSOCIATION, 1860

A title page can say a lot. This voter handbook, printed for a Northern audience, was intended to explain the complex political landscape of the 1860 presidential election. The main issue of the day is summed up in one line: *slavery in the territories*. But disagreement on this issue had caused such widespread fracturing that the race for president became one between four separate political parties: the Republican, in their second-ever presidential contest; the Constitutional Union, in their first; the Southern Democratic, a recent breakaway group; and the old guard (Northern) Democratic.

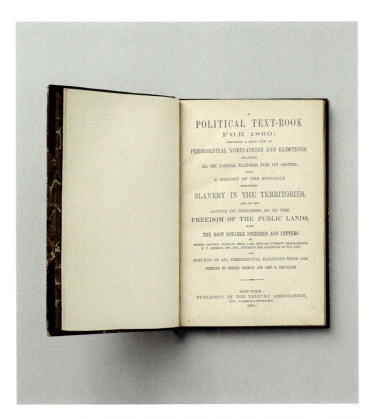

William H. Burleigh (editor), *The Republican Pocket Pistol*

NEW YORK: DAYTON, 1860

The 1860 Republican Party platform, settled on at the Illinois convention, was reprinted in Northern cities for the next few months by aligned publishing mouthpieces. Here it is as a serialized pamphlet for a New York audience. Lincoln was not on the platform-drafting committee, and this pamphlet does not mention his name. But textually the platform's language owes much to Lincoln's thought: the Declaration of Independence has the power of law, the Founders restricted slavery, Union precedes abolition, and new territories and states must be slave-free.

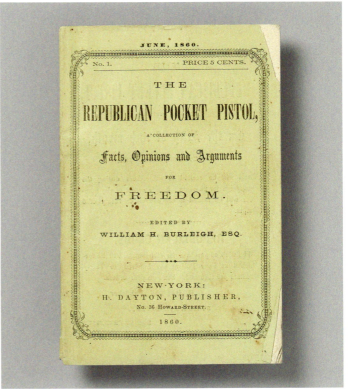

LINCOLN THE CANDIDATE · 1859 TO 1860

For President, Abram Lincoln, Republican Election Ticket, 1860

For President, John Bell, Constitutional Union Ticket, 1860

For President, John C. Breckinridge, Southern Democratic Ticket, 1860

For President, Stephen A. Douglas, Democratic Ticket, 1860

The 1860 presidential election was not merely a choice between political ideas but also one between candidates who were the embodiments of their political parties. To varying levels of success, these parties used print media to differentiate their candidates in a crowded field of four office seekers—or at least to express how they expected voters to regard them.

Paper ballots are one example of print used by political parties in the service of their campaigns. Today's state-overseen "blanket ballots," which list all candidate names, did not exist. In 1860 states could set forth the acceptable dimensions of ballots, but the ticket designs were devised by the parties and distributed not only to their electorate faithful but as a canvassing device.

While evocative imagery in campaigns was not new, the 1860 Republican Party's artful use of symbolism feels surprisingly modern. Lincoln is portrayed dually as sincere and hardworking, as both "Honest Abe" in an anodyne three-quarter portrait and as "The Railsplitter" in a wood-chopping action shot. Homesteader language (i.e., "homeless") is used for political effect.

Often, paper ballots were dealt out on voting day and at voting sites. One ballot dropped in a ballot box counted as a vote. Lincoln's opponents were John C. Breckinridge, of the proslavery Southern Democrats; John Bell, of the antisecession Constitutional Union Party; and Stephen A. Douglas, of the remnants of the Democratic Party, who championed "Popular Sovereignty."

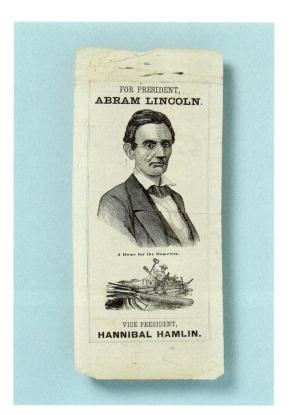
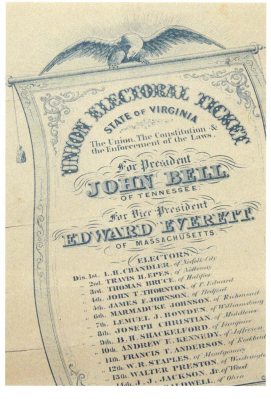
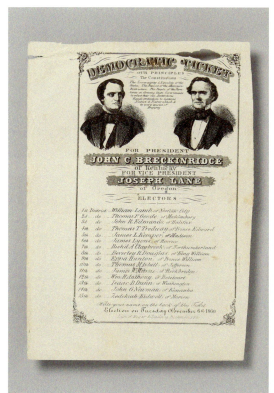
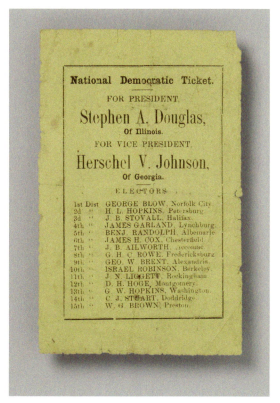

Middleton, Strobridge & Co.

Yours truly
A. Lincoln

The story of Abraham Lincoln was created by book-form campaign biographies printed for his 1860 run for president. Numbering almost thirty distinct issues, they are the first public accounts of his life. They arrived early in the election season, in multiple languages, by both hack and high-minded authors. They originated a mythology around Lincoln, which aided in his victory. Every subsequent treatment of Lincoln's life has had to question or confirm this mythology.

They were printed for two reasons. First, to popularize an insider candidate. Lincoln was not well known outside of Illinois. To the extent he was known in his state, his mere two years in national office restricted him as a backbench Republican paladin. His speeches kept him relevant, but in an era saturated with political oratory, relevancy abounded. That he was a dark horse candidate chosen by convention delegates suggested an air of mysterious origins.

Second, the campaign biographies worked in the service of the Republican Party to speak for the candidate when the candidate himself was not actively campaigning. Election decorum in 1860 typically dictated that those seeking the highest office in the land did not plead for votes. Instead, with electoral victory seemingly certain, the 1860 Republicans sought to keep together their new coalition of aligned Northern interests through the power of patriotic biography.

The biographies weave two threads: that Lincoln's life of toil and poverty was an essential part of the American West, and that he acted virtuously on every political controversy of the 1850s. The implication is one of destiny: Lincoln is on the side of history. "Lincoln himself in his history [and] character is the true offspring of a democracy," wrote one. "Not only in character but in person, is Abraham Lincoln a type of the West…the future Hoosier President," wrote another.

FRONT FLAP

Joseph Hartwell Barrett, *Life of Abraham Lincoln (of Illinois)*
CINCINNATI: MOORE [ET AL.], 1860

TOP ROW

The Life, Speeches, and Public Services of Abram Lincoln. Wigwam Edition
NEW YORK: RUDD & CARLETON, 1860

David W. Bartlett, *The Life and Public Service of Hon. Abraham Lincoln. Authorized Edition*
NEW YORK: DERBY & JACKSON, 1860

Joseph Hartwell Barrett, *Life of Abraham Lincoln (of Illinois)*
CINCINNATI: MOORE [ET AL.], 1860

[Richard J. Hinton], *Life and Public Services of Hon. Abraham Lincoln of Illinois*
BOSTON: THAYER & ELDRIDGE, 1860

Portraits and Sketches of the Lives of All the Candidates for the Presidency and Vice Presidency
NEW YORK: BUTTRE, 1860

Hanes Bywyd Abraham Lincoln, O Illinois, a Hannibal Hamlin, O Maine
POTTSVILLE [PA]: BANNAN, 1860

Elihu B. Washburne, *Abraham Lincoln, His Personal History and Public Record*
N.P.: REPUBLICAN CONGRESSIONAL COMMITTEE, [1860]

Portraits and Sketches of the Lives of All the Candidates for the Presidency and Vice Presidency
NEW YORK: BUTTRE, 1860

MIDDLE ROW

The Life and Public Services of Hon. Abraham Lincoln, of Illinois, and Hon. Hannibal Hamlin, of Maine. Wide-Awake Edition
BOSTON: THAYER & ELDRIDGE, 1860

David W. Bartlett, *The Life and Public Services of Hon. Abraham Lincoln. Authorized Edition*
NEW YORK: DAYTON, 1860

Ichabod Codding, *A Republican Manual for the Campaign*
PRINCETON [IL]: REPUBLICAN BOOK & JOB PRINTING OFFICE, 1860

Leben, Wirken und Reden des Republikanischen Präsidentschafts-Candidaten Abraham Lincoln
NEW YORK: GERHARD, 1860

William Dean Howells, *Life of Abraham Lincoln*
COLUMBUS [OH]: FOLLETT [ET AL.], 1860

BOTTOM ROW

David W. Bartlett, *The Life and Public Services of Hon. Abraham Lincoln. Authorized Edition*
NEW YORK: DERBY & JACKSON, 1860

[John Locke Scripps], *Tribune Tracks.—No. 6. Life of Abraham Lincoln*
NEW YORK: GREELEY, 1860

William Dean Howells, *Lives and Speeches of Abraham Lincoln and Hannibal Hamlin*
COLUMBUS [OH]: FOLLETT [ET AL.], 1860

James Quay Howard, *The Life of Abraham Lincoln: With Extracts from His Speeches*
COLUMBUS [OH]: FOLLETT [ET AL.], 1860

Joseph Hartwell Barrett, *Life of Abraham Lincoln. Barrett's Authentic Edition*
CINCINNATI: MOORE [ET AL.], 1860

The Republican Campaign Songster
CINCINNATI: AMERICAN PUBLISHING HOUSE, 1860

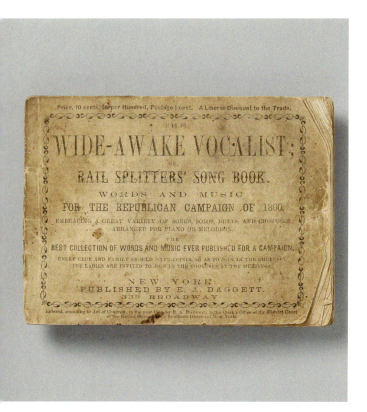

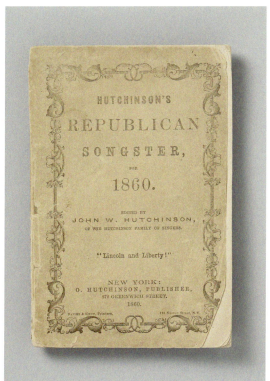

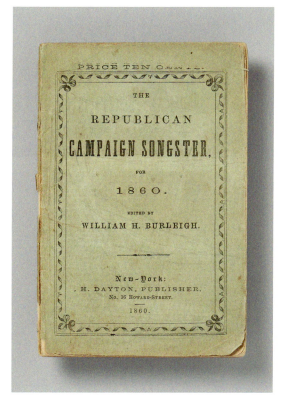

The Wide-Awake Vocalist

NEW YORK: DAGGETT, 1860

John W. Hutchinson, *Hutchinson's Republican Songster*

NEW YORK: HUTCHINSON, 1860

William H. Burleigh, *The Republican Campaign Songster*

NEW YORK: DAYTON, 1860

Republican Song Book

NEW YORK: THAYER & ELDRIDGE, 1860

Political songsters of the 1860 presidential campaign emerged from the popular and vernacular musical traditions of the nineteenth century. In this era before recording technology, nonreligious music was performed publicly for both entertainment and social cohesion. Printed songs could have staff notation (i.e., for instruments) with new musical arrangements, but more often they were low-cost booklets that offered new lyrics set to well-known melodies from the folk ballad and minstrelsy repertoires. Political songsters offered topical lyrics agitating for a cause.

The 1860 Republican songsters boosted their candidate and mocked his rivals, just as songsters for two of Lincoln's rivals, Douglas and Bell, did (we know of none for Breckinridge). In Lincoln's songsters the West plays an outsized role, as in "The Neb-Rascality" and "The Song of the Kansas Emigrant." Lincoln is sung of as the "Western Star" and the "Wood-Chopper of the West." The songs were distributed at rallies and sung by members of the recently formed Republican youth militia called the Wide Awakes, who would serve as bodyguards for antislavery speakers.

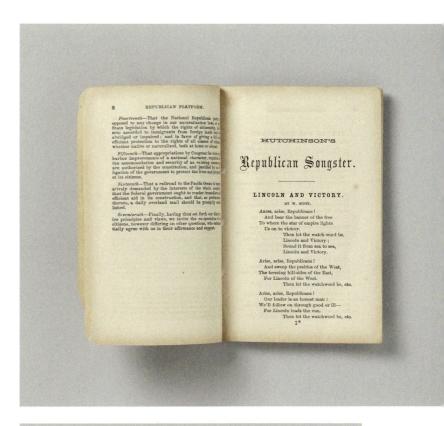

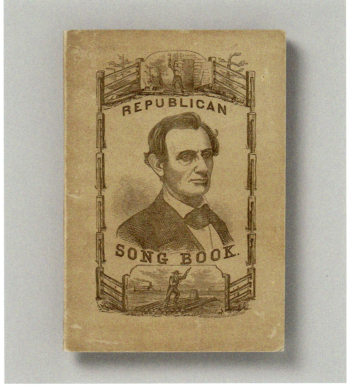

LINCOLN THE CANDIDATE · 1859 TO 1860

Lincoln the Chosen
1860 to 1861

WIGWAM AT CHICAGO,

Republican Ticket.

LINCOLN & HAMLIN.

For Electors of President and Vice-President,

John Sullivan,
Ebenezer Stevens,
David Gillis,
Nathaniel Tolles,
Daniel Blaisdell.

"Faith That Right Makes Might"

HAROLD HOLZER

NOT UNTIL MID-1859 did Abraham Lincoln—by then a twice-failed candidate for the United States Senate—admit that he now aspired to the presidency. "Why don't you run me?" he reportedly told friends. "I can be nominated, I can be elected, and I can run the government."[1] To the skeptical, Lincoln's résumé hardly encouraged such confidence. He had served but a single term in the House of Representatives. His military experience had been so uneventful that he referred to it only jokingly.[2] Other Republicans were better known and better qualified.

Still, Lincoln had earned a strong national reputation during his recent Senate campaign debates with Stephen A. Douglas. Although he had lost the 1858 contest, Lincoln won several 1859 invitations to address Republicans in states neighboring Illinois. Barnstorming through Iowa, Wisconsin, Kansas, Indiana, and Ohio, he declared: "We want, and must have, a national policy, as to slavery, which deals with it as being a wrong."[3] In a fragment composed before speaking in Indianapolis, he added, "Free labor has the inspiration of hope; pure slavery has no hope." His speeches stimulated a new round of press attention. Republicans fared well wherever Lincoln visited. And in mid-October, he returned home to an enthusiastic welcome from a "vast multitude" of local supporters.[4] Awaiting him, too, was a momentum-building invitation to address the Young Men's Central Republican Union at Brooklyn's Plymouth Church.[5] That abolitionist shrine would be hosting a series of lectures by western Republicans auditioning to be potential alternatives to presidential favorite William H. Seward of New York. Some party men believed the senator was too radical to win a general election for the White House, even if Lincoln's own friends believed the nomination was headed irrevocably "Sewardward."[6]

Having never spoken in the New York area, Lincoln seized this opportunity and shrewdly arranged to appear last on the schedule, settling on February 27, 1860. The delay gave him time to research and write a 7,500-word masterpiece that deployed both historical evidence and emotional persuasion to justify limitations on slavery. Lincoln did not know until

The Cooper Institute, New York (n.p., ca. 1859). Wood engraving

his arrival that the location had been shifted from Brooklyn to Manhattan—to the newly opened Cooper Union (or Institute), barely a mile from the city's "Newspaper Row." Before the event, Lincoln visited Mathew Brady's studio on Lower Broadway, where the celebrated photographer made an iconic portrait of Lincoln. Brady's posing emphasized his subject's commanding stature, gauzed over his homely facial features, and placed him evocatively between symbolic props: a pillar to signify statesmanship and a stack of books to suggest wisdom. The result would become the standard image of Lincoln for the 1860 campaign.[7]

The Cooper Union Address proved to be a triumph. Before 1,500 spectators, Lincoln reiterated his opposition to slavery but pledged he would not interfere with it where it already existed. He argued that John Brown's recent abolitionist raid on Harpers Ferry in Virginia did not represent his party's moderate principles and predicted (overoptimistically) that Republicans could compete politically in the South. Above all, he demonstrated that the nation's Founders believed the federal government would always have the power to regulate slavery and restrict its extension into the territories. Lincoln concluded on a moral high note, perhaps inspired by Frederick Douglass's recent editorial comment: "Slavery...shields itself behind *might*, rather than right." Lincoln told his Cooper Union audience, "LET US HAVE FAITH THAT RIGHT MAKES MIGHT."[8]

The elite crowd, dubious at first about the ill-clad speaker with the Hoosier twang, erupted in cheers when he finished. The next day, four local newspapers published Lincoln's magnum opus in full. Horace Greeley, the influential anti-Seward editor of the pro-Republican *New-York Daily Tribune*, added, "No man ever before made such an impression on his first appeal to a New-York audience."[9] Mathew Brady later remembered Lincoln claiming that his photograph "and the Cooper Institute speech made me president."[10]

Following his success, Lincoln headed north for a series of orations in New England, but, except for one more speech at Bloomington, Illinois, he thereafter retreated into unaccustomed public silence.[11] Not until late April, just weeks before Republicans headed to Chicago to choose their standard-bearer, did Lincoln go on record about his White House ambitions. He confided to an ally, "The taste *is* in my mouth a little," but hastened to add, "Let no eye but your own see this."[12]

Pages 88–89: Detail from J. Q. Howard, *The Life of Abraham Lincoln* (Columbus, OH: Follett et al., 1860)

Page 90: 1860 Republican ballot for New Hampshire

Lincoln's reticence masked many months of behind-the-scenes maneuvering. Having locked up the crucial support of the powerful *Chicago Daily Press and Tribune*, Lincoln parlayed its blessing into a favorite-son presidential endorsement from home-state Republicans. Supporters meanwhile argued that Lincoln's log cabin origins and hardscrabble youth provided perfect ingredients for a "hullabaloo" campaign: they put focus on the candidate's personal virtues while minimizing contentious discussion of slavery and equal rights for Blacks (an issue that plagued Lincoln in his recent

92   CHAPTER FIVE

Mathew B. Brady, Abraham Lincoln, photographed hours before delivering his Cooper Union Address, New York City, 1860. Gelatin silver print

senate race). To dramatize his rise from obscurity, his backwoods cousin marched into a party meeting at Decatur, Illinois, toting two log rails allegedly split by a young Lincoln working on the prairie.[13]

Before the 1860 Republican National Convention gaveled into order, Lincoln hit on an ingenious strategy to attract delegates: do nothing to offend their "first love" while remaining within striking distance should Seward falter.[14] Lincoln's backers packed the convention hall with enthusiasts and instructed them to raise the roof at every mention of his name. The plan worked perfectly, facilitated by the last-minute promise of cabinet positions to delegate-rich states.[15] On the third ballot, Lincoln secured the nomination.

LINCOLN THE CHOSEN · 1860 TO 1861

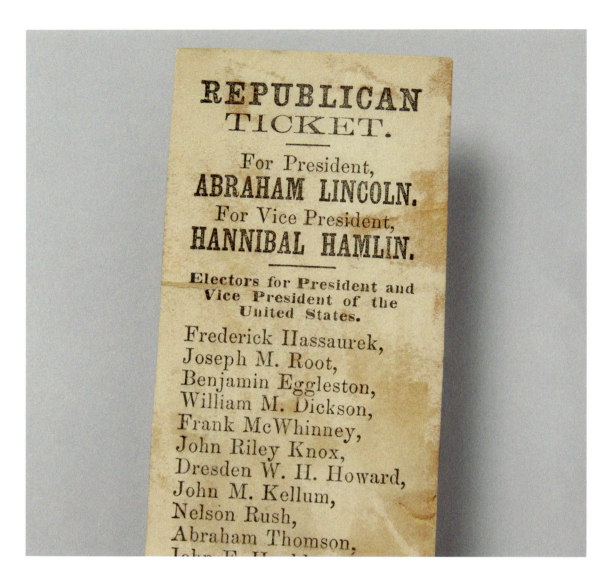

1860 Republican ballot for Ohio

He eagerly embraced the Republican platform, which called for continued immigration, high protective tariffs, free homestead land, a transcontinental railroad, and, above all, an absolute ban on the spread of slavery. While surrogates began campaigning for him tirelessly, the candidate continued holding his tongue, save for when he gave a brief, unplanned greeting in August at a rally in Springfield, Illinois, where he reiterated his vow to "make no speeches."[16] Three months later, on Election Day, with Democratic Party opposition split, Lincoln won a commanding electoral vote majority, though his popular vote total reached only 40 percent and came almost exclusively from the North.

The sectional nature of Lincoln's victory—and the resulting decision by South Carolina to break from the Union—plunged the country into what Henry Adams called the "Great Secession Winter."[17] As additional slave states quit the Union, Lincoln faced the gravest crisis ever to confront a president-elect, but was constitutionally powerless to act and remained personally reluctant to speak.[18] In the void, Northerners wondered about his intentions: Would he conciliate the South? Would he solidify his base by coercing secessionists? Was he even up to the task awaiting him?

Publicly—and ironically, for a politician who had made his reputation as a skilled speaker—Lincoln clung to a strategy that became known as "masterly inactivity," insisting that further comments by him were sure to "excite the contempt of good men, and encourage bad ones to clamor the more loudly."[19] In confidential letters to congressional Republicans, however, Lincoln was steadfast, instructing them to "hold firm, as with a chain of steel" against slavery's extension. He urged Senator Lyman Trumbull: "Let there be no compromise . . . The tug has to come, & better now, than any time hereafter."[20] Had Lincoln agreed to concessions, slavery might have endured to the end of the century with no guarantee that the Union would have endured permanently in return. To yield, Lincoln moreover believed, would suggest "slavery has equal rights with liberty."[21]

Honest old Abe on the Stump. Springfield 1858. Honest old Abe on the Stump, at the ratification Meeting of Presidential Nominations. Springfield 1860, (n.p., ca. 1860). Lithograph on wove paper

John Wood, *Inauguration of Mr. Lincoln, March 4. Washington D.C., 1861*, ca. 1861. Photographic print

In assembling his cabinet, Lincoln did appoint two men from the slave-holding border states of the Upper South: Missourian Edward Bates as attorney general and Maryland's Montgomery Blair as postmaster general. Beyond that, he confidently filled his official family with leading Northerners like Seward as secretary of state, Ohio's Salmon P. Chase as secretary of the treasury, and Pennsylvania's Simon Cameron as secretary of war. All were better-known former rivals for the Republican presidential nod.[22]

Lincoln otherwise spent most of the four-month interregnum conferring with Republican leaders; welcoming visitors bearing gifts, advice, and endless requests for federal patronage jobs; and posing for photographers and artists.[23] Lincoln believed that doing any more—or traveling to Washington, DC, earlier than required, as some had suggested—might imperil the counting of electoral votes in Congress on February 13. That risk-filled joint session was to be presided over by a Southern Democrat who had run against him, outgoing Vice President John C. Breckinridge—a toxic recipe for insurrection. But the much-feared effort to overturn the election never materialized.

After spending his final days in Springfield drafting his inaugural address and modifying his frontier image by growing avuncular whiskers, Lincoln departed on February 11, 1861. Bidding his neighbors an emotional farewell, he asked for God's help but defied political tradition by comparing himself to the first president, asserting that he had "a task before me greater than that which rested upon Washington."[24] At a hundred stops along his thirteen-day rail journey to the White House, out of practice though he may have been, the gifted orator proceeded to delight audiences across the North with charming extemporaneous remarks. ("I have stepped out upon this platform that I may see you and that you may see me," the homely Lincoln joked to one crowd, "and in the arrangement I have the best of the bargain").[25] In all, he appeared in front of more people than had ever before glimpsed an American leader. To his aide John Hay, it seemed as if Lincoln traveled "upon the crest of one continued wave of cheers."[26]

But Lincoln faltered in his first formal speeches, at one point ludicrously questioning whether a crisis truly existed.[27] Regaining his footing once he reached the East, he delivered impassioned remarks at two cradles of American liberty, Trenton and Philadelphia. At Independence Hall on Washington's birthday, he declared, "I would rather be assassinated on this spot than to surrender it."[28] Only a few hours earlier, he had learned that an assassination plot indeed awaited him once he crossed the Mason-Dixon line. Reluctantly, he altered his schedule and proceeded through Baltimore overnight, in secret and, according to an exaggerated report in the *New York Times*, in disguise. Lincoln came to regret the decision to travel incognito, especially after it ignited ridicule, but the deception got him safely to the nation's capital.[29]

Once in Washington, Lincoln reassuringly made his presence known to all three branches of government, as well as the military. He visited outgoing President James Buchanan at the White House, met with General-in-Chief Winfield Scott (who gave assurance that he would safeguard the inauguration), and paid courtesy calls on Congress and even the Supreme Court justices who had issued the baleful Dred Scott decision that he had long criticized. Lincoln also greeted members of the so-called Peace Conference assembled in Washington to explore a compromise between the North and South. The President-elect again made it clear that he remained unwilling to accept the extension of slavery.[30]

Meanwhile, Lincoln invited prominent men to review his inaugural address. William Seward, using red ink, suggested softening elements he thought too bellicose (including the original closing line: "Shall it be peace, or a sword?").[31] As a substitute, Seward drafted a nostalgic call for unity emphasizing the country's shared history. Lincoln embraced the idea but massaged it into near poetry. Seward's prosaic text ended up as Lincoln's oft-quoted appeals to the "mystic chords of memory" and "the better angels of our nature."[32]

The words did nothing to reverse disunion. Instead, the seven seceded states formed a government of their own and chose Jefferson Davis as its president. Lincoln still considered secession a constitutional impossibility but refused to act aggressively to suppress it. For his first five weeks as chief executive, he awaited the South's next move. It came on April 9, 1861, when Confederate forces opened fire on Fort Sumter, a federal citadel in Charleston Harbor that Lincoln had refused to abandon, pledged not to rearm, but craftily decided to resupply, provoking the attack.

THE DAVID M. RUBENSTEIN AMERICANA COLLECTION

Abraham Lincoln, *Tribune Tracts.— No. 4., Speech…Delivered at the Cooper Institute*

NEW YORK: NEW YORK TRIBUNE, 1860

Lincoln's 1860 speech at New York's Cooper Union made him a political star. The event's Republican organizers had already hosted other party names as viable presidential contenders. What the audience heard on the night of February 27 was a tour de force of historical research and political thought, of rhetoric and deduction. In a single speech, Lincoln defined what antislavery Americans were fighting for and essentialized proslavery factions as contrary to the Constitution, the Founders, the Union, political moderation, and moral standards.

This and the following four pamphlets are different printings of Lincoln's 1860 Cooper Union speech.

TRIBUNE TRACTS.—No. 4.

National Politics.

SPEECH
OF
ABRAHAM LINCOLN,
OF ILLINOIS,

DELIVERED AT THE COOPER INSTITUTE, MONDAY, FEB. 27, 1860.

Mr. President and Fellow-Citizens of New York: The facts with which I shall deal this evening are mainly old and familiar; nor is there anything new in the general use I shall make of them. If there shall be any novelty, it will be in the mode of presenting the facts, and the inferences and observations following that presentation.

In his speech last autumn, at Columbus, Ohio, as reported in "The New York Times," Senator Douglas said:

"Our fathers, when they framed the Government under which we live, understood this question just as well, and even better, than we do now."

I fully indorse this, and I adopt it as a text for this discourse. I so adopt it because it furnishes a precise and an agreed starting point for a discussion between Republicans and that wing of Democracy headed by Senator Douglas. It simply leaves the inquiry: "What was the understanding those fathers had of the question mentioned?"

What is the frame of Government under which we live?

The answer must be: "The Constitution of the United States." That Constitution consists of the original, framed in 1787 (and under which the present Government first went into operation), and twelve subsequently framed amendments, the first ten of which were framed in 1789.

Who were our fathers that framed the Constitution? I suppose the "thirty-nine" who signed the original instrument may be fairly called our fathers who framed that part of the present Government. It is almost exactly true to say they framed it, and it is altogether true to say they fairly represented the opinion and sentiment of the whole nation at that time. Their names, being familiar to nearly all, and accessible to quite all, need not now be repeated.

I take these "thirty-nine," for the present, as being "our fathers who framed the Government under which we live."

What is the question which, according to the text, those fathers understood just as well, and even better than we do now?

It is this: Does the proper division of local from federal authority, or anything in the Constitution, forbid our Federal Government to control as to slavery in our Federal Territories?

Upon this, Douglas holds the affirmative, and Republicans the negative. This affirma-

☞ For Sale at the Office of the New York Tribune. Price, per Single Copy, 4c.
Dozen Copies, 25c.; per Hundred, $1 25; per Thousand, $10.

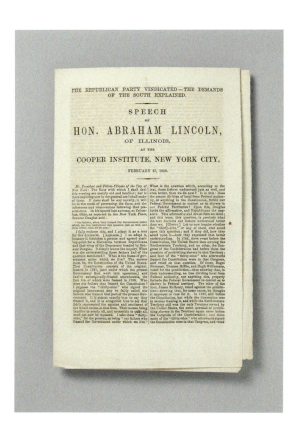

Abraham Lincoln, *The Republican Party Vindicated…Speech of Hon. Abraham Lincoln*

[WASHINGTON]: REPUBLICAN EXECUTIVE CONGRESSIONAL COMMITTEE, 1860

The risk for Lincoln was that an urbane audience would not approve of his style. The opposite happened; the speech's popularity—that night and in print beginning the next day—was due to its strength as a punchy, lawyerly, interrogative deliverance. The speech appeared in newspapers and pamphlets in the North, Midwest, and West Coast. Its logic demonstrated that the creation of the United States, as written in its original laws and as realized by its original statesmen, was linked to the end of slavery by the powers granted to the government to restrict slavery's growth.

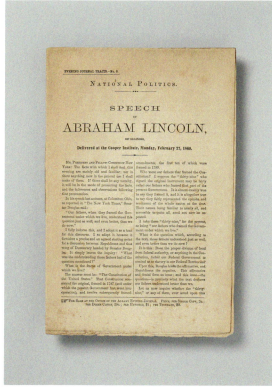

Abraham Lincoln, *Evening Journal Tracts.—No. 5…Speech of Abraham Lincoln*

ALBANY [NY]: ALBANY EVENING JOURNAL, 1860

The first half of Lincoln's 7,500-word Cooper Union speech concluded that most of the Founders were against slavery. Following that, he contrasted the qualities of the parties from the North and South. Lincoln's Republicans follow the Founders' instructions, and so are true conservatives; they wish only for reasonable debate, so they are not extremists like John Brown; they want to be on all ballots, so they cannot be sectionalists. Lincoln had checkmated the South: either be the opposite of conservative, reasonable, and nationalistic or agree with the conclusions of his speech.

Abraham Lincoln, *The Address... Delivered at Cooper Institute*

NEW YORK: YOUNG MEN'S REPUBLICAN UNION, 1860

By speaking in the first-person plural ("We respect that warning of [George] Washington"; "we have constantly protested our purpose"; etc.), Lincoln gave voice to a party yet unified around a logic so eloquent as his. His last 1,000 words spoke directly to Republicans, concluding with the now-famous capitalization, "LET US HAVE FAITH THAT RIGHT MAKES MIGHT." Of the many 1860 pamphlet printings of his speech, perhaps the most interesting is this one, printed by the Young Men's Republican Union, the sponsors of the event, which provides thirty-eight footnotes of legal gloss.

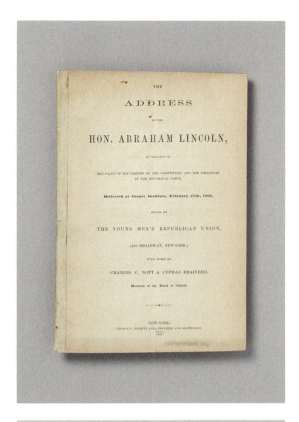

Abraham Lincoln, *Speech...at the Cooper Institute*

[SAN FRANCISCO: DAILY GAZETTE, 1860]

Lincoln had wisely postponed his New York speech to late winter when the 1860 presidential election season began. He premised the speech as a refutation of a recent article written by Stephen A. Douglas (see page 64, bottom). Lincoln's success at Cooper Union not only put him in the offing as a candidate for the Republican Convention in May; it made him an obvious national answer to Douglas's foil as the probable Democratic nominee. Evidence is this 1860 California printing of the speech. After New York, the country realized its need for Lincoln.

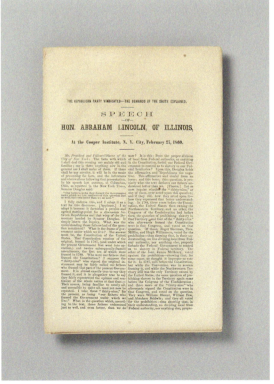

LINCOLN THE CHOSEN · 1860 TO 1861

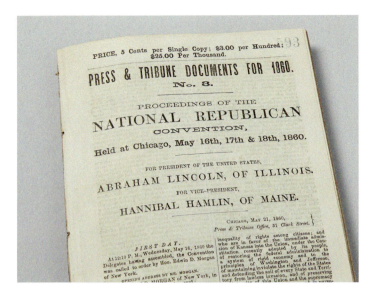

Proceedings of the National Republican Convention

CHICAGO: PRESS & TRIBUNE OFFICE, 1860

At the May 1860 Republican Convention, Lincoln emerged as his party's presidential nominee. He was chosen as a candidate who could appeal to both moderate and radical voters in the North and West. His selection was prudent after the rival Democrats had halved into factions in their convention two weeks earlier, suggesting favorable electoral conditions for a unifying alternative. Lincoln was also the candidate on whom the very geographically diverse delegates could agree; before then, the Republicans were more united in opposition to slavery than behind a leader.

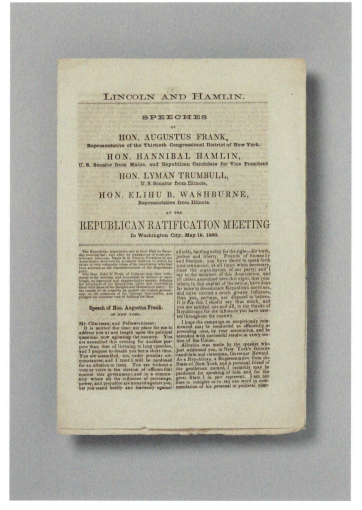

Lincoln and Hamlin. Speeches…at the Republican Ratification Meeting in Washington City

[WASHINGTON: REPUBLICAN ASSOCIATION OF WASHINGTON CITY, 1860]

Lincoln did not attend the convention. His popularity following Cooper Union and his debates against Douglas granted cover for his allies to use tactics to get delegates to vote for him. They promised cabinet positions; they seized chairs reserved for out-of-town contingents; they hired shouters to yell his name. On the third ballot, Lincoln won by receiving nearly all votes except those from delegates backing the man most observers thought would win: Senator William H. Seward of New York. Lincoln was deemed the less radical choice, the less likely to spark a civil war.

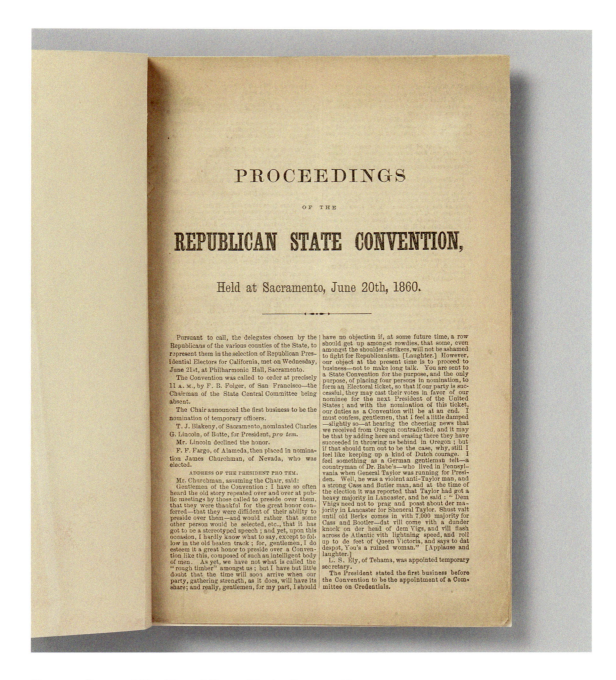

Proceedings of the Republican State Convention
SACRAMENTO: [CALIFORNIA REPUBLICAN PARTY], 1860

These three printings show how Lincoln's momentum emanated from Chicago into the East and West. As various Republican city chapters held their ratification meetings to endorse the party's platform, they read and heard speeches praising Lincoln's virtues. By Election Day on November 6, the party had unified behind him. The result was mathematical inevitability: although Lincoln won only 40 percent of the popular vote, he received all the Electoral College votes from the North (180), while his three opponents split the votes (123) from the Southern and border states.

LINCOLN THE CHOSEN · 1860 TO 1861

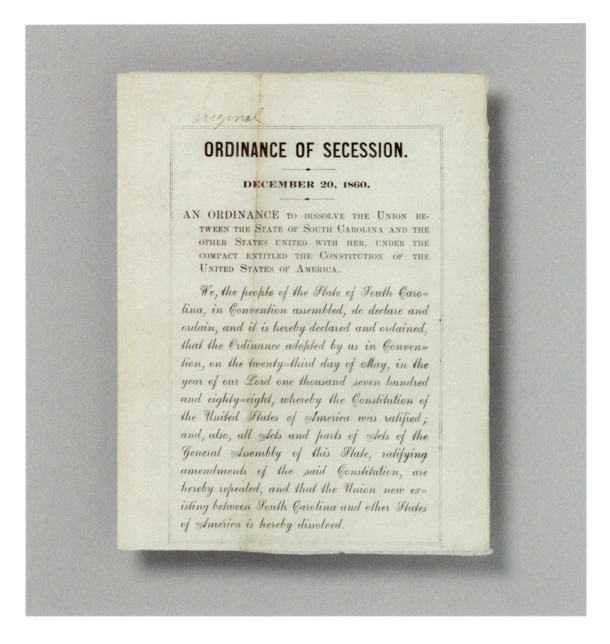

[South Carolina Secession Convention], *Ordinance of Secession*

[CHARLESTON, SC: EVANS & COGSWELL], 1860

No printing from 1860 better represents the consequence of Lincoln's presidential victory than South Carolina's "Ordinance of Secession." It was a fundamentalist, proslavery action. The South had already left the Democrats because the party platform did not include a federal slave code. Now a Southern state premised disuniting from the country because the president-elect opposed slavery. Four days after Lincoln won, South Carolina's two senators withdrew from Congress in protest; on November 13 it began mustering its state militias. The outgoing U.S. president, James Buchanan, did nothing, as his cabinet fractured over Southern sovereignty.

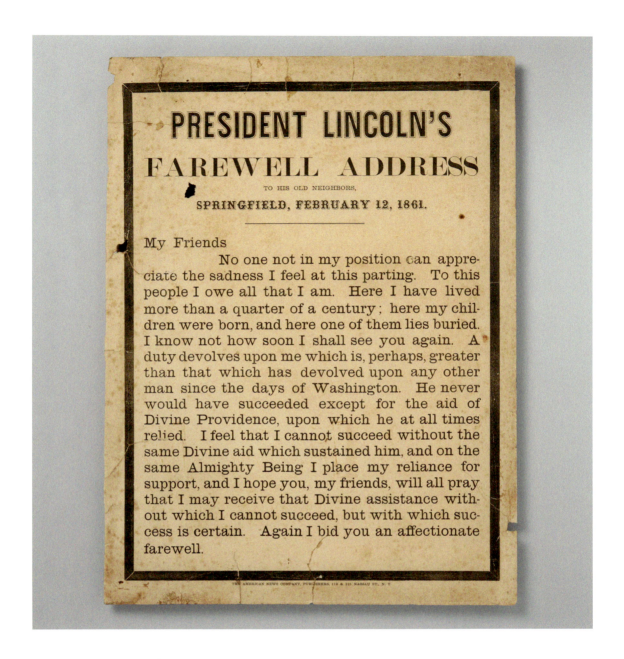

Abraham Lincoln, "Farewell Address"

NEW YORK: AMERICAN NEWS, [PRINTED LATER, CA. 1865]

By the time Lincoln left Illinois for the White House, seven U.S. states had withdrawn from the Union; (federal) Fort Sumter in Charleston Harbor had heard Southern artillery warning shots; four members of Buchanan's cabinet had resigned over his dithering on secession; and the secessionists had formed a "confederacy" with a president and a provisional constitution. Upon embarking at the Springfield, Illinois, railroad station, Lincoln improvised a short speech that acknowledged the challenges awaiting him as president. Three versions exist, as they were either transcribed by journalists or recollected by Lincoln and his staff during their trip by train to Washington.

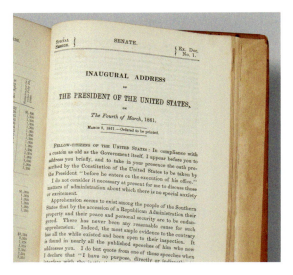

Abraham Lincoln, "Inaugural Address," *Senate Documents*
WASHINGTON: GOVERNMENT PRINTING OFFICE, 1861

Lincoln became president on March 4, 1861. Before being sworn in, he gave his First Inaugural Address, devoting it entirely to the secession crisis. It was the linguistic equivalent of an optical illusion: one could view it two ways. As historians have noted, he seemed to placate the South; he would not "interfere with the institution of slavery in the States where it exists." This language was the old Lincoln—he always said this. The new Lincoln was a resolute executive who had no choice but to enforce the Constitution, a contract that does not allow states to withdraw from it unilaterally. In his enforcement, there would be no bloodshed "unless it be forced upon the national authority." There would be no invasion "beyond what may be necessary" to secure federal posts.

Union Ball 1860 [Inaugural Invitation]
WASHINGTON: PHILP & SOLOMONS, [1860 OR] 1861

The inauguration had an audience of 25,000, mostly well-wishers and dignitaries. However, Lincoln's speech was not meant for them. In attendance was the outgoing president, James Buchanan, who had written that Lincoln's "antecedents...justify the fears of the South." The chief justice swearing in Lincoln was Roger B. Taney, who issued the Dred Scott decision. Also present was Stephen A. Douglas, who, to his disdain, held Lincoln's hat during the speech. Lincoln spoke to the South and barely hid his contempt for their absurdity: The Constitution prohibits fugitive slaves—but also the import of slaves. Secession is "anarchy"—splintered states can only keep splintering into oblivion. And what about geography? The states "can not but remain face to face."

Lincoln & Hamlin Inauguration Ball [Dance Card]
N.P.: N.P., 1861

In the evening of Inauguration Day, guests were invited to a celebration at the so-called Union Ball, held in a massive wooden hall constructed in the weeks since Lincoln's victory. Meant to be temporary, it became an army garrison for the whole of the war to come. Shown here are an invitation to the event, accomplished in ink, and an unused dance card for a lady. As the festivities carried on, the South was busy elsewhere. The Confederacy's first general, P. G. T. Beauregard, had just arrived in Charleston, South Carolina, and began building its defenses. A congress of Confederate delegates had been meeting in Alabama for a month to form their new government. But in Washington the Republicans were celebrating their first president.

President and Cabinet [Albumen Carte de Visite]

N.P.: N.P., CA. 1861

Lincoln formed his government's cabinet the same way he won the nomination and presidency: unifying diverse political power centers under a shared political goal. The top posts in his administration went to the four men with the most delegates (besides Lincoln's) at the Republican Convention. Each was from a different state; each occupied a different position on the political spectrum; and each had been the others' opponent at different times. William H. Seward, senator from New York, was made secretary of state; Salmon P. Chase, governor of Ohio, was secretary of the treasury; Simon Cameron, senator from Pennsylvania, became secretary of war; and Edward Bates, the former Missouri congressman, attorney general.

CONSTITUTION

OF THE

CONFEDERATE STATES OF AMERICA.

We, the people of the Confederate States, each State acting in its sovereign and independent character, in order to form a permanent Federal Government, establish justice, insure domestic tranquility, and secure the blessings of liberty to ourselves and our posterity—invoking the favor and guidance of Almighty God—do ordain and establish this Constitution for the Confederate States of America.

ARTICLE I.

SECTION I.

All legislative powers herein delegated shall be vested in a Congress of the Confederate States, which shall consist of a Senate and House of Representatives.

SECTION II.

1. The House of Representatives shall be composed of members chosen every second year by the people of the several States; and the electors in each State shall be citizens of the Confederate States, and have the qualifications requisite for electors of the most numerous branch of the State Legislature; but no person of foreign birth, not a citizen of the Confederate States, shall be allowed to vote for any officer, civil or political, State or Federal.

2. No person shall be a representative, who shall not have attained the age of twenty-five years, and be a citizen of the Confederate States, and who shall not, when elected, be an inhabitant of that State in which he shall be chosen.

3. Representatives and direct taxes shall be apportioned among the several States, which may be included within this Confederacy, according to their respective numbers, which shall be determined by adding to the whole number of free persons, including those bound to service for a term of years, and excluding Indians not taxed, three fifths of all slaves. The actual enumeration shall be made within three years after the first meeting of the Congress of the Confederate States, and within every subsequent term of ten years, in such manner as they shall

Constitution of the Confederate States of America

RICHMOND [VA]: ELLIOTT, 1861

Exactly one week after Lincoln's inauguration, on March 11, the Confederate states adopted a permanent constitution. The paradox was that the U.S. Constitution, on which it was based, had replaced the flawed charter of an earlier, unsuccessful American confederation. Indeed, this new government was a loose coalition of states unified by the absolutism of slavery (a word used nine times here but never in the federal original). Under the new law, slave owners could travel with their slaves without the risk of forfeiting them. A slave in one state was a slave in all. And if the Confederacy acquired new territory, slavery there was ensured. The Confederate constitution preserved the decrees of the Dred Scott Decision, the Kansas-Nebraska Act, and the Fugitive Slave Act.

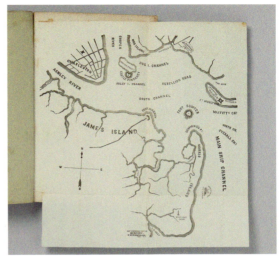

The Battle of Fort Sumter and First Victory of the Southern Troops

CHARLESTON [SC]: EVANS & COGSWELL, 1861

Secession became Civil War on April 12, when the Confederate military fired on Fort Sumter, a partially built island fortification at the mouth of Charleston Harbor, which had been occupied since December by about eighty-five U.S. Army troops. After the last election, the South began seizing federal assets: post offices, lighthouses, mint branches, etc. Fort Sumter was a garrison in the then most northern seceded state, and the Confederates, after surrounding it with over five hundred men, wanted Lincoln to surrender it. To capitulate, Lincoln risked losing the support of the North. To send in the navy, Lincoln would be the aggressor, and so risked losing more slave states to the Confederacy. Lincoln chose a third way: he sent a small squadron captained by a civilian delivering food.

Within Fort Sumter; Or, a View of Major Anderson's Garrison Family

NEW YORK: TIBBALS, 1861

Major Robert Anderson, the commander at Fort Sumter, had supplies to last until April 15. The supply squadron arrived in the early morning of April 12. Just as it entered the harbor, the South fired the first shots; learning of it ahead of time, they viewed the convoy as a Northern aggression. What followed was thirty-four hours of continued Confederate cannon fire, punctuated by the occasional return volley of an outgunned army. By the 14th, the fort was demolished, but before there were casualties, Anderson evacuated his troops. He was ferried back to New York by the squadron's ships and was received as the Union's first hero of the conflict. The Confederacy celebrated the defense of its self-declared sovereign territory. The Civil War had begun within forty days of Lincoln's presidency.

LINCOLN THE CHOSEN · 1860 TO 1861

Lincoln the Wartime President, Part I
1861 to 1863

FOURTH AND FINAL ROUND.
Ab am ca ches Jeff "in chancery," and pummels Secession out of him

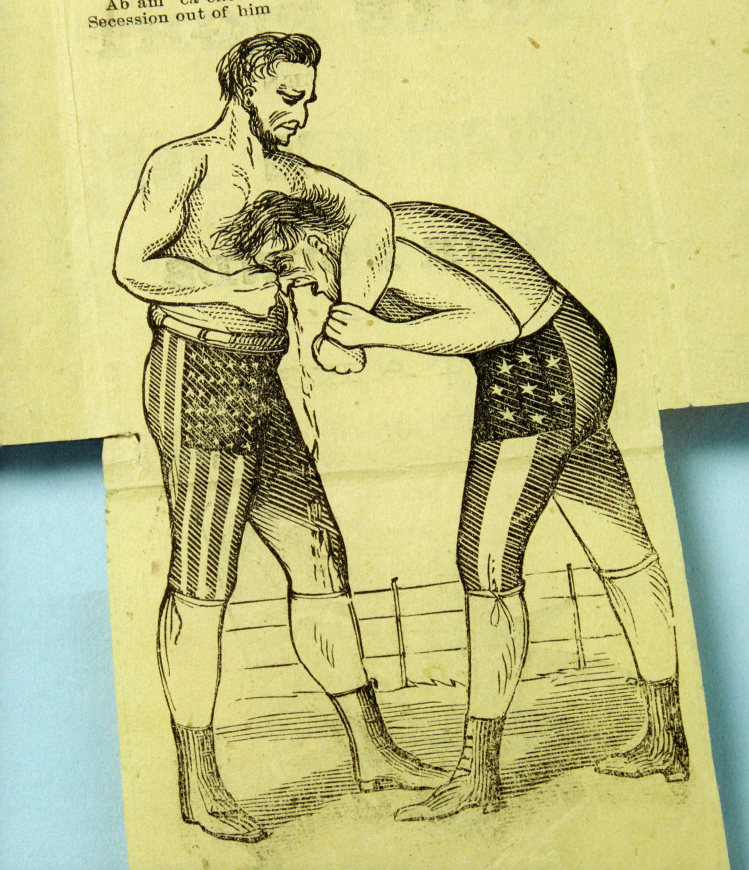

"The Sharp Discipline of Civil War"

CHANDRA MANNING

PRIOR TO BECOMING PRESIDENT, Abraham Lincoln's thinking on his country's central problems was that he despised slavery, loved the Union, and accepted, in a nod to conventional wisdom, that preserving the latter depended on tolerating the former. When he ran for president in 1860, Lincoln's campaign platform promised to stop the expansion of slavery but also to leave the authority over its future to the states where it already existed. Even when states seceded from the United States rather than accept the election of a candidate opposed to slavery's growth, Lincoln continued to acknowledge that saving the Union and ending slavery were separate—even opposite—goals. Then came the Civil War, which swept away this false distinction. From his position in office, President Lincoln's observations of slaves and freedpeople in the nation's capital intensified his longstanding antislavery principles and persuaded him that saving the Union could only be achieved by removing the cause of its breakup: slavery. The new clarity did not come gently. Instead, Lincoln's abiding willingness to face the suffering and loss caused by war shaped his emerging conviction that saving the Union and ending slavery were inseparable and enabled him to lead the nation through the crisis that did both.

Lincoln consistently hated slavery, even as he held complicated views on race. "If slavery is not wrong, then nothing is wrong," he insisted.[1] Slavery concentrated wealth and power and made a mockery of the nation's Founders and their ideals. Most of all, Lincoln reviled slavery "because of the monstrous injustice of slavery itself."[2] However, hatred of slavery did not mean belief in racial equality. Before the war, Lincoln admitted, "I am not in favor of negro citizenship," even though several states recognized African Americans as citizens.[3] Additionally, he was plagued by a fatalistic presumption that white people's prejudice, "harsh as it may be," made peaceful coexistence between Black and white people impossible.[4] In sum, Lincoln's conservatism on race complicated but did not negate his opposition to slavery.

Lincoln's love for the Union, in contrast, was *un*complicated and sprung from his certainty that the survival of America's system of representative

Bombardment of Fort Sumter, Charleston Harbor: 12th & 13th of April, 1861 (New York: Currier & Ives). Hand-colored lithograph

Pages 112–13: Detail from "Birds Eye View of Louisiana, Mississippi, Alabama, and Part of Florida," *Panorama of the Seat of War* (New York: John Bachmann, 1861). Chromolithograph. (see pages 134–35)

Page 114: Detail from *Prize Fight between Abram and Jeff, in Four Rounds*, ca. 1861. (see page 125)

Page 117: *Charleston Mercury* broadside, Dec. 20, 1860. This appeared within hours of South Carolina's vote to separate from the country and repeal the Constitution.

self-rule mattered for people everywhere. In his First Message to Congress, Lincoln affirmed that the war "embraces more than the fate of these United States. It presents to the whole family of man, the question, whether a constitutional republic, or a democracy—a government of the people, by the same people—can, or cannot" succeed. The Union had to survive to prove the viability of elected self-government as designed by the Founders on the Declaration of Independence's stated principles of liberty and equality. If the Union was destroyed, humans everywhere would conclude that a democratic republic created out of the Declaration's ideals was a failure. For proof, Lincoln drew listeners' attention to the contrasting "declarations of independence," meaning the ordinances of secession adopted by the Confederate states, "in which, unlike the good old one, penned by Jefferson, they omit the words 'all men are created equal.'"[5]

When secession first happened, Lincoln downplayed slavery for strategic reasons. Four slaveholding states elected not to secede, and retaining their loyalty was vital for the Union's survival. "To lose Kentucky is nearly the same as to lose the whole game," Lincoln confided to a friend, and with "Kentucky gone, we can not [*sic*] hold Missouri, nor, as I think, Maryland. These all against us, and the job on our hands is too large for us." Nothing, Lincoln felt sure, would propel Kentucky, Missouri, or Maryland out of the Union faster than threatening slavery.[6] Further, Lincoln believed that most white Southerners secretly opposed secession; temporarily misled by a few hotheads, they would rush back to the Union as long as the federal government did not come for their slaves. With this conciliatory strategy in mind, Lincoln maintained a strict separation between the war's stated objective of preserving the Union and the issue of slavery. In his First Inaugural Address, he assured listeners that he had "no purpose, directly or indirectly, to interfere with slavery in the States where it exists."[7]

The abrupt ferocity of the Civil War added a human element to the abstract dichotomy between the Union and slavery when Lincoln saw the

CHAPTER SIX

CHARLESTON
MERCURY

EXTRA:

Passed unanimously at 1.15 o'clock, P. M., December 20th, 1860.

AN ORDINANCE

To dissolve the Union between the State of South Carolina and other States united with her under the compact entitled "The Constitution of the United States of America."

We, the People of the State of South Carolina, in Convention assembled, do declare and ordain, and it is hereby declared and ordained,

That the Ordinance adopted by us in Convention, on the twenty-third day of May, in the year of our Lord one thousand seven hundred and eighty-eight, whereby the Constitution of the United States of America was ratified, and also, all Acts and parts of Acts of the General Assembly of this State, ratifying amendments of the said Constitution, are hereby repealed; and that the union now subsisting between South Carolina and other States, under the name of "The United States of America," is hereby dissolved.

THE
UNION
IS
DISSOLVED!

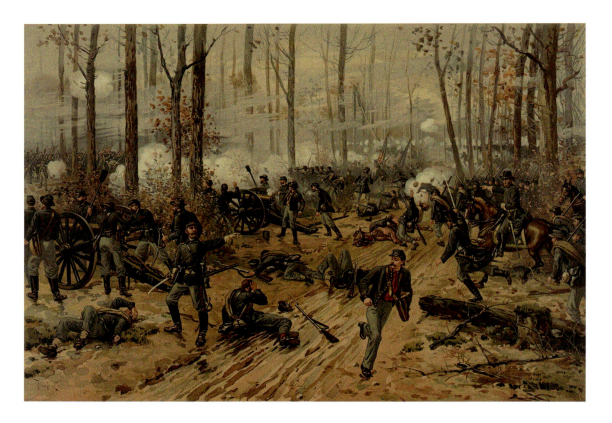

Thure de Thulstrup, *Battle of Shiloh* (Boston: Prang, ca. 1880s). Chromolithograph

Abraham Lincoln's summer home, Washington, DC, 1863. Stereograph

toll taken by those fighting for their country and those suffering underfoot the schismatic institution. The North's casualties mounted. The Battle of Shiloh, fought in Tennessee in the spring of 1862, had over 13,000 Union casualties; Second Manassas, in Virginia that August, also had over 13,000; and Antietam, in Maryland that September, had over 12,000. Lincoln's beloved Willie had died of typhoid fever in early 1862, so he knew all too well what the loss of a son was like. And day after day, as Lincoln made his way from the White House to his family's summer lodgings at the Soldiers' Home on the outskirts of Washington, DC, he passed a cemetery where 8,000 newly dug graves brought wartime loss literally to his doorstep.[8]

Amid constant reminders of death, Lincoln's awareness of freedom-seeking former slaves in the nation's capital united with his own antislavery principles to convince him that slavery and the Union could no longer be treated as separate causes. His route to the Soldier's Home passed by Camp Barker, a so-called "contraband camp" where formerly enslaved people who had fled bondage took refuge with the army. Lincoln stopped to "visit and talk" there, including with Mary Dines, an erstwhile runaway, who sang for him "Nobody Knows What Trouble I See," "Free at Last," and other songs of heartbreak and liberation. Dines reported that Lincoln seemed "so sad" but that the music moved

118   CHAPTER SIX

Camp Barker, Washington, DC, 1862. Newly freed slaves from the South, who sought refuge in Washington. Photograph

him to return.[9] The fortitude to endure slavery, courage to escape it, and determination to fight it that Lincoln witnessed at Camp Barker demanded that slavery remain no mere abstraction. These endurances clarified his growing conviction that a Union which mattered for all could only be saved through liberty for all.

During the summer of 1862, Lincoln began composing the Preliminary Proclamation, the precursor to the Emancipation Proclamation and the first directive from his administration that linked preserving the Union with ending slavery. He knew that before he could issue it, he had to prepare both his cabinet and the public for the enormity of its effect. His department heads' responses varied, from the martial endorsement of Secretary of War Edwin Stanton to the measured blessing of Secretary of the Treasury Salmon Chase to the conspicuous silence of Secretary of the Interior Caleb Smith. In an open letter to editor Horace Greeley in August, Lincoln cleverly worked to link the goals of the Union and emancipation in the public mind. "If I could save the Union without freeing *any* slave I would do it, and if I could save it by freeing *all* the slaves, I would do it; and if I could save it by freeing some and leaving others alone I would also do that. What I do about slavery, and the colored race, I do because I believe it helps to save the Union," he wrote, even as the text of the Preliminary Emancipation Proclamation sat in his desk while he waited for the right moment to release it.[10] When he finally did, on September 22, 1862, it announced that all enslaved people in states in rebellion would be "forever free." In December, in this Second Annual Message to Congress, Lincoln, ever the communicator, reasoned to the public that emancipation would help save the Union because it "would shorten the war."[11]

The war felt anything but shortened to Lincoln in 1863. The year began with the issuance of the Final Emancipation Proclamation on January 1, but what followed was a period of bloody military equilibrium between the two sides that would not tilt easily to the advantage of Lincoln's forces. In April the Union navy failed to capture Charleston Harbor. In May the Union Army was routed at Chancellorsville, with over 17,000 casualties against the Confederate's 12,000. However, on July 4, Vicksburg, Mississippi, fell to Union forces, thus returning control of the Mississippi River to the North. And on the same day, Confederate General Robert E. Lee's Army of Northern Virginia retreated after losing at the Battle of Gettysburg. The twin victories were momentous, but Lincoln was "distressed immeasurably" when, after Gettysburg, Union General George Meade failed to pursue and crush Lee's forces.[12] That same month, deadly riots in New York protested the draft, terrorized and killed African Americans, and burned down an orphanage for Black children. In addition, Lincoln's wife was so severely injured in a carriage accident that their eldest son, Robert, was called home, only to arrive at the White House to find his father with his head down on his desk, crying.[13] All that summer, observers described Lincoln as "careworn."[14]

It was a careworn Lincoln who accepted an invitation to offer "appropriate remarks" at the ceremony to dedicate a cemetery for soldiers who died at Gettysburg, remarks that further linked the survival of the Union to emancipation by honoring the pain and loss of the servicemen who battled for both.[15] The opening clause of the Gettysburg Address invoked the Declaration of Independence as the moment when the Union, "conceived in liberty and dedicated to the proposition that all men are created equal," came into being. Now Union soldiers fought to demonstrate "whether that nation, or any nation so conceived, and so dedicated, can long endure." The conclusion of the address clearly stated that saving the nation so boldly begun in 1776 depends on emancipation—a "new birth of freedom." But to get from an opening about the Union to the culminating lines about freedom, Lincoln took the public through an intermediate section about struggle, suffering, and the insignificance of human effort. One rarely encounters this middle section quoted, but we cannot get to the speech's resonant conclusion without wading through it, any more than we can leap over the loss brought by war.[16] As 1863 drew to a close, Lincoln told Congress that "under the sharp discipline of civil war, the nation is beginning a new life."[17]

In March 1865 Lincoln gave his Second Inaugural Address, which proclaimed that a just God would not allow the Union to be saved until the sin of slavery had been atoned for by the whole nation. Calling American slavery an "offence," Lincoln posited that God "gives to both North and South, this terrible war, as the woe due to those by whom the offence came." The Second Inaugural Address made sense of the war by viewing every drop of blood "drawn with the sword" as national penance for "every drop of blood drawn with the lash." Without suffering to end and atone for slavery, there could be no Union, nor could there be "just and lasting peace, among ourselves and with all nations," Lincoln told listeners.[18]

Lincoln's words retain relevance today. His words tell us that the survival of the nation depends upon each generation's willingness to face the darkness of our past without being immobilized by it and on each generation's commitment to the understanding that the system of government our Founders created for us is inherently connected to freedoms not just for some, but for all.

NOTES

1. Lincoln to Albert G. Hodges, Apr. 4, 1864, in Roy P. Basler, ed., *The Collected Works of Abraham Lincoln*, 8 vols. (hereafter *Collected Works*) (New Brunswick, NJ: Rutgers University Press, 1953), 7:281–82.

2. "Speech at Peoria, Illinois," Oct. 16, 1864, in *Collected Works*, 2:255.

3. "Debate at Charleston, Illinois," Sept. 18, 1858, in *Collected Works*, 3:180.

4. "Address on Colonization to a Deputation of Negroes," Aug. 14, 1862, in *Collected Works*, 5:372.

5. "Message to Congress in Special Session," July 4, 1861, in *Collected Works*, 4:426, 438.

6. Lincoln to Orville Browning, Sept. 22, 1861, in *Collected Works*, 4:533. The fourth slaveholding Union state was Delaware.

7. "First Inaugural Address," Mar. 4, 1861, in *Collected Works*, 4:251.

8. Matthew Pinsker, *Lincoln's Sanctuary: Abraham Lincoln and the Soldiers' Home* (New York: Oxford University Press, 2003), 94.

9. "The Contrabands at Camp Barker," *Evening Star*, Aug. 12, 1862, 1; Mary Dines in *They Knew Lincoln*, ed. John Washington, with new intro. by Kate Masur (New York: Oxford University Press, 2018), 83–88.

10. Lincoln to Horace Greeley, Aug. 22, 1862, in *Collected Works*, 5:388–89.

11. "Annual Message to Congress," Dec. 1, 1862, in *Collected Works*, 5:537.

12. Lincoln to General George Meade, written July 14, 1863 [unsent], Washington, DC, in *Collected Works*, 6:237–29.

13. Pinsker, *Lincoln's Sanctuary*, 106.

14. Walt Whitman in *Walt Whitman's Memoranda during the War & Death of Abraham Lincoln*, ed. Roy P. Basler (Bloomington: Indiana University Press, 1962), 6–7. Many Union soldiers who saw Lincoln also used the word "careworn."

15. David Wills to Abraham Lincoln, Nov. 2, 1863, quoted in Douglas L. Wilson, *Lincoln's Sword: The Presidency and the Power of Words* (New York: Alfred A. Knopf, 2006), 209.

16. "Gettysburg Address," Nov. 19, 1863, in *Collected Works*, 7:23.

17. "Annual Message to Congress," Dec. 8, 1863, in *Collected Works*, 8:40.

18. "Second Inaugural Address," Mar. 4, 1865, in *Collected Works*, 8:332–33.

THE DAVID M. RUBENSTEIN AMERICANA COLLECTION

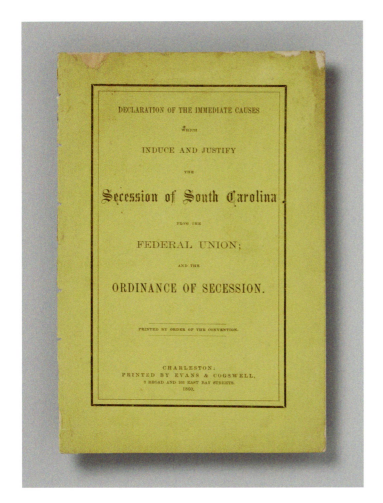

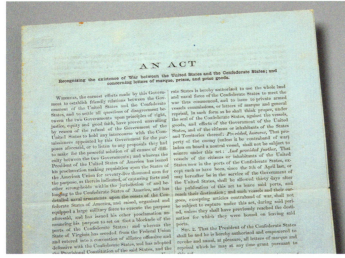

Declaration of the Immediate Causes Which Induce and Justify the Secession of South Carolina from the Federal Union

CHARLESTON [SC]: EVANS & COGSWELL, 1860

The seven states that seceded from the Union after Lincoln's presidential victory in 1860 were joined by four states that seceded after the Battle of Fort Sumter in April 1861. Initially secession was a Constitutional matter; South Carolina's declaration of it, famously printed in the *Charleston Mercury* (see page 117), was a legal statement similar to what the *Mercury* had peddled in the 1850s. A fuller legal justification for secession, printed in the Evans & Cogswell pamphlet shown here, was that Lincoln and the North's willingness to end slavery violated a "compact between the states." After Fort Sumter the basis for secession devolved into one of military inevitability.

An Act Recognizing the Existence of War between the United States and the Confederate States

[MONTGOMERY, AL]: N.P., 1861

Three days after South Carolina attacked Fort Sumter, Lincoln issued a proclamation that called for 75,000 militiamen, labeled the seceding states an insurrectionary collective, and declared his intention to repossess federal property within state borders. Virginia left the Union two days later, on April 17, 1861; the visceral political reaction to a central government possibly battling its own citizens bolstered the cause of prosecession forces in the Virginia Convention. On May 6 the now eight-strong Confederacy issued this act "recognizing" that they were at war with the United States given Lincoln's intentions to raise troops and capture Confederate "strong-holds."

The Massacre at Baltimore
HARTFORD [CT]: KELLOGG, CA. 1861

The first casualties of the Civil War were in Baltimore, where, on April 19, the 6th Massachusetts Infantry, following Lincoln's summoning of state militaries, passed through the city on its way to protect Washington, DC. Because the north and south rail lines there did not connect, the troops had to transfer their train cars by horse between two stations on either side of the Patapsco River (now the Inner Harbor). A rowdy, pro-Confederate crowd thwarted the last two (of seven) cars. The remaining 200 to 250 troops were forced to march. The crowd grew into a mob; it began throwing stones and then shooting at the soldiers. The troops, in turn, were ordered to fire into the mob. By the time the police arrived, four servicemen and twelve civilians had died.

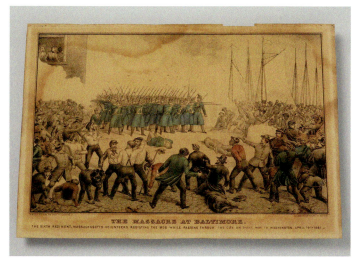

"Rebellious Excitement in Maryland and Virginia," *Herald Extra* (Calais, ME)
APR. 23, 1861

Following the Baltimore Riot, the North was galvanized into a war footing. As shown by this 1861 Maine newspaper supplement, towns and cities held civic meetings, promised personnel and funds for the war, and voraciously consumed news telegraphed from Maryland and Virginia, the earliest sites of interstate combat. One significant development of the war is buried here in the bottom headline: Lincoln's naval blockade of Southern ports, issued by executive decree four days prior to this printing. A military and economic measure, the blockade was designed to prevent importing weapons to and exporting goods from the seceding states (see page 126, top).

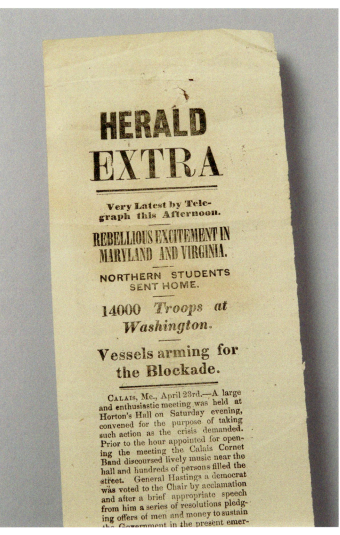

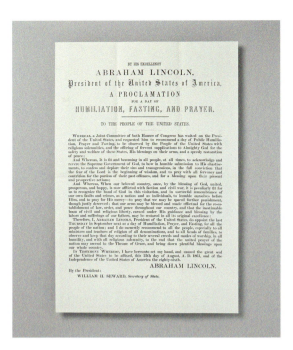

Abraham Lincoln, A Proclamation for a Day of Humiliation, Fasting, and Prayer
N.P.: N.P., [1861]

President Lincoln issued nine Thanksgiving proclamations during the Civil War. This, his first, did not follow a Union victory, as did his more famous one from October 1863, after the Battles of Gettysburg and Vicksburg (which began the nationwide tradition of reserving the last Thursday of November to express gratitude to God). This proclamation, from August 1861, arrived in the wake of the First Battle of Bull Run, the first significant land battle of the war and the Confederacy's first victory. Bull Run was a turning point, revealing to both sides that there would be no quick end to the conflict. Here Lincoln requests prayers for a "speedy restoration of peace."

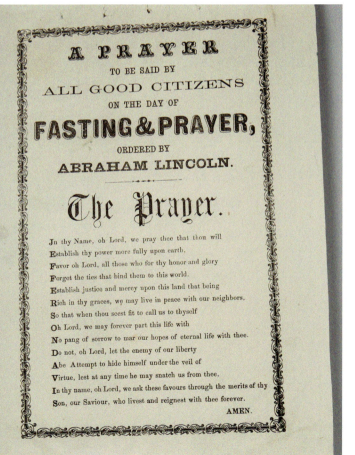

A Prayer to Be Said by All Good Citizens
N.P.: N.P., [1861]

This anti-Lincoln broadside mocks the president's Thanksgiving proclamation with an acrostic poem that spells out the name of Jefferson Davis, the leader of the Confederacy. On November 6, 1861, on the first anniversary of Lincoln's election, Davis was voted to a six-year term in the only presidential election the South would hold. Davis had been Mississippi's senator but resigned when it seceded. This parody asks, "Do not, oh Lord, let the enemy of our liberty / Abe Attempt to hide himself under the veil of / Virtue." Davis did issue his own Thanksgiving proclamation that year, which in part asked to "preserve our homes and altars from pollution."

Prize Fight Between Abram and Jeff, in Four Rounds

N.P.: N.P., [CA. 1862]

By July 1861 all eleven states had seceded from the nation, and in the second half of the year, nearly thirty skirmishes and armed encounters took place between U.S. and Confederate forces. The constant news of military deployments and the widening of the war to areas as far south as Florida (Santa Rosa Island) and west as Missouri (Rich Mountain; Wilson's Creek) altered the social landscape in the North as the reality of war set in. Some former adversaries, like Stephen A. Douglas, began to endorse Lincoln as the embodiment of the Union, and the public began to view Lincoln as the personification of the country, as shown by this paper metamorphosis toy.

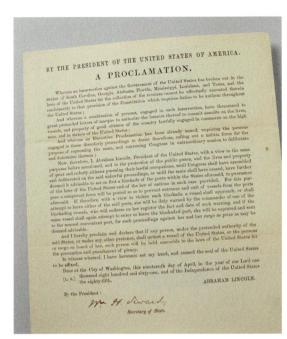

Abraham Lincoln, William H. Seward [countersigned], By the President of the United States of America. A Proclamation. [Blockade of Confederate Ports]

[WASHINGTON: GOVERNMENT PRINTING OFFICE, 1861]

The Union blockade of maritime traffic into and out of Southern ports was the earliest military decision by Lincoln with the longest impact on the war. It arrived swiftly: on April 19, within a week of the Battle of Fort Sumter. It was very ambitious: by July it covered all 3,500 miles of Confederate coastline. It was risky: it forced European nations to reconsider the economic benefits of allegiances with American states. It pushed the limits of executive authority: it was a proclamation of war powers, an authority granted to the legislative branch (indeed, Lincoln issued it when Congress was not in session), against states that Lincoln considered inherently part of the Union. It was a targeted, sustained blow against the South's agricultural economy.

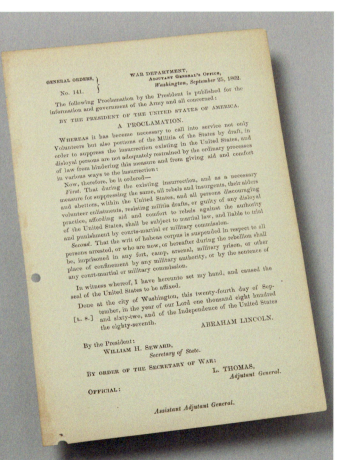

Abraham Lincoln, By the President of the United States of America. A Proclamation. [Suspension of the Writ of Habeas Corpus], *General Orders* [No. 141]

WASHINGTON: [GOVERNMENT PRINTING OFFICE], 1862

Lincoln suspended the writ of habeas corpus three times during the Civil War. By doing so he exercised the power granted in the Constitution, "in cases of rebellion," to arrest individuals without warrant and detain them without needing to prove sufficient cause to a judge or court. Shown here is his third proclamation, which imposed martial (i.e., military) law across the country in 1862. This declaration was controversial, not only because the writ of habeas corpus is so fundamental to Anglo-American liberties and jurisprudence but also because the Constitution is ambiguous on whether the power to suspend it is reserved for Congress or the president.

Roger B. Taney, *The Merryman Habeas Corpus Case*
JACKSON [MS]: POWER, 1861

On April 27, 1861, Lincoln suspended the writ of habeas corpus for the first time, specifically for the corridor of travel between Philadelphia and Washington—namely, for Maryland. He believed it was a military necessity because after Virginia seceded, the nation's capital became surrounded by hostile forces, as witnessed in the Baltimore Riot. In May, John Merryman, a pro-Confederate Marylander, was arrested for sabotage and incitement but held in a military jail with no charges or legal representation. The chief justice, Roger Taney, intervened by issuing a writ for Merryman and delivering an opinion that the power to suspend the writ rested only with Congress. Lincoln ignored Taney and continued to allow military arrests for the remainder of the war.

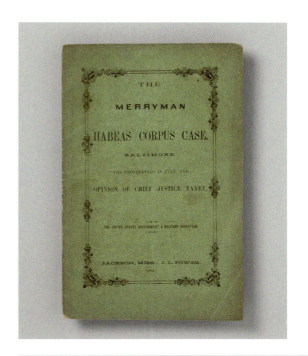

Abraham Lincoln, *Letter from President Lincoln: Military Arrests Vindicated*
N.P.: N.P., 1863

This open letter written by Lincoln to defend military arrests was one of his presidency's most well-received public statements. In March of 1863, Congress authorized Lincoln's suspension of habeas corpus, which the Union army then used against Confederate sympathizers in the North. An Ohio politician named Clement Vallandigham was arrested after a subversive speech, and fellow Democrats from New York, led by Erastus Corning, an Albany congressman, drafted a censure of Lincoln. In rebuttal, Lincoln interpreted the Constitution to imply that the greater a rebellion is, the less suited "ordinary" courts are to handle it, adding, "Ours is . . . a clear, flagrant, and gigantic case of Rebellion."

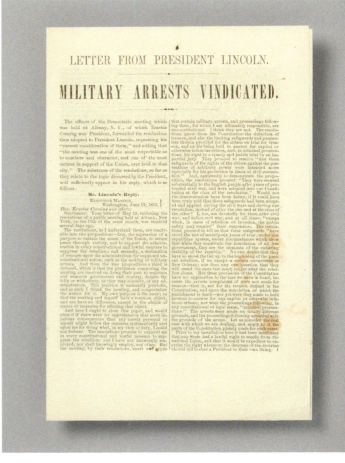

[Edward A. Pollard], *The Seven Days' Battles in Front of Richmond*

RICHMOND [VA]: WEST & JOHNSTON, 1862

The absence of a major Union military victory into 1862 and a string of Confederate battlefield successes weighed heavily on Lincoln and indicated that he had a general problem: his generals. To goad them into a more aggressive posture, Lincoln issued his War Order No. 1, which instructed all Northern forces to attack on a single day: February 22. One general did not comply: George B. McClellan, head of the newly formed Army of the Potomac. Instead, in March, McClellan led his men toward Richmond, Virginia. By May, after inconclusive clashes in Yorktown and Williamsburg, they were ten miles from the South's capital—where they sat for a month. In June, in a reverse, McClellan was attacked and forced to retreat, as recounted in this Richmond-printed pamphlet.

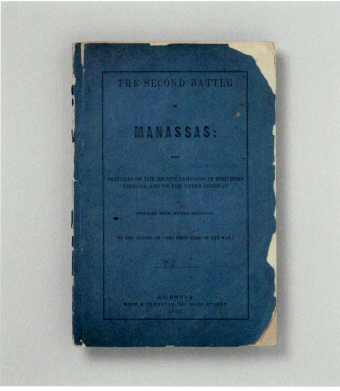

[Edward A. Pollard], *The Second Battle of Manassas*

RICHMOND [VA]: WEST & JOHNSTON, 1862

The Union defeat at Richmond was executed by a newly installed general leading the South's Army of Northern Virginia: Robert E. Lee. Following his victory against McClellan, Lee directed his troops one hundred miles north toward Manassas, where Union general John Pope was camped. If McClellan erred toward inaction, Pope was the opposite and was baited by Lee into launching several ill-conceived, messy attacks against various Confederate positions. The results were disastrous: Lee took advantage of Pope's army's disarray and routed them back in the direction of Washington, DC, to a stream named Bull Run (the second battle in the area that the Union lost). Alas, McClellan, believing the fight unwinnable, sent too few reinforcements to Pope too late.

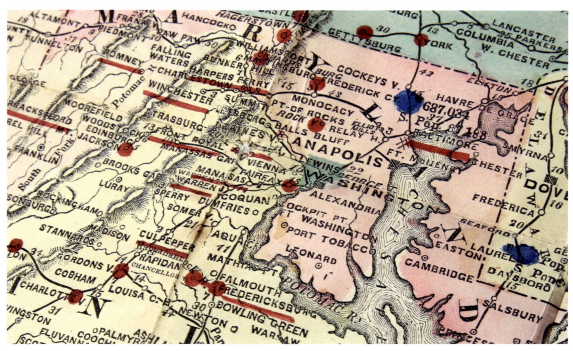

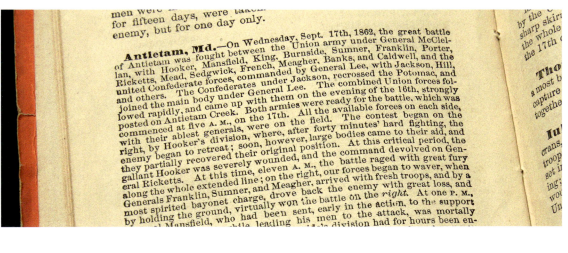

Historical and Military Map of the Border and Southern States

NEW YORK: PHELPS & WATSON, 1863

General Lee next marched into Maryland. It was a Confederate invasion of Union territory. For him, capturing the state would provide both needed resources and a foothold toward the greater goal of overtaking Washington. What followed was the deadliest day of the war: the Battle of Antietam, on September 17, 1862. A copy of Lee's battle plan had come into McClellan's possession, enabling him to move his units into optimal position on the opposite side of a cornfield from Lee's. From about 5:30 a.m. to 5:30 p.m., enough direct crossfire was shot to result in over 3,600 dead and over 17,000 wounded. Although the Union side shed more blood, Lee retreated, allowing Lincoln to claim victory. But McClellan did not pursue the withdrawing Lee, angering Lincoln.

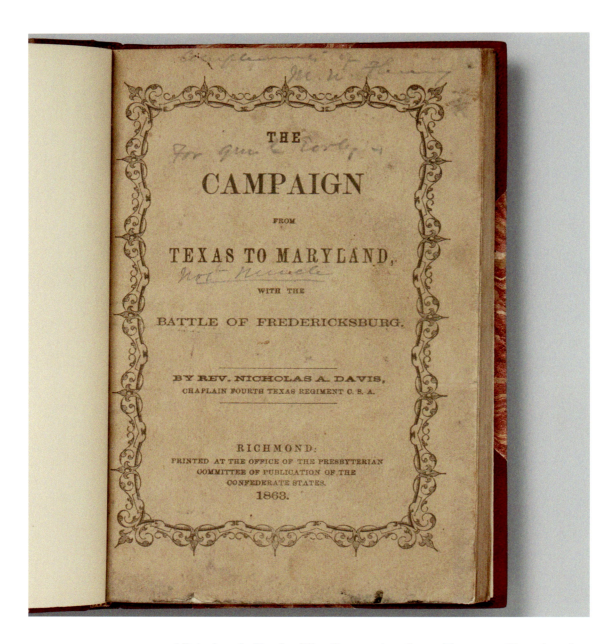

Nicholas A. Davis, *The Campaign from Texas to Maryland*
RICHMOND [VA]: PRESBYTERIAN COMMITTEE OF PUBLICATION, 1863

In November 1862 Lincoln relieved McClellan of his command of the Army of the Potomac and promoted Major General Ambrose Burnside to the position. Heeding Lincoln's urgency for a Union offensive, Burnside marched his men again to Richmond on a southeast course that required crossing the Rappahannock River. On the riverbanks near Fredericksburg, about sixty miles short of their target, over four days in December, they met intense Confederate resistance. Burnside and his men were repelled, horrifically so, with over 12,000 casualties (more than double their opponents). The defeat outraged the North, including Republicans, who fixed blame on Lincoln's cabinet. Shown here is a rare war history of a Confederate unit that fought at Fredericksburg.

Volunteers Wanted for Nine Months Service
[PHILADELPHIA: N.P., 1862]

This Pennsylvania recruitment broadside illustrates the staffing realities of the Civil War before the national draft appeared. Servicemen already in the regular army were kept in their own regiments. Separate volunteer units, such as the one shown here, were mustered from each state. The Militia Act of 1862, which Lincoln signed in July, stipulated that shortages in a state's volunteer quotas must be made up by impressments into the state's militias. Bounties (signing incentives) were paid to enlistees; this encouraged fraud in the form of "bounty jumpers," who disappeared with the money before serving. Volunteer levels began to diminish after the Union losses of 1862.

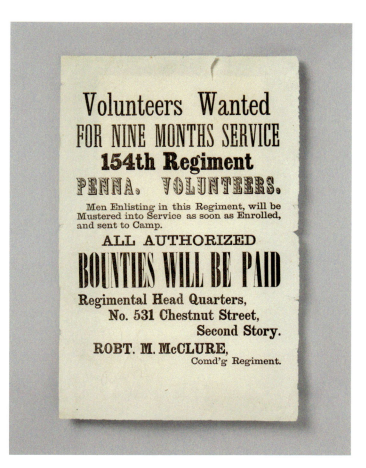

"The Draft," *Journal Extra* (Southbridge, MA)
MAY 17, 1864

This newspaper extra from south-central Massachusetts lists the men drafted in May 1864 to "supply the deficiency" of recruited volunteers from four adjoining towns (given that enrollment districts were created out of congressional districts). The woodcut illustration is a reversible "portrait" that, when viewed one way, shows a worried "fellow that was drafted" and, when viewed 180 degrees inverted, shows a happy "fellow that wasn't drafted." The illustration also imparts the Janus-like thinking the public had of the law's expensive deferral system for the privileged few. For some it proved that this was "a rich man's war, but a poor man's fight."

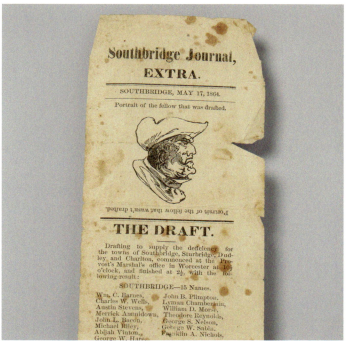

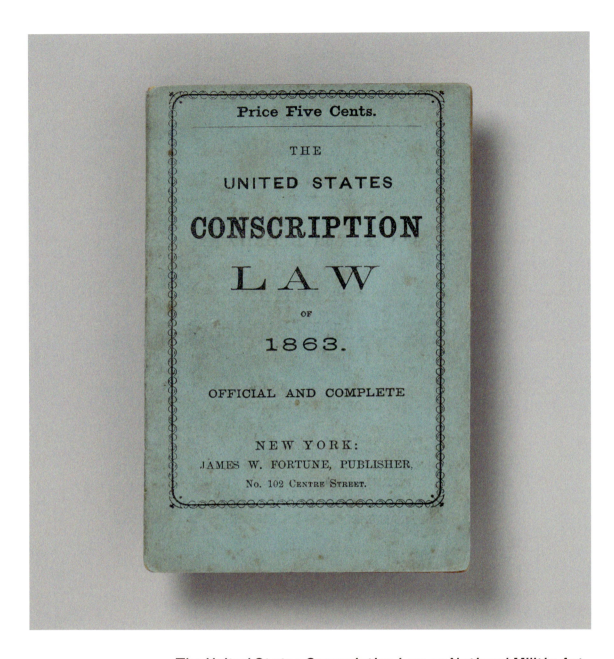

The United States Conscription Law or National Militia Act
NEW YORK: FORTUNE, 1863

The first military draft in U.S. history was passed by Congress in early 1863 and signed by Lincoln in March. The U.S. Enrollment Act, shown here in pamphlet form with one of several lay renamings, ordered that all male citizens and would-be naturalized immigrants between ages twenty and forty-five be "declared to constitute the national forces" and ready to fight "when called out by the President." There were exceptions: those not able-bodied, sons of infirm parents, widowers, and eldest brothers of parentless children. Also exempt were those who could pay $300 (equal to over $7,000 today) or find an "acceptable substitute" to fight in their place.

David M. Barnes, *The Draft Riots in New York*
NEW YORK: BAKER & GODWIN, 1863

Early on July 13, the second day of the draft lottery, protesters stormed New York City's enrollment office on East 47th Street, burning it to the ground. Quickly the crowd became an unchecked, many-thousands-strong horde. It attacked policemen and soldiers. It attacked the *New York Times* and Brooks Brothers. It turned overtly racist, attacking Black men on the streets, Black workers on the piers, Black businesses—as well as the homes of abolitionists and even the Colored Orphan Asylum, pillaging it of supplies. The police were overwhelmed. Fifty buildings were destroyed. Only when federal troops arrived three days later was order restored in the city.

The Bloody Week! Riot, Murder & Arson
NEW YORK, COUTANT & BAKER, [1863]

New York City was a tinderbox of political anger in 1863, and the Enlistment Act ignited it into the four days of violent mob destruction and murder that we call the Draft Riots. The instigators were at both ends of the social spectrum: the powerful political- and business-class elites who opposed the war, and the working-class, mostly Irish immigrant poor whose names began being called into service on July 11. For months anti-Lincoln newspapers and pontificators had stoked the fear of a Union victory, claiming it would lead to an influx of Southern Blacks and thus cheaper competition for jobs. Other cities had draft riots (Detroit, Boston), but nothing like New York's.

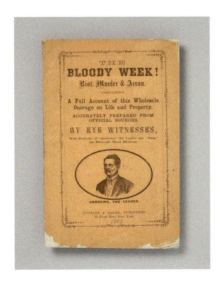

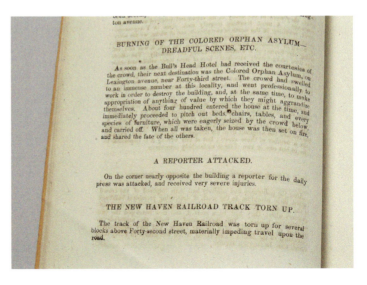

Panorama of the Seat of War

BIRDS EYE VIEW OF VIRGINIA, MARYLAND, DELAWARE AND THE DISTRICT OF COLUMBIA

BIRD[S EYE VIEW] OF NORTH AND SOUTH C[AROLINA]

BIRDS EYE VIEW OF KENTUCKY AND TENNESSEE SHOWING CAIRO AND PART OF THE SOUTHERN STATES

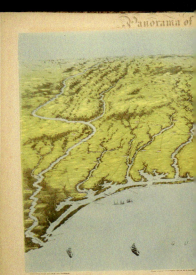

BIRD[S EYE VIEW] OF TEXAS A[ND ...]

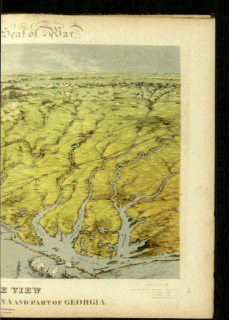

Panorama of the Seat of War
NEW YORK: JOHN BACHMANN, 1861

The "bird's eye view," a form of interpretive cartography, was one of the wonders of nineteenth-century printmaking, made possible by the new graphical precision of lithography or flat stone printing. When these views first appeared in America, their subjects were primarily the burgeoning cities of the East Coast and Midwest. John Bachmann, a Swiss-born artist and publisher known for producing much-admired views of New York City, turned his attention to the Civil War and created this monumental series of avian-altitude perspectives of the main theaters of battle. The prints were meant to be displayed continuously, and the effect was one of geographical scale that corresponded with Lincoln's blockade of Southern ports. Shown in this chapter is a rare suite of six plates, covering the Chesapeake Bay to the Gulf of Mexico (the image on pages 112–13 shows the sixth view from this suite). This is their first-issue printings of 1861–62, at the early stages of the conflict. Bachmann later issued additional plates with imagery of battles as the war progressed.

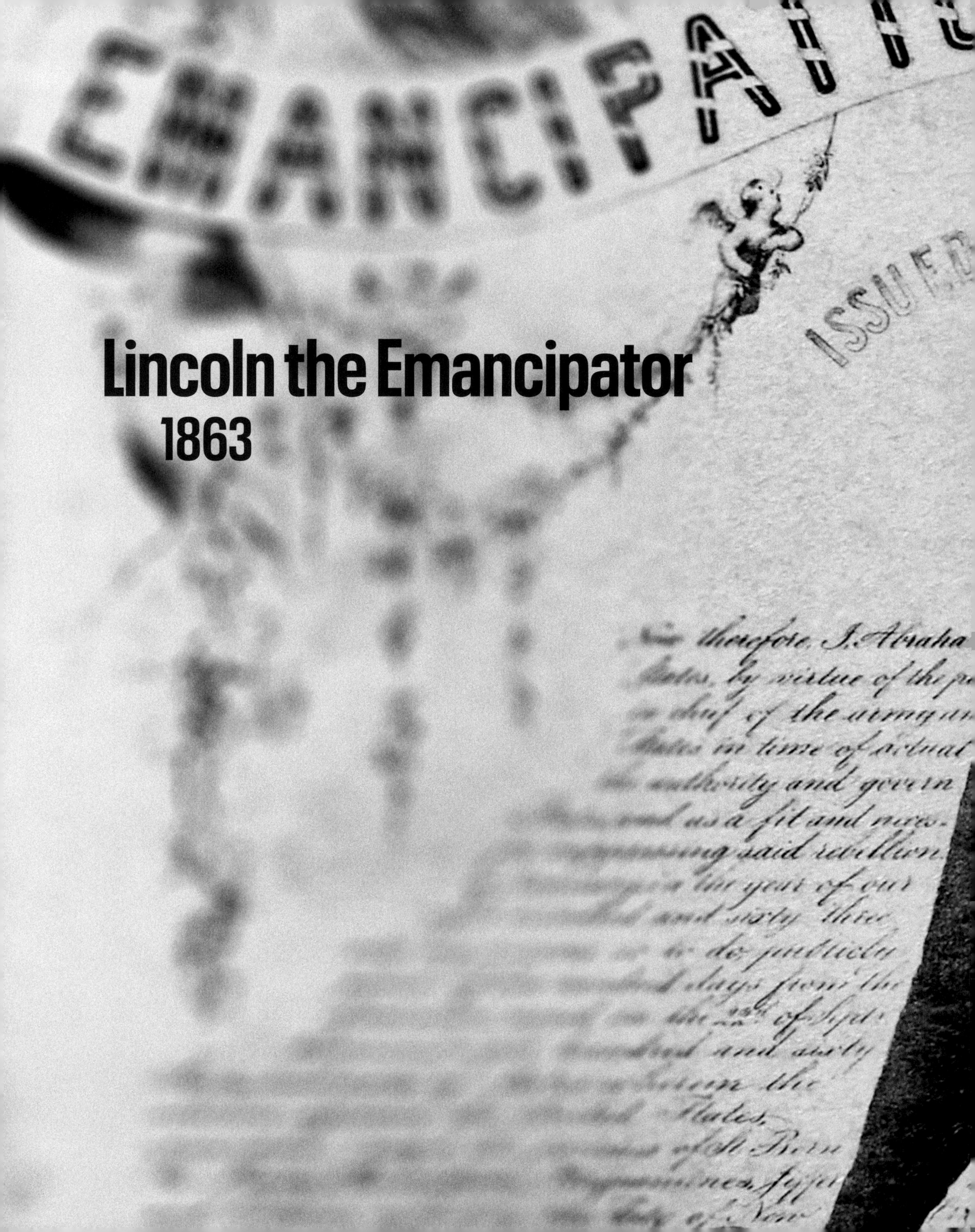

Lincoln the Emancipator

1863

PROCLAMATION
JANUARY 1st 1863

...Lincoln... President of the United
...   ...vested as commander
...   ...macy of the United
...   ...rebellion against
...   ...ment of the United
...   ...my war measure
...   ...& on this first day
...   ...Lord one thousand
...   ...and in accordance
...   ...claimed for the full
...   day ...mentioned in my pro
...   ...the year of our Lord one
...   ...order and designate as the
...   ...people thereof respectively are
...   ...following to wit: Arkansas, Tex
...   Assumption, Terre Bonne, Lafou
...   St. John, St. Charles, St. Jam
...   Mississippi, Alabama, Florida

"The Central Act of My Administration"

LUCAS E. MOREL

THE MOST ENDURING HONOR given to Abraham Lincoln, since at least the year of his death, has been to call him "the Great Emancipator." During the Civil War, he issued the Emancipation Proclamation and lobbied to get the Thirteenth Amendment passed.[1] Historically, and perhaps increasingly, two notions have disturbed this portrait in the discourse on Lincoln: the charge that he had ulterior motives for emancipating slaves, and the greater emphasis remedially placed on the contributions of the enslaved to their liberation.[2] Lincoln did not emancipate because it was morally right, the argument goes, but because he needed more men to fight to preserve the Union. Moreover, viewing Lincoln as the Great Emancipator minimizes the efforts of enslaved Black people in gaining their freedom. Should we retire the notion that "Lincoln freed the slaves"?

Lincoln actually resolved this debate in the very documents that credit him with emancipation. His Preliminary Emancipation Proclamation of September 22, 1862, required both the authority of the federal government and the initiative of the enslaved to achieve emancipation. As Lincoln declared, "the executive government of the United States, including the military and naval authority thereof, will recognize and maintain the freedom of such persons, and will do no act or acts to repress such persons, or any of them, in any efforts they may make for their actual freedom."[3] The explicit mention of "efforts" toward freedom promised an enormous reversal of federal policy toward escaped slaves.

The Fugitive Slave Act of 1793 empowered slaveowners "to seize or arrest such fugitive from labor" and "upon proof . . . remov[e] the said fugitive from labor to the State or Territory from which he or she fled."[4] Revised in 1850 to provide more detailed and punitive federal enforcement, the Fugitive Slave Act remained official government policy in the opening year of the Civil War. But when Lincoln issued his Final Emancipation Proclamation on January 1, 1863, he became the first president to tell American slaves he was on their side. Only with a federal government committed

Pages 136–37: Detail from "Emancipation Proclamation, Issued January 1st, 1863," ca. 1865. Albumen carte de visite

Page 138: *Abraham Lincoln and His Emancipation Proclamation* (Cincinnati: Strobridge, 1888)

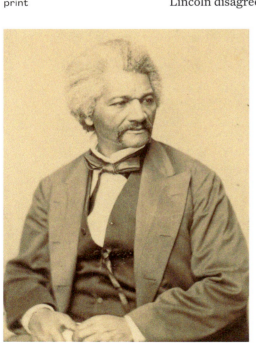

George Francis Schreiber, Frederick Douglass, head-and-shoulders portrait, facing right, 1870. Albumen print

to protecting, rather than returning, escaped slaves would any efforts at self-emancipation be successful.

To maintain the loyalty of the four slaveholding states that had not seceded from the Union, Lincoln's Emancipation Proclamation defined his action as "a fit and necessary war measure for suppressing said rebellion."[5] Regardless of its necessity, it required the support of loyal Americans, in and out of the military, to ensure its successful implementation. To gain this, Lincoln tied the controversial act of liberating the legal property of rebellious citizens to the uncontroversial aim of preserving the Union. As the abolitionist Frederick Douglass said of Lincoln in 1876, "Had he put the abolition of slavery before the salvation of the Union, he would have inevitably driven from him a powerful class of the American people and rendered resistance to rebellion impossible."[6] By freeing slaves to help preserve the Union, Lincoln made his reputation not only as the Great Emancipator but also as the Savior of the Union.

Lincoln's concern that emancipation be predicated on preserving the Union has led some critics to call him a "reluctant emancipator."[7] To be sure, he assumed the presidency disavowing any "lawful right" or "inclination" to "interfere with the institution of slavery in the States where it exists."[8] Like most Americans, Lincoln believed the federal Constitution did not empower the president or Congress to regulate any state's domestic institutions, which included chattel slavery. But when Confederate forces bombarded Fort Sumter less than six weeks into Lincoln's presidency, abolitionists thought the moment was ripe for emancipation. In Douglass's words, "this slaveholding rebellion...demands the instant liberation of every slave in the rebel states."[9]

Lincoln disagreed. Seeking to keep the war from "degenerat[ing] into a violent and remorseless revolutionary struggle," he said in his December 3, 1861, First Annual Message to Congress, he "thought it proper to keep the integrity of the Union prominent as the primary object of the contest."[10] Lincoln's explanation to his countrymen was that, in his reading of the law, preserving the Union was a constitutional duty of the chief executive, and so emancipation should be pursued in service of that presidential prerogative. This line of reasoning continued the assertion he had put forth in March of that year, in his First Inaugural Address, when he spoke directly to the dissatisfied among the seceding states. "*You* have no oath registered in heaven to destroy the Government," whereas the Presidential Oath of Office required Lincoln to "preserve, protect and defend the Constitution."[11] We should remember that the Constitution was created, its preamble tells us, to "form a more perfect Union, establish Justice, [and] insure domestic Tranquility."

Lincoln said as much in an open letter to newspaper editor Horace Greeley on August 22, 1862. His response to Greeley's demand for a more vigorous enforcement of the Confiscation Acts of 1861 and 1862, which allowed for the Union seizure of Confederate property, has become the *locus classicus* for critics of Lincoln's tardiness on emancipation. He made his priority clear to Greeley and the rest of the nation: "I would save the Union. I would save it the shortest way under the Constitution.... My paramount object in this struggle *is* to save the Union, and is *not* either to save or to destroy slavery."[12] Unbeknownst to all but his cabinet, Lincoln had already drafted the Preliminary Emancipation Proclamation but awaited a military victory to issue it from a position of strength rather than desperation.

Horace Greeley 1811–1872, n.d. Photographic print

Simply put, as president, to emancipate slaves Lincoln had to turn a humanitarian end into a constitutional means. This way, emancipation would be not only "an act of justice," as Lincoln stated in the Emancipation Proclamation, but also "warranted by the Constitution."[13] Emancipating slaves because it was morally right but in a manner that violated consent (by violating the Constitution) would undermine the very self-government that American slaves needed. By finding a constitutional way to liberate slaves, Lincoln sought to make both his means and his ends as president a faithful expression of the consent of the American people. This explains why Lincoln consistently argued that the survival of self-government, not the abolition of slavery, was why he was fighting the war. He believed that the Union war effort would achieve its objective if it reinforced the conviction among the American people that a constitutional republic was worth defending. A week before issuing the Preliminary Emancipation Proclamation, Lincoln said to a gathering of pro-emancipation ministers that "we already have an important principle to rally and unite the people in the fact that constitutional government is at stake. This is a fundamental idea, going down about as deep as any thing."[14]

In the secession winter of 1860–61, disloyal Americans rejected the legitimate outcome of a federal election—and with it, majority rule as a governing principle. Their secession from the Union may have felt like freedom, but on Inauguration Day, Lincoln taught the nation that this was actually "the essence of anarchy."[15] And unwarranted, he counseled: "No administration, by any extreme of wickedness or folly, can very seriously injure the government, in the short space of four years." In his July 4, 1861, Message to Congress in Special Session, Lincoln further explained, "When ballots have fairly, and constitutionally, decided, there can be no successful appeal, back to bullets; that there can be no successful appeal, except

Facsimile of a portion of President Lincoln's draft of the Preliminary Proclamation of Emancipation, reprinted in *History of the United States* (New York: C. Scribner's Sons, 1894–1903)

to ballots themselves, at succeeding elections."[16]

The rebelling states should have followed the example of the Republicans in the previous presidential election. When they failed to elect their candidate, John C. Frémont of California, they accepted the "doughface Democrat" (or Northern appeaser of slaveholders and the South) James Buchanan of Pennsylvania as the president of the United States, despite his receiving only 45 percent of the popular vote. They did not preach resistance to the new administration, chant "not my president," or consider secession a valid response to losing an election. Instead, over the next four years, they sought to convert fellow citizens to the Republican cause by making resonant political arguments and appealing once again for votes. We have them to thank for the election of Lincoln in 1860.

Lincoln became the Great Emancipator by issuing the Emancipation Proclamation, which he called "the central act of my Administration, and the great event of the nineteenth century."[17] That reputation was bolstered by his efforts to get the Thirteenth Amendment passed in Congress before the end of the Civil War. This not only ensured that enslaved people would be liberated but also that slavery itself would be abolished throughout the entire United States. Lincoln hoped that winning a war that liberated three-to-four million slaves would enable the nation to experience, in the words of his immortal Gettysburg Address, "a new birth of freedom."[18] By finding a constitutional means to secure freedom for the enslaved, Lincoln helped Americans make sure that government "of the people, by the people, for the people, shall not perish from the earth."

NOTES

1. For a history of Lincoln's various steps to emancipate American slaves, see Allen C. Guelzo, *Lincoln's Emancipation Proclamation: The End of Slavery in America* (New York: Simon & Schuster, 2004). For Lincoln's support of the Thirteenth Amendment, see Michael Vorenberg, *Final Freedom: The Civil War, the Abolition of Slavery, and the Thirteenth Amendment* (New York: Cambridge University Press, 2001), 123–27, 180–85, 194, 198–202, 208–10; cf. 70–71, 113–14.

2. For a sampling of seminal works advancing the self-emancipation thesis, see James M. McPherson, "They Chose Freedom," *New York Review of Books* (Mar. 20, 2008): 47. McPherson cites the following: Vincent Harding, *There Is a River: The Black Struggle for Freedom in America* (New York: Harcourt Brace Jovanovich, 1981); *Freedom: A Documentary History of Emancipation, 1861–1867*, ser. 1, vol. 1, *The Destruction of Slavery*, ed. Ira Berlin et al. (Cambridge, UK: Cambridge University Press, 1985); and Barbara J. Fields, "Who Freed the Slaves?," in *The Civil War: An Illustrated History*, Geoffrey C. Ward with Ric Burns and Ken Burns (New York: Knopf, 1990).

3. "Preliminary Emancipation Proclamation," Sept. 22, 1862, in Roy P. Basler, ed., *The Collected Works of Abraham Lincoln*, 8 vols. (hereafter *Collected Works*) (New Brunswick, NJ: Rutgers University Press, 1953), 5:434.

4. "An Act Respecting Fugitives from Justice, and Persons Escaping from the Service of Their Masters," Feb. 12, 1793, Sec. 1, *Annals of Congress*, 2nd Congress, 2nd Session, Appendix, 1414, A Century of Lawmaking for a New Nation: U.S. Congressional Documents and Debates, 1774–1875, https://memory.loc.gov/cgi-bin/ampage?collId=llac&fileName=003/llac003.db&recNum=702 (accessed Nov. 27, 2023).

5. "Emancipation Proclamation," Jan. 1, 1863, in *Collected Works*, 6:29.

6. "Oration of Frederick Douglass Delivered on the Occasion of the Unveiling of the Freedmen's Monument in Memory of Abraham Lincoln," Apr. 14, 1876, in *The Essential Douglass: Selected Writings and Speeches*, ed. Nicholas Buccola (Indianapolis: Hackett, 2016), 245.

7. See, for example, Lerone Bennett Jr., *Forced into Glory: Abraham Lincoln's White Dream* (Chicago: Johnson Publishing Company, Inc., 2000). For a critique of Bennett's thesis, see Lucas E. Morel, "Forced into Gory Lincoln Revisionism," *Claremont Review of Books* 1, no. 1 (Fall 2000), https://claremontreviewofbooks.com/forced-into-gory-lincoln-revisionism/ (accessed Nov. 27, 2023).

8. "First Inaugural Address," Mar. 4, 1861, in *Collected Works*, 4:263.

9. "Substance of a Lecture [on Secession and the Civil War]," June 16, 1861, in *The Essential Douglass*, 163.

10. "Annual Message to Congress," Dec. 3, 1861, in *Collected Works*, 5:49.

11. Abraham Lincoln, "First Inaugural Address" (March 4, 1861), *Collected Works*, 4:271 (emphasis in original).

12. Lincoln to Horace Greeley, Aug. 22, 1862, in *Collected Works*, 5:388 (emphasis in original).

13. "Emancipation Proclamation," Jan. 1, 1863, in *Collected Works*, 6:30.

14. "Reply to Emancipation Memorial Presented by Chicago Christians of All Denominations," Sept. 13, 1862, in *Collected Works*, 5:424.

15. "Reply to Emancipation Memorial," 4:268.

16. "Message to Congress in Special Session," July 4, 1861, in *Collected Works*, 4:439.

17. Abraham Lincoln quoted in Francis B. Carpenter, "The Emancipation Proclamation: Interesting Sketch of Its History by the Artist," *New York Times*, June 16, 1865, col. 4, 1.

18. "Address Delivered at the Dedication of the Cemetery at Gettysburg," Nov. 19, 1863, in *Collected Works*, 7:23.

Abraham Lincoln, "The Letter to Horace Greeley," *The Letters of President Lincoln on Questions of National Policy*
NEW YORK: LLOYD, 1863

The Emancipation Proclamation, issued by Lincoln on January 1, 1863, was his most significant executive decision. It declared that slaves were free—in areas that were then "in rebellion." The decision was radical, its consequences considerable. Before its being issued, Lincoln did not publicly endorse emancipation. When Horace Greeley, the radical abolitionist publisher of the *New-York Tribune*, printed an appeal for Lincoln to free certain slaves, Lincoln replied cautiously and cannily: "If I could save the Union without freeing *any* slave I would do it, and if I could save it by freeing *all* the slaves I would do it; and if I could save it by freeing some and leaving others alone I would also do that. What I do about slavery...I do because I believe it helps to save the Union."

Abraham Lincoln, By the President of the United States: A Proclamation. [Preliminary Emancipation Proclamation]

[BOSTON: ATTRIB. TO JOHN MURRAY FORBES, 1862]

Lincoln's conditional statements in 1862 on freeing slaves hid a secret: he had already written a draft of what became the Preliminary Emancipation Proclamation. This was the setup for the more famous proclamation; emancipation was a two-part process. He issued it on September 22, soon after the Union victory at Antietam. The printing shown here is the earliest obtainable broadside version. At its heart, Lincoln (a) affirmed his objective: to restore the Union. He (b) offered to compensate states which "voluntarily adopt...abolishment." He then gave an ultimatum: if, come 1863, a state (a) was still rebelling and (b) still had slaves, then (c) those slaves, by executive authority, military policy, and congressional ruling, shall be "thenceforward, and forever free."

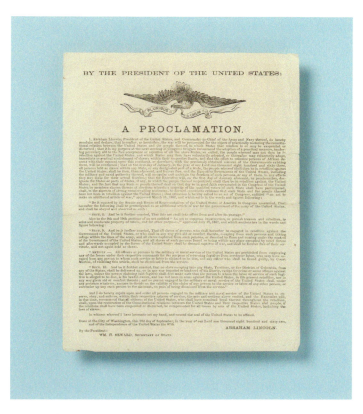

Abraham Lincoln, "The Decree of Emancipation" [Preliminary Emancipation Proclamation], *The New South* (Port Royal, SC)

OCT. 4, 1862

This newspaper printing of the Preliminary Emancipation Proclamation from Union-controlled Port Royal, South Carolina, puts the balancing act that Lincoln achieved into context. Crushing the rebellion required taking its lifeblood: slavery. South Carolina and the Confederacy had three months to show they were "not in rebellion"; the certainty that they would not do so meant their slaves would be deemed free. However, the four border states of Kentucky, Maryland, Missouri, and Delaware could keep their slaves, provided these states stayed in the Union. Also, no escaped slave would be returned—the Fugitive Slave Act was nullified. As to where the formerly enslaved could go, Lincoln offered to "colonize persons of African descent...upon this continent, or elsewhere."

LINCOLN THE EMANCIPATOR · 1863

BY THE PRESIDENT OF THE UNITED STATES OF AMERICA.

A Proclamation.

Whereas, on the twenty-second day of September, in the year of our Lord one thousand eight hundred and sixty-two, a proclamation was issued by the President of the United States, containing, among other things, the following, to wit:

"That on the first day of January, in the year of our Lord one thousand eight hundred and sixty-three, all persons held as slaves within any State or designated part of a State, the people whereof shall then be in rebellion against the United States, shall be then, thenceforward, and forever, free; and the Executive government of the United States, including the military and naval authority thereof, will recognize and maintain the freedom of such persons, and will do no act or acts to repress such persons, or any of them, in any efforts they may make for their actual freedom.

"That the Executive will, on the first day of January aforesaid, by proclamation, designate the States and parts of States, if any, in which the people thereof, respectively, shall then be in rebellion against the United States; and the fact that any State, or the people thereof, shall on that day be in good faith represented in the Congress of the United States, by members chosen thereto at elections wherein a majority of the qualified voters of such State shall have participated, shall, in the absence of strong countervailing testimony, be deemed conclusive evidence that such State, and the people thereof, are not then in rebellion against the United States."

Now, therefore, I, ABRAHAM LINCOLN, PRESIDENT OF THE UNITED STATES, by virtue of the power in me vested as commander-in-chief of the army and navy of the United States, in time of actual armed rebellion against the authority and government of the United States, and as a fit and necessary war measure for suppressing said rebellion, do, on this first day of January, in the year of our Lord one thousand eight hundred and sixty-three, and in accordance with my purpose so to do, publicly proclaimed for the full period of one hundred days from the day first above mentioned, order and designate as the States and parts of States wherein the people thereof, respectively, are this day in rebellion against the United States, the following, to wit: ARKANSAS, TEXAS, LOUISIANA, (except the Parishes of St. Bernard, Plaquemines, Jefferson, St. John, St. Charles, St. James, Ascension, Assumption, Terre Bonne, Lafourche, St. Mary, St. Martin, and Orleans, including the City of New Orleans,) MISSISSIPPI, ALABAMA, FLORIDA, GEORGIA, SOUTH CAROLINA, NORTH CAROLINA, AND VIRGINIA, (except the forty-eight counties designated as West Virginia, and also the counties of Berkeley, Accomac, Northampton, Elizabeth City, York, Princess Ann, and Norfolk, including the cities of Norfolk and Portsmouth,) and which excepted parts are for the present left precisely as if this proclamation were not issued.

And by virtue of the power and for the purpose aforesaid, I do order and declare that all persons held as slaves within said designated States and parts of States are and henceforward shall be free; and that the Executive government of the United States, including the military and naval authorities thereof, will recognize and maintain the freedom of said persons.

And I hereby enjoin upon the people so declared to be free to abstain from all violence, unless in necessary self-defence; and I recommend to them that, in all cases when allowed, they labor faithfully for reasonable wages.

And I further declare and make known that such persons, of suitable condition, will be received into the armed service of the United States, to garrison forts, positions, stations, and other places, and to man vessels of all sorts in said service.

And upon this act, sincerely believed to be an act of justice warranted by the Constitution upon military necessity, I invoke the considerate judgment of mankind and the gracious favor of Almighty God.

In witness whereof I have hereunto set my hand and caused the seal of the United States to be affixed.

[L. S.]   Done at the CITY OF WASHINGTON this first day of January, in the year of our Lord one thousand eight hundred and sixty-three, and of the Independence of the United States of America the eighty-seventh.

Abraham Lincoln

By the President:

William H. Seward, *Secretary of State.*

A true copy, with the autograph signatures of the President and the Secretary of State.

Jno. G. Nicolay,
Priv. Sec. to the President.

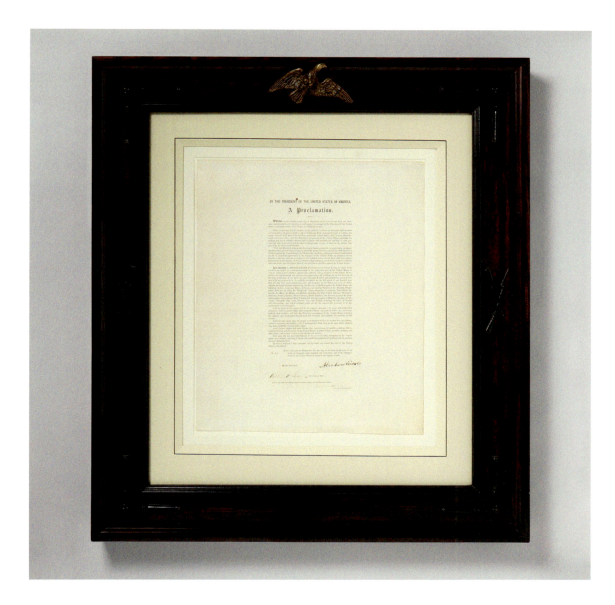

Abraham Lincoln, By the President of the United States of America. A Proclamation. [Emancipation Proclamation, "Great Central Fair Edition," signed]

[PHILADELPHIA: BOKER & LELAND, 1864]

Seen here is the only edition of the Emancipation Proclamation that Lincoln signed. It was one of forty-eight copies printed for Philadelphia's Great Central Fair in June 1864 and sold to raise money for the United States Sanitary Commission. "Sanitary Fairs" were the combination of two nineteenth-century trends: rising concern over germ-borne disease and charity bazaars. The USSC was a mostly women-run civilian relief organization that assisted the medical and hygiene efforts of an ill-equipped U.S. War Department. Two men were responsible for this printing: George Henry Boker, a poet and future diplomat active in pro-Union projects, and Charles Godfrey Leland, a journalist and future linguist who soon fought at Gettysburg. Its price in 1864 was ten dollars.

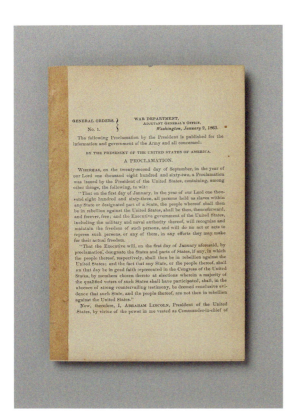

Abraham Lincoln, By the President of the United States of America. A Proclamation. [Final Emancipation Proclamation], *General Orders* [No. 1]

WASHINGTON: [GOVERNMENT PRINTING OFFICE], 1862

The profound implications of the Emancipation Proclamation are demonstrated by this early printing of it in the War Department's general orders. If slaves only in areas of rebellion were declared free, then each Union victory in these areas resulted in the liberation of people held in bondage there. The freeing of slaves became equal to beating the rebellion; a slave's freedom entailed not just the legal protection of the North but the military victory of the Union. Most saliently, the proclamation let ex-slaves fight in the service of victory by affirming that they "will be received into the armed service of the United States." Lincoln's proclamation tied the human rights effect of emancipation to the military effect of his armed forces being strengthened.

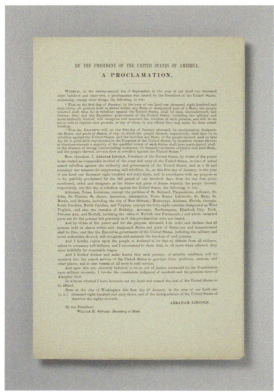

Abraham Lincoln, By the President of the United States of America. A Proclamation. [Final Emancipation Proclamation]

[WASHINGTON: GOVERNMENT PRINTING OFFICE, 1863]

The Emancipation Proclamation became law on January 1, 1863, as Lincoln promised. As seen in this first State Department printing, the two ultimatums from September were quoted in full. Its wording started with a justification: Lincoln, as "Commander-in-Chief, of the Army and Navy," issued this as a "necessary war measure for suppressing [the] rebellion." Ninety words were spent precisely naming the states and districts Lincoln considered rebellious. For this continued treason, "all persons held as slaves within said designated States, and parts of States, are, and henceforward shall be free." The language echoed the earlier decree, which promised that come January, all slaves in the Confederacy would be "thenceforward, and forever free."

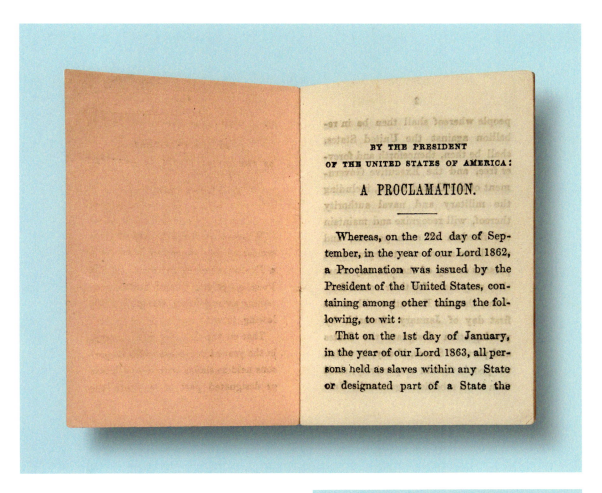

Abraham Lincoln, *Proclamation of Emancipation by the President of the United States*

[BOSTON: FORBES, 1863]

This pocket-sized Emancipation Proclamation was printed in Boston by the industrialist John Murray Forbes, who, in the words of Ralph Waldo Emerson, "was not born to confine himself to matters of private business." Forbes, an abolitionist, also led the Loyal Publication Society, a pro-Union propaganda concern. He helped fund African American fighting units, such as the famed 54th and 55th Massachusetts Regiments. This edition of the proclamation had a purpose. As explained by Forbes's daughter, it was "distributed among the Northern soldiers at the front, who scattered them about among the blacks, while on the march." In 1863, Forbes, with the moral superiority gained by the proclamation, sailed to England to pressure it not to help the South.

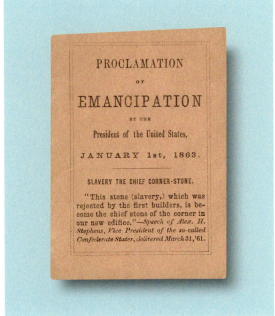

LINCOLN THE EMANCIPATOR · 1863

[Attrib. to Mathew Brady Studio], ["A Group of Contrabands"]

[HARTFORD, CT: TAYLOR & HUNTINGTON, CA. 1870S]

Before the Emancipation Proclamation, the status of slaves who crossed into areas that the North controlled evolved from fugitive to qualified freedom. In May 1861, in Union-occupied Fort Monroe, Virginia, Major General Benjamin Butler refused to return three runaways, observing that because the slaveholders were in rebellion, because the slaves were considered property, and because their labors would aid the enemy's defense, he was in the right to consider them "contraband of war." The Lincoln administration tacitly approved Butler's decision. In August Congress passed the First Confiscation Act, holding Confederate property as the "lawful subject of prize and capture wherever found." Later in August Butler wrote that his fort had received nine hundred escaped slaves.

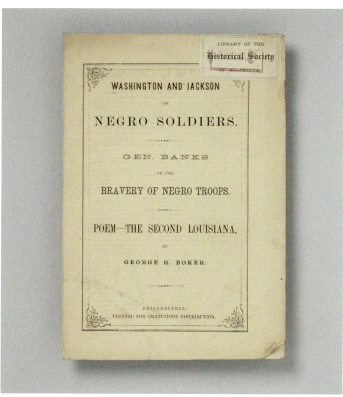

Nathaniel Banks, "[Letter to Major General Henry Halleck]"

PHILADELPHIA: N.P., [1863]

From contraband to combatants: in two years African Americans went from being subordinate to the secession dilemma to being instrumental in the Union's victory. Initially, the Militia Act of 1862 allowed them only to "perform camp service." Likewise, 1862's Second Confiscation Act stated vaguely that Lincoln could employ "persons of African descent [for] suppression of this rebellion." But the Emancipation Proclamation put Black fighters squarely on the front lines, as this 1863 pamphlet recounts. During the long Siege of Port Hudson, Louisiana, Union general Nathaniel Banks wrote of the "First regiment of Louisiana Engineers, composed exclusively of colored men," noting, "Their conduct was heroic. No troops could be more determined or more daring."

John H. Taggart, *Free Military School for Applicants for Command of Colored Troops*

PHILADELPHIA: KING & BAIRD, 1864

Eligible but not equal: the arrival of African Americans into the military was marred by prejudice and inadequacy. Commanders often assigned them drudgery. Their regiments were segregated and their weapons often inferior. Their wages were less than their white counterparts. Congress fixed this with an appropriations act in 1864 that also pledged back pay to the start of the year. The most persistent problem was the lack of advancement: Black servicemen generally could not rise past enlisted ranks, although about one hundred surgeons and chaplains eventually became commissioned officers. White officers wishing to command Black regiments needed specialized training, as this rare pamphlet delineated, on the assumption that their troops would be poorly disciplined.

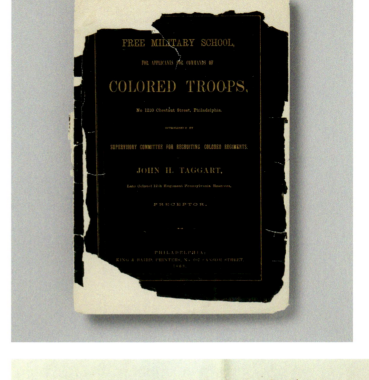

Rufus Saxton, *A Happy New Years Greeting*

N.P.: N.P., 1864

Following the Emancipation Proclamation, over 200,000 African Americans served in the U.S. military during the Civil War. Nearly 20 percent of them were killed or died of disease. They fought in over 40 major battles and over 400 skirmishes, firefights, and small combats. Their legions formed numerous volunteer units from both slave and free states, and in 1863 the War Department formed the Bureau of Colored Troops, which marshaled over 150 infantry, artillery, and cavalry regiments. One of these, the 33rd, was raised in South Carolina by General Rufus Saxton. Shown here is his invitation to celebrate the first anniversary of Lincoln's decree. To many freed Blacks, January 1st had long been known as "Heartbreak Day," for the annual slave auctions held then.

Lincoln the Wartime President, Part II
1863 to 1865

WOUNDED

and many thousands yet
in the field!

G! THEY ARE DYING!!

HAPEL,

THE

d Spring Garden Streets,

FROM 2 P. M. UNTIL 10 P. M.

"Let the Thing Be Pressed"

GLENN W. LAFANTASIE

IN EARLY JANUARY 1863, as the American Civil War raged on, James M. Winchell, a *New York Times* correspondent, interviewed Abraham Lincoln in the White House and found him anxious about a string of defeats suffered by the Union armies. Winchell, who otherwise doubted Lincoln's suitability as commander in chief, later remembered the interview with more sentiment and reverence than he ever displayed while Lincoln was alive. The president, he said, looked "grave and careworn," but carried himself with "simplicity, kindness, and dignity." Lincoln's "apparent knowledge of military science," Winchell said, was "surprising in a man who had been all his life a civilian." He could only conclude that Lincoln "had profoundly studied the war in its military aspect."[1]

Winchell was not alone in recognizing and praising Lincoln's military acumen; observers marveled at his knowledge of warfare and how deeply he comprehended strategy and tactics. These attributes led Lincoln, as leader of the Union, to win a stunning victory over the Confederate states. Our modern estimate of Lincoln as a wartime president differs little from how his contemporaries saw him—except, of course, that his political opponents and Southern enemies harped on his shortcomings and mistakes throughout his four years in office, and war-weariness often made Northerners wonder about his competency and policies, especially after Lincoln embraced the idea of emancipation. After his assassination, when his national apotheosis began, views of his prowess as a commander in chief continued to be praiseworthy, often excessively so. Three years after the president's death, the publisher Horace Greeley, whose statements about Lincoln had run hot and cold during the war, applauded him for his unshakable determination. "Mr. Lincoln," said Greeley, "accepted war as a stern necessity, and stood ready to fight it out to the bitter end."[2]

To educate himself on military matters, Lincoln read army manuals borrowed from the Library of Congress and formulated his own ideas about the principles of war. One of his personal secretaries, John Hay, remarked, "The President was a man of great aptitude for military studies." Hay

Pages 152–53: Detail from *The Battle Rages More Fiercely Than Ever!* (n.p., 1864). Printed handbill

Page 154: *U.S. Grant, Lt. Gen* (New York: E. & H. T. Anthony, ca. 1863). Albumen carte de visite

recalled that Lincoln "gave himself, night and day, to the study of the military situation. He read a large number of strategical works. He pored over the reports from the various departments and districts of the field of war."[3] It is more likely, though, that Lincoln—equipped with a superior intellect and, as a close friend from Illinois put it, "an immense stock of common sense"[4]—came up with his own strategic notions, which, in the end, amounted to one important goal: to worry less about conquering the enemy's territory or Richmond, the Confederacy's capital, but instead to concentrate on destroying Confederate armies in the field. It was a direct, aggressive, counterforce approach that solidified the partnership between Lincoln and his commanding general, Ulysses S. Grant, in the final year of the war.

Lincoln knew he had to appoint competent generals to lead the Union armies, but the search for field commanders who possessed proficiency, initiative, and a willingness to engage the enemy became an immense, almost insoluble challenge. It seemed no one fit the bill, not West Pointers, graduates of state military academies, or politicians whom the president naively hoped would learn on the job. From the start, Union defeats defined the war effort, and Lincoln witnessed a parade of misfit generals march in and out of the White House during the first two years of conflict: Brigadier General Irvin McDowell, who lost the first major battle of the war on July 21, 1861, near Bull Run Creek, north of Manassas, Virginia; Major General George B. McClellan, who expended eight months getting the Army of the Potomac ready for combat but, when he finally launched a campaign on Virginia's Tidewater Peninsula in June 1862, was easily outgeneraled by Robert E. Lee, the Confederate commander; Major General John Pope, who, when placed in command of the Union Army of Virginia, ignominiously lost to Lee in the Second Battle of Bull Run, fought over the last three days of August. To Hay, Lincoln said: "Well, John, we are whipped again, I am afraid."[5]

As Lee continued his northward campaigns, Lincoln cashiered Pope and reluctantly called on McClellan to halt Lee's progress. The showdown came at Sharpsburg, Maryland, on September 17, 1862, the bloodiest single day in the war and American history, when Lee held firm his battle lines along a high ridge overlooking Antietam Creek. Aghast at McClellan's failure to pursue a battered enemy, Lincoln at last fired him on November 5 after tolerating the general's incompetency for far too long. Major General Ambrose E. Burnside, next appointed by Lincoln to take command of the Army of the Potomac, was also not up to the job and suffered one of the worst Union losses at the Battle of Fredericksburg, Virginia, on December 13. Then, from April 30 to May 6, 1863, Major General Joseph Hooker took

Major General George Thomas (left) and Major General George McClellan (right), n.d. Collotype

CHAPTER EIGHT

Glass plate photograph by Alexander Gardner of Abraham Lincoln on his visit to Antietam, MD, two weeks after the battle, ca. 1862

Paul Philippoteaux, *Battle of Gettysburg* (New York: Manhattan Art, 1898). Chromolithograph

over the army and experienced defeat brought on by his lack of nerve as well as the skillful flank attacks made by Lee and Lieutenant General Thomas J. "Stonewall" Jackson during the Battle of Chancellorsville, Virginia. Lincoln, in anguish, cried out: "My God! My God! What will the country say?"[6]

Hooker finally resigned on June 27, as Lee once more led his Army of Northern Virginia northward on a raid that he hoped would threaten Washington, DC. To replace Hooker, the president appointed Major General George Gordon Meade, a smart and competent leader whose military mettle was put to the test from July 1 to July 3, 1863, at Gettysburg, Pennsylvania. Although the president was happy enough with the victory won by his beleaguered Army of the Potomac, he was sharply displeased with Meade. He could not understand why the general let Lee avoid a crushing blow and retreat unmolested to Virginia. In this case, however, Lincoln misunderstood Meade's good sense. His regiments were in shambles. The president's desire to annihilate Lee's army was totally unrealistic.

As Lincoln groused about his generals in the Eastern Theater, the picture was not nearly as bleak in the West. In January 1862 Brigadier General George H. Thomas defeated Confederate forces at Mill Springs, Kentucky. That set the stage for then Brigadier General Ulysses S. Grant to capture the Confederate Forts Henry and Donelson on February 6 and 16. At Donelson, the Confederates surrendered an entire army to Grant, giving him the popular nickname "Unconditional Surrender Grant," befitting his initials. Grant's army, now called the Army of the Tennessee, followed the Confederate retreat southward. On April 6, 1862, Confederate General Albert Sidney Johnston surprised Grant with an attack at Shiloh Church near Pittsburg Landing, Tennessee. The next day, after Union reinforcements arrived, Grant ordered a counterattack that effectively rolled the enemy back to their defenses in Corinth, Mississippi. Instead of praising Grant's victory, Major General Henry W. Halleck, his superior, shelved him for minor infractions while believing rumors that Grant was up to his "old habits," which meant he was drinking heavily (though he was not). When a friend urged the president to remove Grant, Lincoln's answer was to the point: "I can't spare this man; he fights."[7]

When Grant regained command of the Army of the Tennessee, he set his sights on capturing Vicksburg, Mississippi, something Lincoln devoutly desired. Given the terrain of steep hills and plunging ravines, swampy bayous and thick woods, and the serpentine turns of the Mississippi River, Grant encountered great difficulty carrying out the mission. After trying for several months to approach Vicksburg by digging canals and advancing through impenetrable bayous, which caused the Northern press to doubt Grant's military acumen, the general decided that the only feasible option was to get his army and navy flotilla south of Vicksburg, and then cross his battalions over to the east bank of the Mississippi by using ironclads and transports. Despite Lincoln's misgivings about the strategy, Grant accomplished what was believed impossible: his gunboats and transports ran the Confederate batteries, his army marched south down the west bank of the river and was ferried to the east, and he outflanked Vicksburg by laying siege to it from the rear. Ignoring orders and attacking contrary to accepted military practice, Grant led his army northeast toward Jackson, the capital of Mississippi.

Beginning April 29, 1863, over nineteen days, with no available means to communicate with Washington, Grant won five battles and ultimately captured Jackson. His Army of the Tennessee then marched west to the foot of the Confederate earthworks defending Vicksburg. After two unsuccessful assaults against the Confederates, on May 19 and 22, Grant realized that he must conduct a siege of attrition against the enemy. On July 4, the day after Meade's Union victory at Gettysburg, the Confederate garrison surrendered Vicksburg to Grant. With this news, the Northern states celebrated the victories and the generals who had achieved them. In Washington, Lincoln said solemnly, referring to the Mississippi River, "The Father of Waters again flows unvexed to the sea." On July 13 the president congratulated Grant by disclosing some of his own worries during the campaign. "When you turned Northward East of the Big Black [River]," wrote Lincoln, "I feared it was a mistake. I now wish to make the personal acknowledgment that you were right, and I was wrong."[8]

In early March 1864, after his victory in the Chattanooga Campaign, Grant was summoned to Washington to receive a commission as lieutenant general—the only general other than George Washington to hold this highest rank—and General-in-Chief of all Union armies. Grant claimed that Lincoln promised not to interfere with military operations, but the reality was that the commander in chief watched this general as closely as he had the others. Nevertheless, after a search of three years, Lincoln had finally enemy armies in detail. An Indiana soldier wrote home: "I am like the fellow that got his house burned by the guerillas. [H]e was in for emancipation subjugation extermination and hell and damnation. We are in war and anything to beat the south."[13] The Emancipation Proclamation gave a moral underpinning to the Union's prosecution of this kind of escalated, "hard" war, a term borrowed by military historians from Major General William Tecumseh Sherman's phrase "hard hand of war" to differentiate it from the modern term "total war."

In the decades following the war, Lincoln and Grant were hailed as the saviors of the Union. But it is Lincoln who rightly stands above Grant. As the commander in chief, Lincoln originated a many-sided strategy—a grand design—that was military, political, and social. If we look to the Gettysburg Address, his most famous speech, and certainly the finest words spoken by an American to honor the war dead, we learn of the responsibility those who did not fight must have to "the unfinished work" of those who fought and died on Civil War battlefields. The speech's occasion was the dedication ceremony for Soldiers' National Cemetery, where the North's casualties at Gettysburg were given proper graves. Yet Lincoln's universalizing message in the speech was for the public "rather to be dedicated" to the twofold war aims of safeguarding the American Union and ending the bondage of people. "The great task remaining before us," he said, is "devotion to that cause for which they here gave the last full measure of devotion," a cause that shall bring both "a new birth of freedom" and "government of the people, by the people, for the people." The war against secession and slavery had to be won; there was no future for democracy or freedom if separatists and enslavers gained victory. To win such a war against one's fellow countrymen required the power of Lincoln's leadership—in wielding his understanding of the military, confounding the doubts of his detractors, staying the course as his command structure changed, and leading an army of men willing to make the ultimate sacrifice.

NOTES

1. James M. Winchell, "Three Interviews with President Lincoln," *The Galaxy* 16 (July 1873): 34–35.

2. Horace Greeley, "Greeley's Estimate of Lincoln" [ca. 1868], *Century* 42 (July 1891): 377.

3. John Hay, "Washington Correspondence," Nov. 2, 1861, in Michael Burlingame, ed., *Lincoln's Journalist: John Hay's Anonymous Writings for the Press, 1860–1861* (Carbondale: Southern Illinois University Press, 1998), 130; John G. Nicolay and John Hay, *Abraham Lincoln: A History*, 10 vols. (New York, 1890), 5:155.

4. Harold Holzer, ed., *Lincoln as I Knew Him* (Chapel Hill, NC: Algonquin Books of Chapel Hill, 1999), 38.

5. T. Harry Williams, *Lincoln and His Generals* (New York: Alfred A. Knopf, 1951), 124. See also James Ford Rhodes, *History of the Civil War, 1861–1865* (New York: MacMillan, 1919), 160.

6. Noah Brooks, *Washington in Lincoln's Time* (New York: The Century, 1895), 56–58.

7. Alexander K. McClure, *Abraham Lincoln and Men of War-Times* (Philadelphia: Times, 1892), 180.

8. Roy P. Basler, ed., *The Collected Works of Abraham Lincoln*, 8 vols. (hereafter *Collected Works*) (New Brunswick, NJ: Rutgers University Press, 1953), 6:326.

9. *Collected Works*, 8:392.

10. Isaac N. Arnold, *The Life of Abraham Lincoln* (Chicago, 1885), 375.

11. Schuyler Colfax, in Allen Thorndike Rice, ed., *Reminiscences of Abraham Lincoln by Distinguished Men of His Time* (New York, 1886), 342–43.

12. Lincoln to Andrew Johnson, Mar. 26, 1863, in *Collected Works*, 6:149–50.

13. Amory K. Allen to Delphany Allen, Jan. 8, 1863, "Civil War Letters of Amory K. Allen," *Indiana Magazine of History* 31 (Dec. 1935): 361.

THE DAVID M. RUBENSTEIN AMERICANA COLLECTION

> The dedicatory remarks were then delivered by the President, as follows:
>
> PRESIDENT LINCOLN'S SPEECH.
>
> Four score and seven years ago our fathers brought forth upon this continent a new nation, conceived in Liberty, and dedicated to the proposition that all men are created equal. (Applause.) Now we are engaged in a great civil war, testing whether that nation or any nation so conceived and so dedicated can long endure. We are met on a great battle-field of that war. We are met to dedicate a portion of it as the final resting-place of those who here gave their lives that that nation might live. It is altogether fitting and proper that we should do this. But in a larger sense we cannot dedicate, we cannot consecrate, we cannot hallow this ground. The brave men living and dead who struggled here have consecrated it far above our power to add or detract. (Applause.) The world will little note nor long remember what we say here, but it can never forget what they did here. (Applause.) It is for us, the living, rather to be dedicated here to the unfinished work that they have thus far so nobly carried on. (Applause.) It is rather for us to be here dedicated to the great task remaining before us, that from these honored dead we take increased devotion to that cause for which they here gave the last full measure of devotion; that we here highly resolve that the dead shall not have died in vain, (applause;) that the nation shall, under God, have a new birth of freedom; and that governments of the people, by the people and for the people, shall not perish from the earth. (Long-continued applause.)
>
> The exercises were closed by a song from the choir present. The procession then returned to the town. Crowds, however, hung about the Diamond and around the house where were stopping the prominent public men.

Abraham Lincoln and Edward Everett, *An Oration Delivered on the Battlefield of Gettysburg*

NEW YORK: BAKER & GODWIN, 1863

The most acclaimed speech by an American president is Lincoln's Gettysburg Address, so named for the land on which a massive three-day military encounter was won by the Union in the first days of July 1863. The victory came at a cost: the Battle of Gettysburg bore the most casualties of any Civil War conflict, with over 23,000 from the North and 28,000 from the South. Lincoln gave his speech at the dedication of the cemetery built from the battlefield's graves, and the acclaim it has received since is owing to his reflective restraint following such carnage. Speeches are insufficient for the task of honoring the war dead, Lincoln said. Dedication must be more than an event, but rather an "increased devotion" to the very reason why the war was fought.

Abraham Lincoln, "The President's Dedication Address at Gettysburg"

[NEW YORK]: MILLER & MATHEWS, [1864]

The Gettysburg Address reframed the basis for winning the war: to ensure the continuance of American democracy. It then improved the definition of democracy to include the Lincolnian concepts of a "new birth of freedom" and "government of the people, by the people, for the people." Clearly Lincoln meant a more equitable, postslavery society. He did this in under 280 words, spoken in less than five minutes. Lincoln was not the featured speaker for the ceremony; that honor went to Edward Everett, who in the 1850s was secretary of state and a senator from Massachusetts but who by the 1860s was a touring heavyweight orator. His speech preceded Lincoln's, included over 13,000 words, lasted two hours, and is scarcely remembered today.

David Wills [et al.], *Report of the Select Committee Relative to the Soldiers' National Cemetery*

HARRISBURG [PA]: SINGERLY & MYERS, 1864

The Gettysburg ceremonies were on November 19, four months after the battle. Perhaps by then Lincoln could sense that 1863 was the year when the war would turn in the North's favor after additional Union victories in Tennessee, Mississippi, and Virginia. The first item shown here is the first book-form edition of the day's speeches, printed six days after the event, in a rare cloth variant that betrays the top billing given to Everett (Lincoln's speech was tucked onto page 40 and not mentioned on the title page). Shown next is the first separate broadside printing of the Gettysburg Address. The third item is the report of the committee which built the cemetery. Lincoln made final edits to his speech when lodging at the residence of the report's editor.

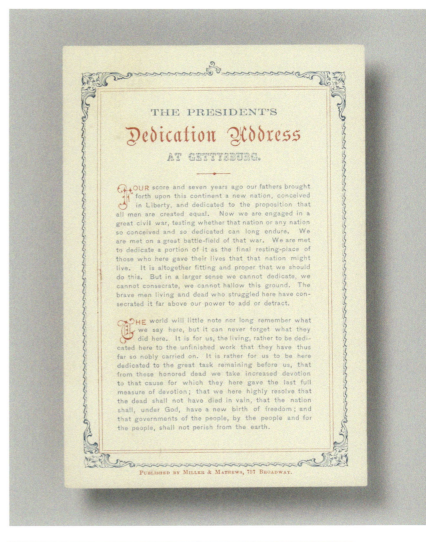

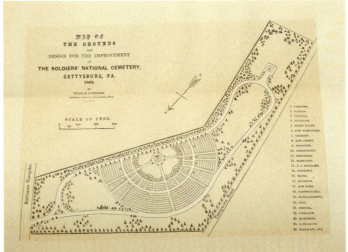

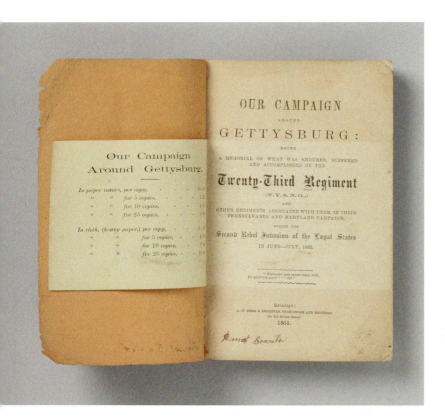

John Lockwood, *Our Campaign around Gettysburg*

BROOKLYN: ROME BROTHERS, 1864

Gettysburg was the largest of over fifteen battles during Confederate General Lee's second campaign to attack the North. Lincoln had appointed George Meade as commanding general of the Union's Army of the Potomac four days earlier. Battle-hardened and meticulous, Meade moved his battalions into tight defensive positions resembling a fishhook to keep the rebel army from gaining any elevation on the field. Repeated Confederate assaults were repulsed, bloodily so, and, on the fourth day, when no Union counterattack came, Lee retreated to Virginia. Lincoln was enraged that Meade did not chase Lee. But Meade was, in the words of the author of this early Gettysburg battle history, "engaged in succoring the wounded and burying the dead."

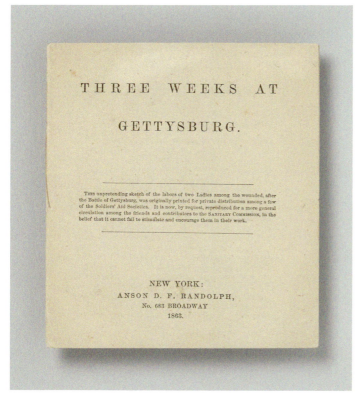

Georgeanna Woolsey Bacon, *Three Weeks at Gettysburg*

NEW YORK: RANDOLPH, 1863

Georgeanna Woolsey wrote one of the war's more well-known female nursing narratives based on her time at Gettysburg after the battle. She came from a New York abolitionist family, one of seven sisters dedicated to volunteerism and a brother who served in the Union army. Woolsey worked for the U.S. Sanitary Commission, which, as a civilian medical aid society assisting the military, gave her nursing training and often asked her to transport supplies to the field. Her privately printed *Three Weeks at Gettysburg* was so well-received that the USSC reissued it for fundraising and recruitment. Woolsey served as a nurse for the whole war. Her description of the army's recently implemented tiered treatment structure remains a source for American medical history.

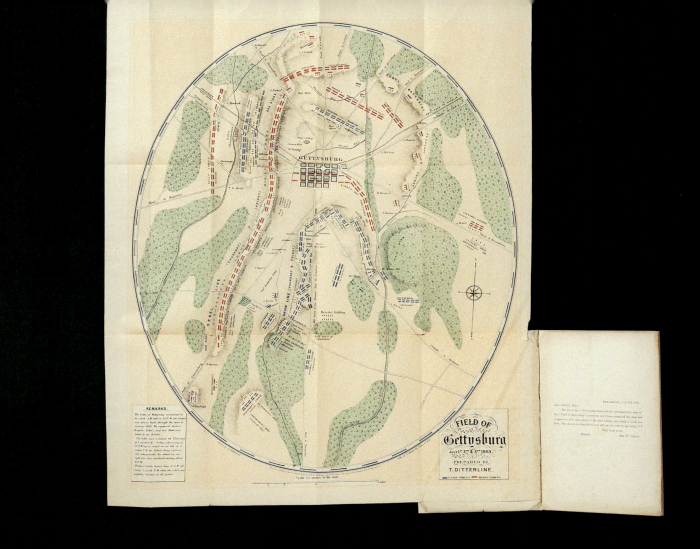

Theodore Ditterline, *Sketch of the Battles of Gettysburg*
NEW YORK: ALVORD, 1864

This is the first map printed of the Battle of Gettysburg, done by a local amateur cartographer named Theodore Ditterline, who was a career office clerk both in Pennsylvania at the time and eventually in Washington at the War Department. He drew the locations of both forces—Union in blue and Confederate in red—based on his personal observations, those of other residents, and the earliest dispatches of war correspondents. The Ditterline map represents a moment in print history when portrayals of Civil War battles, in minute detail, gained cultural currency as expressions of valorization. One can see not only troop and artillery positions but also labels for buildings and infrastructure. By 1864 the history of the war was concurrent with the war itself.

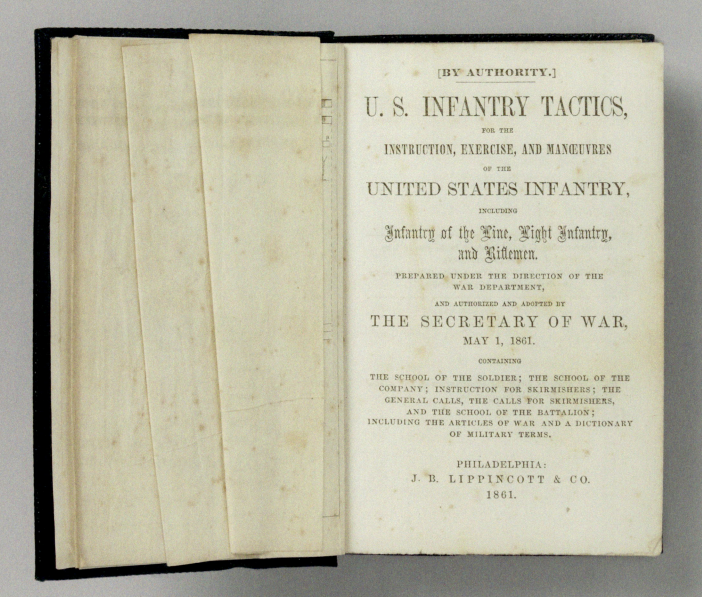

[War Department], *U.S. Infantry Tactics*

PHILADELPHIA: LIPPINCOTT, 1861

We have no record of Lincoln reading this edition of the army's infantry handbook, published by the War Department in the first year of his presidency. We know that Lincoln was an assiduous student of military tactics and strategy, enough eventually to match his top generals in understanding field maneuvers and to surpass his Confederate counterparts in having a national plan that linked military aims with policy advances. Thirty years earlier Lincoln had been elected captain of his militia battalion during the Black Hawk War. Now he was commander in chief during the largest (and costliest, and deadliest) war fought on American soil. The preservation of the Union depended on Lincoln demonstrating that he was an assertive *wartime* president above all else.

Abraham Lincoln, *The President to General McClellan*

[WASHINGTON]: N.P., 1862

Lincoln's grasp of military matters—movement, men, materiel—was evident in this published telegram from early in the war during McClellan's Peninsula Campaign, so named for the sea-land approach up Virginia's coastal plain that the Union general took to the Confederate capital of Richmond. McClellan had complained of inadequate soldiers. Actually, Lincoln explained, McClellan's numbers were commensurate with other divisions and, importantly, spared troops to defend the nation's capital. The letter exposed the reason for McClellan's posturing: personnel was his excuse not to attack aggressively. "By delay, the enemy will readily gain on you," Lincoln wrote here, adding, "Once more let me tell you, it is indispensable to you that you strike a blow."

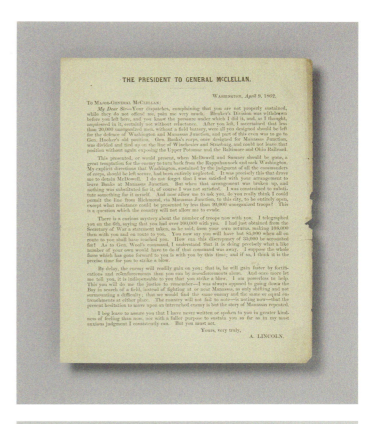

Frederick Petersen, *Military Review of the Campaign in Virginia & Maryland*

NEW YORK: TOUSEY & DEXTER, 1862

McClellan's failures in Virginia showed not only that he was irredeemably uncooperative and inherently unaggressive but that targeting the South's capital would be less effective than targeting its forces. This split in strategy had its parallel in public opinion, where criticism of the war went either to the generals or Lincoln's administration. Lincoln's insistence on giving direct orders to his generals, as he sharpened his national strategy, was exoneration for those on the generals' side. Consider the assertion of this pro-McClellan pamphlet printed for the 1862 midterm elections. "What reason had the President to interfere personally with the affairs of the army?" it wrote. "It cannot be want of confidence in...McClellan's capacity or loyalty[.]"

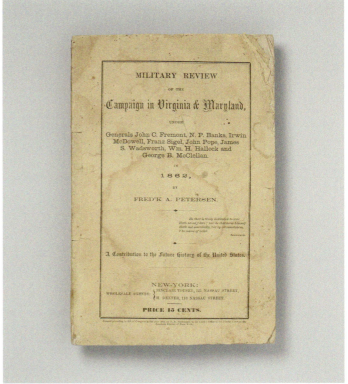

CAMPAIGN IN VIRGINIA.

GENERAL POPE'S OFFICIAL REPORT.

New York, January 27th, 1863.

General:

I have the honor to submit the following report of the operations of the army under my command during the late campaign in Virginia:

Several of the reports of Corps Commanders have not yet reached me, but so much time has elapsed since the termination of the campaign, that I do not feel at liberty to withhold this report longer.

The strange misapprehension of facts concerning this campaign, which, though proceeding from irresponsible sources, has much possessed the public mind, makes it necessary for me to enter more into detail than I should otherwise have done, and to embody in the report such of the dispatches and orders sent and received as will make clear every statement which is contained in it.

On the 26th day of June, 1862, by special order of the President of the United States, I was assigned to the command of the Army of Virginia. That army was constituted as follows:

First Corps, under Major-Gen. Fremont.
Second Corps, under Major-Gen. Banks.
Third Corps, under Major-Gen. McDowell.

In addition to these three Corps, a small unorganized force under Brig.-General Sturgis was posted in the neighborhood of Alexandria, and was then in process of being organised for field service. The forces in the entrenchments around Washington were also placed under my command. All the disposable moveable forces consisted of the three Corps first named. Their effective strength of infantry and artillery as reported to me was as follows:

Fremont's Corps, eleven thousand five hundred strong; Banks' Corps, reported at fourteen thousand and five hundred, but in reality only about eight thousand; McDowell's Corps, eighteen thousand four hundred—making a total of thirty-eight thousand men.

The cavalry numbered about five thousand, but most of it was badly mounted and armed, and in poor condition for service. These forces were scattered over a wide district of country, not within supporting

---

John Pope, *The Campaign in Virginia, of July and August 1862*

MILWAUKEE: JERMAIN & BRIGHTMAN, 1863

For his army to win, Lincoln made personnel changes. In September 1862 he relieved General John Pope of his command of the Army of Virginia. In November he removed General McClellan as leader of the Army of the Potomac. In December Lincoln ordered General Nathaniel B. Banks, recently dismissed from the Army of the Shenandoah, to be transferred to New Orleans to take over the Department of the Gulf from General Benjamin Butler, who then formed the 1st Louisiana Native Guard (the first Black regiment). In January Lincoln relocated General Ambrose Burnside to Ohio after the disaster at Fredericksburg. All this created some stupefaction among the generals. The first one, Pope, wrote this defense of his leadership of so "difficult" and "thankless" a mission.

I.

THE WAR.

When President LINCOLN issued his first call for 75,000 men, we read in the newspapers that the announcement of this Proclamation was received by the rebel Congress—then sitting at Montgomery—with shouts of laughter. Our indignation was justifiable at the time, but experience soon taught us that we had underrated the strength, harmonious unity and resources of the South, and we now admit that they had reason to smile at the pigmy army of 75,000 men, with which we proposed to enforce the laws of the United States. After discovering our mistake, a gigantic and patriotic North has, for the last two years, poured out its wealth, men and immense resources, at the many-headed Dragon; and we are to-day, to all practical purposes, no nearer the re-establishment of the Union than when it first broke asunder. True, we are in possession of more Southern soil than we could boast of two years ago, but the armies and defenses of our enemy are as strong and seemingly impregnable as ever, and our conquests have merely increased the already enormous expenses of transportation and subsistence, without any adequate benefit whatsoever.

Obedience and discipline are the paramount duties of a soldier, without which an army is but a powerless mob. The Volunteers of the United States can boast of having practiced these military virtues in a degree never before witnessed in the world. It is a historical fact that the armies of the old world owed their existence to a despotic rule, that reduced the soldiery to a mere machinery of brutal force that had no voice in the destinies of their respective nations, and to whom patriotism meant nothing but military vain-glory. But the soldiery of the United States is entirely differently constituted.

[Anonymous], *West Point and the War*
ST. LOUIS: N.P., 1863

The American Civil War was fought in separate theaters of conflict, each with named armies and high commands. The initial string of Union defeats was in the Eastern Theater. The scenario was different in the Western Theater, which covered Tennessee, Mississippi, and Georgia. There the Union armies had an unrelenting general named Ulysses S. Grant who, by 1863, had won key strategic battles across a swath of West Tennessee and was put in charge, by Lincoln, of all volunteer forces. This East-West discrepancy was provocatively plumbed by the author of this fascinating, anonymous pamphlet, who blamed the "mismanagement" and "slow progress" in the east on the incompetence of non-volunteer officers from West Point, the military academy.

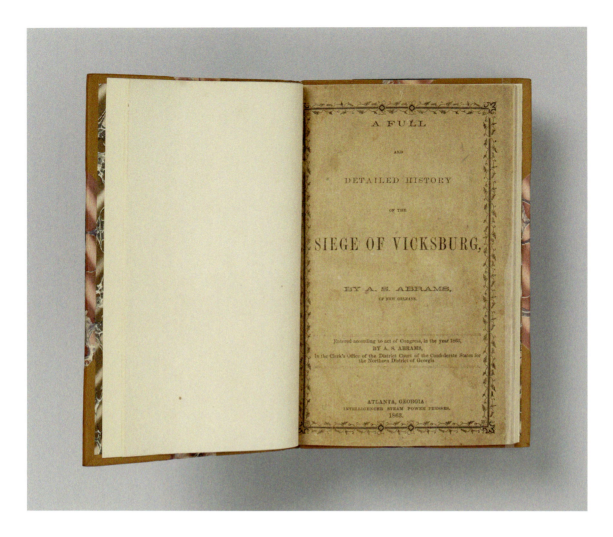

Alexander S. Abrams, *A Full and Detailed History of the Siege of Vicksburg*

ATLANTA: INTELLIGENCER STEAM POWER PRESSES, 1863

General Grant's western battlefield successes in 1862 pleased Lincoln; they arrived sequentially and seized important interior and waterway lines for the Union. He captured Fort Henry on the Tennessee River and Fort Donelson on the Cumberland River. His enemy weakened (and greatly imprisoned), Grant moved up the Tennessee, where, on April 6, a Confederate attack led to the savage Battle of Shiloh. That evening Grant received a reinforcement of men; the next morning he repulsed the rebels deep into Mississippi. There, a month later, was one of the Union's greatest victories: the forty-odd-day Siege of Vicksburg, won by Grant's military ingenuity. With Vicksburg in Union hands, the North controlled the Mississippi River, and the South was split in two.

Ulysses S. Grant, *Report of Lieutenant-General U.S. Grant*
NEW YORK: APPLETON, 1865

In Grant, Lincoln had found a general who was inventive, inspiring, and aggressive. This report by Grant to Congress tracked his feats after his 1864 promotion by Lincoln to lieutenant general, putting him in charge of all Union forces. It was the highest achievable rank, one held only once before, by George Washington. With this authority Grant put all his Northern armies to work in a simultaneous, multipronged attack on the South's forces in Virginia—his Overland Campaign. "I [used] the greatest number of troops practicable," he wrote, to "hammer continuously against the armed force of the enemy...until by mere attrition, if in no other way, there should be nothing left to him but an equal submission with the loyal section of our common country to the Constitution and laws of the land."

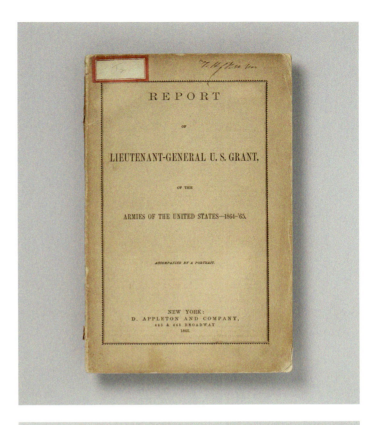

Lincoln's Treatment of Gen. Grant
[NEW YORK]: DEMOCRATIC NEWSPAPER OFFICES, 1864

The progress of the Civil War mattered politically for Lincoln, as 1864 was a presidential election year. The North's electorate knew of the Gettysburg and Vicksburg victories; the policy debate was whether prosecuting the war was worth the lives lost. Lincoln's Democratic challenger emerged as George McClellan, his former irresolute general, who promised his party that he could negotiate peace with the South. His past failures as a military leader were imputed to Lincoln, who he said had interfered with and impaired his command. This pamphlet is Democratic propaganda and cites fifteen directives from Lincoln to McClellan meant to show meddlesomeness compared to the freedom Lincoln gave Grant. For Lincoln to be vindicated, he needed Grant to triumph.

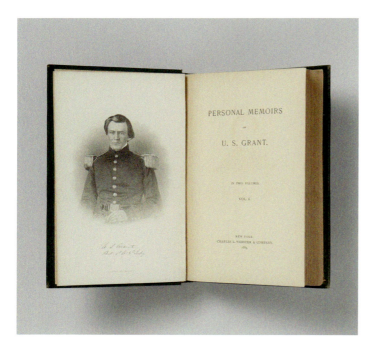

Ulysses S. Grant, *Personal Memoirs*
NEW YORK: WEBSTER, 1885

From Grant's *Memoirs* we learn of his first meeting with Lincoln in Washington in May of 1864. "He stated to me," Grant wrote about Lincoln, "that he had never professed to be a military man or to know how campaigns should be conducted, and never wanted to interfere with them: but that procrastination on the part of commanders...forced him into issuing his series of 'Military Orders'[.] All he wanted or had ever wanted was some one who would take the responsibility and act....Assuring him that I would do the best I could with the means at hand, and avoid as far as possible annoying him or the War Department, our first interview ended." Leaving the White House early, Grant asked to skip dinner, saying, "Time is very important now." Grant's army's final push would begin in June.

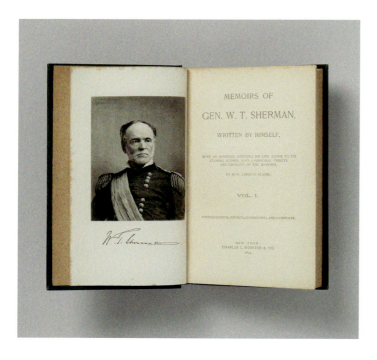

William T. Sherman, *Memoirs of W. T. Sherman*
NEW YORK: WEBSTER, 1891

Sherman took over Grant's operations in the West. In his *Memoirs* he printed his September 1864 letter to Grant: "If you can whip Lee and I can march to the Atlantic, I think Uncle Abe will give us a twenty days' leave of absence." Sherman's *Memoirs* tells us he was aware of the war's reflection on Lincoln: "Success to our arms [was] a political necessity; and it was all-important that something startling in our interest...occur before the election in November. The brilliant success at Atlanta filled that requirement, and made the election of Lincoln certain." Capturing Atlanta was not a set-piece battle but rather a cordoning of the Confederate's manufacturing center. On September 3 Sherman telegraphed Washington, "Atlanta is ours, and fairly won."

Philip H. Sheridan, *Personal Memoirs*

NEW YORK: WEBSTER, 1888

The Confederacy, mired defensively in Virginia, sent forces north to goad the Union's guard into diversionary skirmishes near Washington. The political alarm this caused in 1864 forced Lincoln to resurrect the Army of the Shenandoah and put the thirty-three-year-old Philip Sheridan in charge of it. In his *Memoirs* Sheridan recounts being "remind[ed] that positive success was necessary to counteract the political dissatisfaction existing in some of the Northern States." Grant's orders were more acerbic: "If the war is to last another year, we want the Shenandoah Valley to remain a barren waste." When Sheridan, a cavalryman, heroically rode to lead his men to an unlikely victory near Washington, Lincoln wrote him a letter of thanks, which was reprinted in the book.

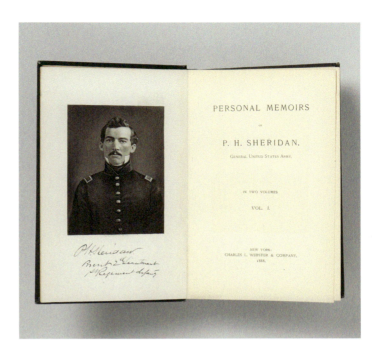

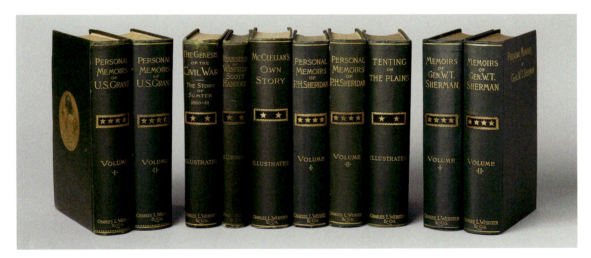

Ulysses S. Grant et al., ["Shoulder Strap" Civil War series]

NEW YORK: WEBSTER, 1885–92

Lincoln owed his 1864 reelection to the war victories of three men leading the Union armies (in ascending order of rank): General Philip Sheridan, for the Battles of Winchester and Cedar Creek (May–June); General William Tecumseh Sherman, for the capture of Atlanta (May–September); and General Grant, for his Virginia standoffs against Confederate General Lee in Spotsylvania, the Wilderness Campaign, and the Siege of Vicksburg. Years later the three generals wrote their memoirs for an imprint owned by Mark Twain, the American novelist. A brief publishing venture operated by Twain's nephew Charles Webster, it printed seven Civil War titles that together are colloquially called the "shoulder strap" set for the rank insignias on their spines.

LINCOLN THE WARTIME PRESIDENT, PART II · 1863 TO 1865

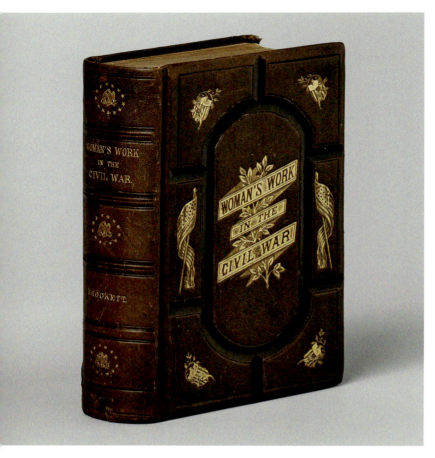

Linus P. Brockett and Mary C. Vaughan, *Woman's Work in the Civil War*

PHILADELPHIA: ZEIGLER, MCCURDY, 1867

A biographical work printed soon after the Civil War was this nearly 800-page compendium of the "Heroism, Patriotism and Patience" of women in the conflict, written by a male doctor and a female temperance worker. It named hundreds of women but devoted extra coverage to Dorothea Dix and Clara Barton. Both women eventually gained lasting recognition for their life's calling, but they were serving as nurses as early as the 1861 Baltimore Riot. Dix became superintendent of army nurses, in charge of recruiting all volunteers. With Lincoln's blessing, Barton formed the Missing Soldiers Office to assist with inquiries from despairing family members. Dix later established the country's first hospitals for the mentally ill. Barton later founded the Red Cross.

Frank Moore, *Women of the War*

HARTFORD [CT]: SCRANTON, 1866

Another early history of women in the Civil War is this by a journalist-anthologist. It tried in part to satisfy the public's fascination with women who passed as men and saw fighting in the war. One chapter tells of a nineteen-year-old Brooklynite who "disguised herself as a boy, and joined the drum corps of a Michigan regiment." Alas, she was killed in Grant's counterattack at Chattanooga. Another profile concerns Lincoln and one of his more liberal policies: pardoning deserters. Mary Morris Husband earned praise for her work with casualty transports near the front lines. Here we learn that, upon noticing court martials done in haste or error, Husband took to Lincoln a regular caseload of soldiers to receive absolution, months before his Proclamation Offering Pardon to Deserters did it nationally.

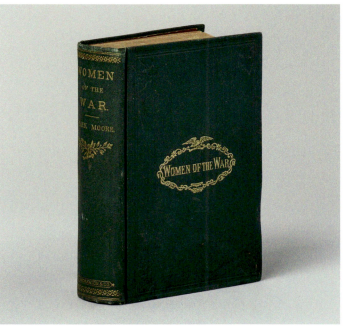

LINCOLN THE WARTIME PRESIDENT, PART II · 1863 TO 1865

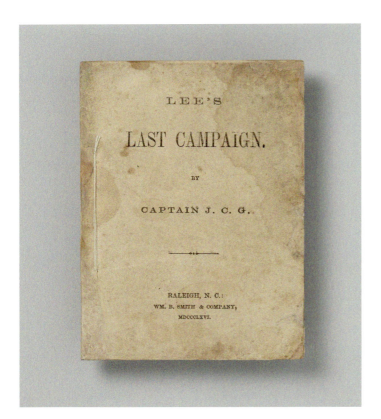

John Gorman, *Lee's Last Campaign*
RALEIGH [NC]: SMITH, 1866

In November 1864 Sherman marched his army 285 miles from Atlanta to the coast, destroying railways, businesses, and crops along the way. He telegraphed Lincoln, "[I] present you as a Christmas gift the city of Savannah." Meanwhile, Sheridan undertook the similarly destructive Shenandoah Campaign, where farms and homes were destroyed. Sheridan then spent the early part of 1865 with Grant chasing Confederate General Lee. The author of this pamphlet, a member of the 2nd North Carolina Regiment, described Lee's army: "I was greatly depressed at the sad state [of] the whole army. Desertions were very numerous, both to the enemy and to the rear, and I found that the army had at last succumbed, not to the enemy . . . but to the discontent."

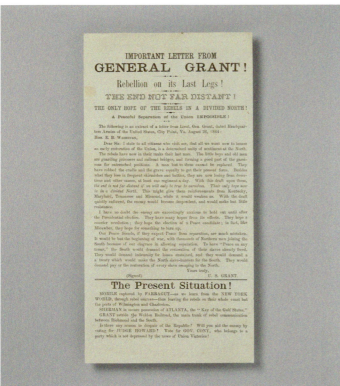

Ulysses S. Grant, *Important Letter… Rebellion on Its Last Legs!*
N.P.: N.P., [1864]

As the Union closed in, news from the front lines was distributed in print channels for domestic effect, as this rare handbill from 1864 shows. Originally a letter from General Grant to Elihu B. Washburn (a congressman from Illinois, who had endorsed Grant's earliest appointments and, when Grant became president, served as his secretary of state), it placed Grant, once a Democrat, into the antislavery folds of the Republican Party, where he remained. The letter was printed nationally in newspapers to counter the peace plank of the Democratic Party in the election. It was then repurposed in at least five known broadside forms for political candidates—here for Abner Cony of Maine, helping ensure that the governorship remained in Republican hands.

"Peace," *Daily Star Extra* (New London, CT)

FEB. 4, 1865

At the heart of the Union's might was the partnership of Lincoln and Grant, built on the mutual respect each had for the other's value to the country. They communicated regularly and bore a virtuous circle of national consequence, where Grant's battlefield wins aided Lincoln's political ones, and Lincoln's statecraft savvy assured Grant a supply of manpower and armaments. This supply allowed Grant to (1) impair the power of the Confederacy and its army and (2) bring the war to the South's citizenry through attrition tactics. Hit the military, hit the people, and the politicians will follow. In turn, Lincoln arranged to meet rebel leadership at the Hampton Roads Conference, described here. It ended in an impasse: Lincoln would not budge on the need for reunification.

Richmond Has Fallen!

N.P.: N.P., [1865]

Victory!…We Celebrate the Fall of Richmond

N.P.: N.P., [1865]

Victory Will Lead to Peace

N.P.: N.P., [1865]

George P. Hardwick, ***Capture of Richmond and Petersburg***

WASHINGTON: HARDWICK, 1865

On March 27 and 28, Lincoln, Grant, and Sherman met at the Union army's headquarters at the mouth of the James River in Virginia. Grant requested the meeting, Lincoln eagerly obliged, and Sherman fortuitously joined soon after his subduing of the Georgia countryside was complete. The agenda was to eliminate the Confederate army. Grant's motive was strategic: allowing them to regroup would prolong the war. Lincoln's was humanistic: he wanted the casualties to cease.

Since June 1864 the Union had battled Confederate forces in Virginia along a thirty-mile sweep of trenches between Richmond and Petersburg. The target was always Richmond, the Confederate capital, but Petersburg was its transportation hub and supply center. The army that controlled one city controlled both. The Union's final attack on these two cities occurred while Lincoln was in Virginia, on a trip that lasted about a week, no farther than ten miles from the fighting.

After meeting with Lincoln, Grant made his move. On April 1 he ordered Sheridan to capture a vital intersection of five roadways near Petersburg. Then, at dawn on the 2nd, Grant sent men from five corps into the city, overtaking it. With Petersburg gone, Richmond was defenseless, and the Confederate government evacuated by train. Their army and General Lee fled soon as well. As the Union army gave chase to the rebels, Lincoln was present to tour the fallen capital by foot.

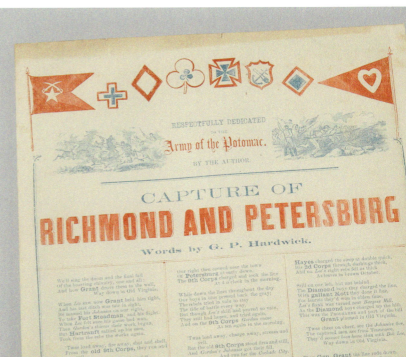

> # LATEST NEWS BY TELEGRAPH.
>
> ---
>
> WASHINGTON, April 7, 10 A. M.
> Major General Dix, New York:
>
> Gen. Sheridan attacked and routed Lee's army yesterday, capturing Gens. Ewell, Kershaw and Button, and many other general officers, and several thousand prisoners, and expects to force Lee to surrender all that is left of his army. Details will be given as speedily as possible, but the telegraph is working badly.
>
>   E. M. STANTON,
>   Secr'y of War.

Latest News by Telegraph

N.P.: N.P., [1865]

The ending of the Civil War began with Confederate General Lee's surrender at the Appomattox Court House, about ninety miles west of Richmond. On his march there, Lee realized the debilitated state of his forces, which were severely in need of food. His path was desperate and winding, constantly met by Union pressure. As this newspaper extra reports, General Sheridan was particularly effective at exploiting fissures in Lee's line—whole divisions dissolved. Sheridan told Grant, "If the thing is pressed I think Lee will surrender." Lincoln, learning of this, messaged Grant: "Let the thing be pressed." When Lee surrendered at Appomattox Court House on April 9, 1865, it was in part because Sheridan had beat him to the nearby station, depriving him of a resupply of rations.

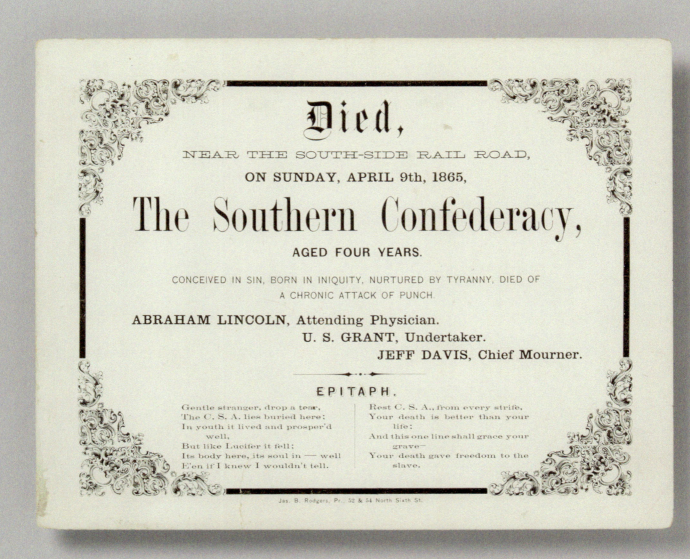

Died, Near the South-Side Rail Road… the Southern Confederacy

[PHILADELPHIA]: RODGERS, 1865

This irreverent broadside made the understandable mistake of assuming that Lee's surrender meant the war—and secession—was over. It only meant that Lee's Army of Northern Virginia, the Confederacy's greatest military force, was defeated; there were other Southern armies in North Carolina, Alabama, and parts west. However, Lee's surrender and the terms provided by Lincoln and Grant would serve as the model for the capitulation of those other forces in the months of May, June, and July. Only in August 1866 did the Civil War officially come to an end after Lincoln's assassination. More than a year after replacing Lincoln, his vice president, Andrew Johnson, issued a proclamation that "peace, order, tranquility, and civil authority now exists."

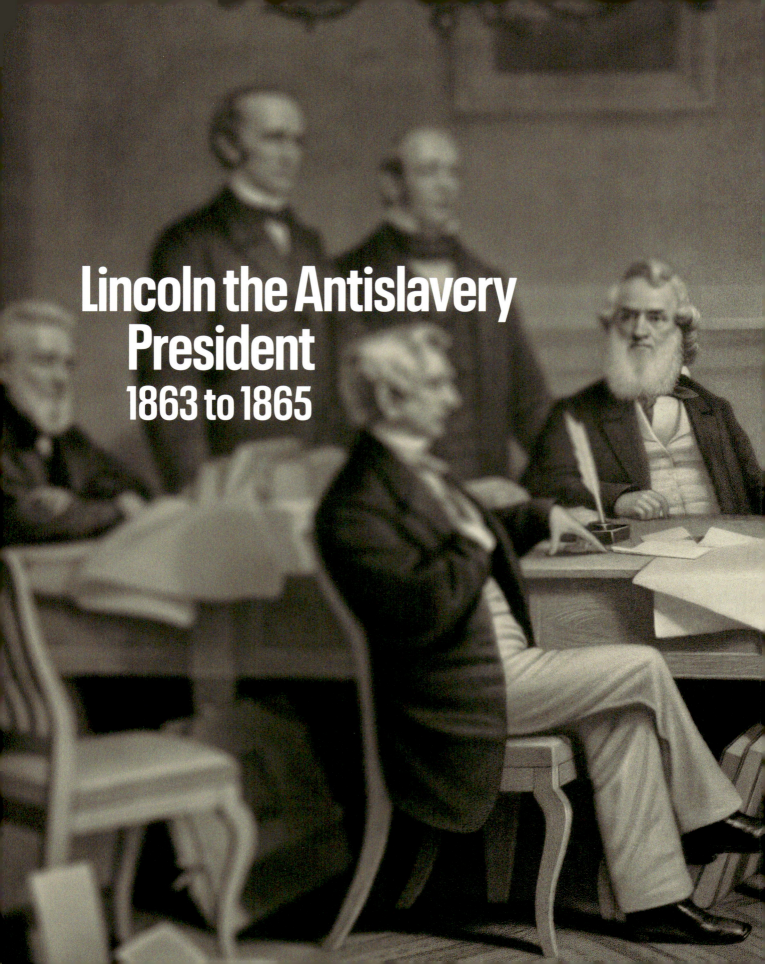

Lincoln the Antislavery President
1863 to 1865

It is hard to say that anything has been more bravely and well done than at Antietam, Murfreesboro, Gettysburg, and on many fields of lesser note.

Nor must Uncle Sam's web-feet be forgotten. At all the watery margins they have been present. Not only on the deep sea, the broad bay, and the rapid river, but also up the narrow, muddy bayou, and wherever the ground was a little damp, they have been and made their tracks.

Thanks to all for the great Republic, for the principle it lives by and keeps alive—for man's vast future—thanks to all.

Peace does not appear so distant as it did. I hope it will come soon, and come to stay, and so come as to be worth the keeping in all future time.

It will then have been proved that among free men there can be no successful appeal from the ballot to the bullet, and that they who take such appeal are sure to lose their case, and pay the cost.

And then there will be some black men who can remember that, with silent tongue, and clenched teeth, and steady eye, and well-poised bayonet, they have helped mankind on to this great consummation; while I fear there will be some white ones unable to forget that, with malignant heart and deceitful speech, they have strove to hinder it.

Still, let us not be over sanguine of a speedy final triumph. Let us be quite sober. Let us diligently apply the means, never doubting that a just God, in his own good time, will give us the rightful result.

Yours, very truly,

A. LINCOLN.

"If My Name Ever Goes into History"

EDNA GREENE MEDFORD

> I think slavery is wrong, morally, and politically. I desire that it should be not further spread in these United States, and I should not object if it should gradually terminate in the whole Union.¹

ABRAHAM LINCOLN did not count himself, nor did his contemporaries consider him, a member of the abolitionist camp. Abolitionists viewed slavery as a national sin and a stain on America's character. In the decades before the Civil War, they lectured throughout the free states and submitted petitions to Congress urging legislators to outlaw the ownership of human beings. Lincoln shared their sentiment that slavery was wrong and a detriment to national honor. Like many Americans of his day, however, he also believed that the abolitionists were a dangerous lot whose agitations fed discord and propelled the nation closer to disunion.² Yet when war threatened to tear apart the Union irrevocably, he looked for a way to ensure that slavery would never again cause division.

Although he stood apart from the abolitionists for most of his life, Lincoln hated slavery. He thought the institution was "a monstrous evil" that deprived America of being a model for republicanism to the rest of the world.³ It also prevented a whole class of people from the opportunity to advance in society. At the same time, he understood that the Constitution protected the right to own human beings, and it could not be easily removed.

Lincoln's prewar solution to the problem of slavery was to prevent its expansion, thus allowing it to die a natural death. He believed this was the original intent of the Founders: while they could not agree to eradicate the institution at the nation's birth, they put it on a path to extinction through containment. The process of emancipation would be gradual to prevent undue financial distress for the slaveholder while supposedly protecting the enslaved;⁴ since enslaved laborers were property, they would be freed only with the consent of the slaveholders, who would be compensated for their loss. Finally, Lincoln suggested that emancipation should be accompanied by "voluntary deportation" of the freedmen and -women. Believing that

Pages 184–85: Detail from Francis Bicknell Carpenter, *The first reading of the Emancipation Proclamation before the cabinet*, ca. 1866. Mezzotint

Page 186: Detail from Abraham Lincoln, "War Policy of the Administration. Letter of the President to the Union Mass Convention at Springfield," *Evening Journal Documents* (Albany, NY: Albany Journal, 1863) (see page 194)

the two races could never coexist as equals on American soil, he encouraged Black Americans to leave the United States and settle in a place where, presumably, they would be able to participate fully in society.[5] It was a position roundly criticized by abolitionists, especially those of color.

As a moderate antislavery man, Lincoln earned the Republican Party nomination in the 1860 presidential election by defeating more radical candidates. He won the general election with just under 40 percent of the popular vote in a four-way race. By the time he took office in March 1861, seven Southern states had seceded. Within a month, four more joined their slaveholding sisters in rebellion. To reassure the seceded states that he had no intention of interfering with slavery, the new president declared his commitment to uphold the existing laws of the nation, including protection of states' domestic institutions, and to enforce the Fugitive Slave Act of 1850. Determined that the Union hold on to the four border states, which permitted slavery but had not seceded, Lincoln initially ignored the hopes for freedom of both the enslaved and those who spoke on their behalf.

After failed attempts at conciliation and the protracted war that followed, Lincoln realized that a new approach had to be devised to secure victory and protect the nation from similar challenges in the future. The solution came in the form of emancipation of the enslaved population in the seceding states. Lincoln believed that he and Congress had no constitutional authority to touch slavery where it already existed; hence, he pressed the border states to adopt plans of emancipation and thus destroy the expectation that the Confederacy would expand. He supported congressional action that ended slavery in the District of Columbia and the Western territories and championed legislation that appropriated funding for colonization. Only after his calls for state action had failed did he embrace the idea of military emancipation. His plan to liberate out of "military necessity" went into effect on January 1, 1863, after he unsuccessfully appealed one last time to the seceded states to end their rebellion. Recognizing the gravity of his actions, he purportedly stated: "If my name ever goes into history it will be for this act, and my whole soul is in it."[6]

The Emancipation Proclamation declared freedom for enslaved people in the states or parts of states still in rebellion. It also authorized the enlistment of Black soldiers into the Union army. In doing so, Lincoln gave African American men the opportunity to fight for their own freedom and to serve as an army of liberation for those who remained in slavery. The enlistment of African Americans boosted the Union's military effort and played a significant role in the outcome of the Civil War.

Lincoln's decision to emancipate was met with fierce criticism on both sides of the political divide. Certain Democrats, such as Governor Horatio Seymour of New York, argued that freeing enslaved people and arming them was inviting rape and murder and the butchery of women and children.[7] A few abolitionists saw the decree as flawed because it exempted certain areas already under the control of the Union army. Even some of Lincoln's Republican friends encouraged him to rescind the decree. In response to such calls, he declared: "You say you will not fight to free

William Morris Smith, *District of Columbia. Company E, 4th U.S. Colored Infantry, at Fort Lincoln*, between 1863–66. Glass plate

negroes. Some of them seem willing to fight for you ... If they stake their lives for us, they must be prompted by the strongest motive—even the promise of freedom. And the promise being made, must be kept."[8]

Lincoln's Emancipation Proclamation freed roughly 3.1 million enslaved men, women, and children in those states or portions of states still in rebellion. It did not touch the more than 800,000 still enslaved in the border states, and it left open the possibility that slavery might be reintroduced in the future. Lincoln and supporters of Black freedom were concerned that his proclamation might be ruled unconstitutional after the war ended. To thwart such a challenge, Republicans in Congress sought to pass a constitutional amendment that would ensure that slavery would be abolished forever.

The struggle for universal emancipation and abolition by constitutional means quickly passed through the Senate but made its way much more slowly through the House. While Congress debated the merits of the measure, Lincoln remained in the background, preferring abolition by state action rather than through federal intervention. By the summer of 1864, however, he supported the Republican Party's platform, which called for a constitutional amendment that would "terminate and forever prohibit the existence of Slavery within the limits of the jurisdiction of the United States."[9]

After he won reelection—a result that was far from certain—Lincoln unreservedly backed the proposed constitutional amendment. Securing passage was not easy. The president insisted on holding a vote in the current term, even though it would have had much greater support when the new Congress was seated in March 1865. On January 31, after intense debates and promises of political favors (presumably sanctioned by the

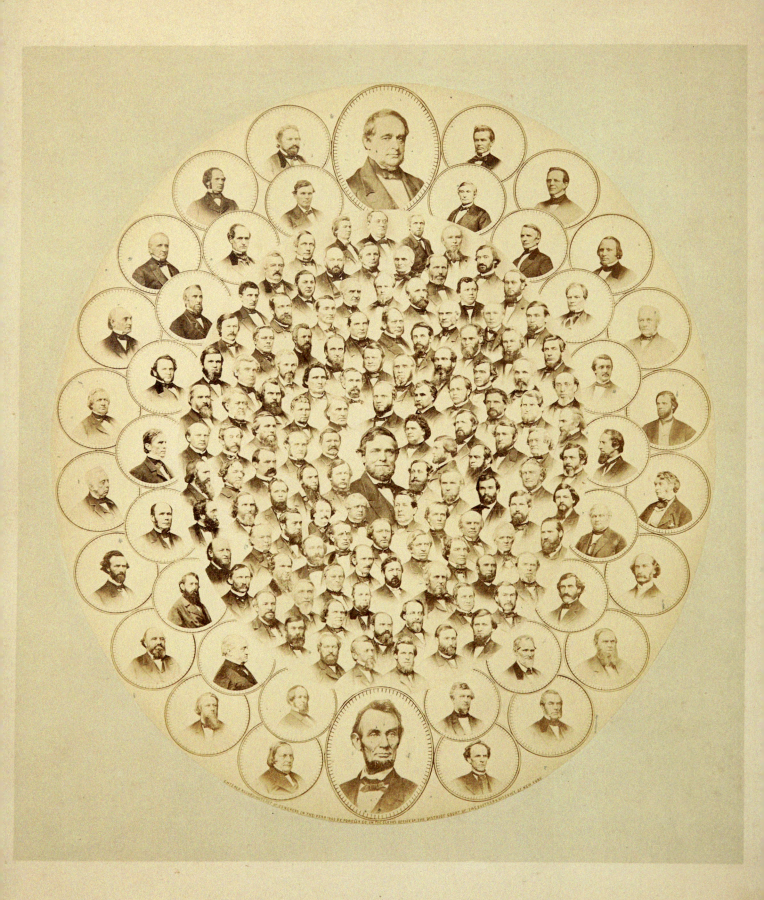

president), the House barely secured the two-thirds majority vote needed for passage.[10] Although he was not required to do so, he indicated his strong support for the amendment by signing it before it was sent out to the states for ratification.

Lincoln embraced the abolitionists' position only after the war made emancipation a military necessity. For some, he moved too quickly; for others, he acted with unnecessary delay. But in issuing the proclamation and working with abolitionists to secure passage of the Thirteenth Amendment, he strengthened America's commitment to freedom for all. His actions affirm the presidency's power for good and exemplify that effective leadership requires a balance between caution and boldness.

Albumen collage (New York: Powell, 1865). The collage shows portraits of the 159 men responsible for the passage at the federal level of the Thirteenth Amendment to the Constitution. On page 192: the identification key provides their names.

KEY TO POWELL & CO'S. PHOTOGRAPHS
of
ABRAHAM LINCOLN, HANNIBAL HAMLIN AND OF THE SENATORS AND REPRESENTATIVES

who voted "AYE" on the resolution submitting to the Legislatures of the several States a proposition to amend the constitution of the United States so as to prohibit
SLAVERY.
Passed in Senate, April 8, 1864. Passed in House of Representatives, Jan 31, 1865
Said resolution being as follows
ARTICLE 14:
Sect. 1. Neither Slavery nor involuntary servitude, except as a punishment for crime, whereof the party shall have been duly convicted, shall exist within the United States or any place subject to their jurisdiction.
Sect. 2. Congress shall have power to enforce this article by appropriate legislation.

1	Abraham Lincoln	of	Ills.		2	Hannibal Hamlin	of	Me.
	SENATORS.					SENATORS.		
151	Anthony H.B.	of	R.I.		123	Howe Timothy O.	of	Wis.
133	Brown B. Grats.	"	Mo.		134	Johnson Reverdy	"	Md.
139	Chandler Zachary	"	Mich.		129	Lane Henry S.	"	Ind.
128	Clark Daniel	"	N.H.		149	Lane James H.	"	Kansas.
143	Collamar Jacob	"	Vt.		148	Morgan Edwin D.	"	N.Y.
140	Conness John	"	Cal.		156	Morrill Lot M.	"	Me.
126	Cowan Edgar	"	Pa.		136	Nesmith J.W.	"	Oregon.
131	Dixon James	"	Conn.		152	Pomeroy Samuel C.	"	Kansas.
159	Doolittle Jas. R.	"	Wis.		127	Ramsey Alexander	"	Min.
135	Fessenden Wm. Pitt.	"	Me.		144	Sherman John	"	Ohio.
157	Foote Solomon	"	Vt.		125	Sprague Wm.	"	R.I.
146	Foster L.F.S.	"	Conn.		145	Sumner Charles	"	Mass.
158	Grimes J.W.	"	Iowa.		134	Ten Eyck J.C.	"	N.J.
155	Hale John P.	"	N.H.		141	Trumbull Lyman	"	Ill.
139	Harding B.F.	"	Oreg.		132	Van Winkle P.G.	"	W.Va.
147	Harlan Jas.	"	Iowa		124	Wade Benjamin	"	Ohio.
150	Harris Ira	"	N.Y.		138	Wilkinson M.S.	"	Min.
153	Henderson J.B.	"	Mo.		137	Willey W.T.	"	W.Va.
122	Howard Jacob M.	"	Mich.		142	Wilson Henry	"	Mass.

REPRESENTATIVES.

76	John B. Alley	Mass.					96	John H. Rice	Me.
103	William B. Allison	Iowa.					37	Edward H. Rollins	N.H.
65	Oakes Ames	Mass.					19	James S. Rollins	Mo.
95	Lucien Anderson	Ky.					14	Robert C. Schenck	Ohio.
80	Isaac N. Arnold	Ill.					91	Glenni W. Scofield	Penn.
8	James M. Ashley	Ohio.					109	Thomas B. Shannon	Cal.
38	Joseph Baily	Penn.					69	Ithamar C. Sloan	Wis.
42	Augustus C. Baldwin	Mich.					117	Green Clay Smith	Ky.
115	John D. Baldwin	Mass.					27	Nathaniel B. Smithers	Del.
41	Portus Baxter	Vt.					67	Rufus P. Spalding	Ohio.
64	Fernando C. Beaman	Mich.	62	Ignatius Donnelly	Minn.	100	Walter D. McIndoe	Wis.	98	John F. Starr	N.J.
26	James G. Blaine	Me.	101	John F. Driggs	Mich.	104	Samuel F. Miller	N.Y.	97	John B. Steele	N.Y.
30	Jacob B. Blair	West Va.	77	Ebenezer Dumont	Ind.	75	James K. Moorhead	Penn.	33	Thaddeus Stevens	Penn.
29	Henry T. Blow	Mo.	52	Ephraim R. Eckley	Ohio.	40	Justin S. Morrill	Vt.	63	M Russell Thayer	Penn.
18	George S. Boutwell	Mass.	78	Thomas D. Eliot	Mass.	118	Wells A. Hutchins	Ohio.	59	Francis Thomas	Md.
121	Sempronius H. Boyd	Mo.	53	Ebon C Ingersoll	Ill.	71	Daniel Morris	N.Y.	47	Henry W. Tracy	Penn.
85	Augustus Brandegee	Conn.	113	John F. Farnsworth	Ill.	108	Amos Myers	Penn.	34	Charles Upson	Mich.
56	John M. Broomall	Penn.	4	Augustus Frank	N.Y.	23	George W. Julian	Ind.	9	Leonard Myers	Penn.
49	William G. Brown	West Va.	114	John Ganson	N.Y.	13	John A. Kasson	Iowa.	102	Homer A. Nelson	N.Y.	65	Rob B. Van Valkenburgh	N.Y.
106	Ambrose W. Clark	N.Y.	107	James A. Garfield	Ohio.	22	William D. Kelley	Penn.	72	Jesse O. Norton	Ill.	15	Elihu B. Washburne	Ill.
17	Freeman Clarke	N.Y.	11	Daniel W. Gooch	Mass.	43	Francis W. Kellogg	Mich.	84	Moses F. Odell	N.Y.	88	William B. Washburn	Mass.
57	Amasa Cobb	Wis.	5	Josiah B. Grinnell	Iowa.	45	Orlando Kellogg	N.Y.	10	Charles O'Neill	Penn.	21	Edwin H. Webster	Md.
86	Alexander H. Coffroth	Penn.	81	John A. Griswold	N.Y.	70	Austin A. King	Mo.	89	Godlove S. Orth	Ind.	58	William H. Wadley	West Va.
94	Cornelius Cole	Cal.	82	James T. Hale	Penn.	120	Samuel Knox	Mo.	28	James W. Patterson	N.H.	105	Ezra Wheeler	Wis.
74	John A.J. Creswell	Md.	51	Anson Herrick	N.Y.	92	De Witt C. Littlejohn	N.Y.	48	Sidney Perham	Me.	82	Thomas Williams	Penn.
7	Henry Winter Davis	Md.	61	William Higby	Cal.	116	Benjamin F. Loan	Mo.	112	Frederick A. Pike	Me.	110	A. Carter Wilder	Kansas.
83	Thomas T. Davis	N.Y.	12	Samuel Hooper	Mass.	39	John W. Longyear	Mich.	99	Theodore M. Pomeroy	N.Y.	32	James F. Wilson	Iowa.
50	Henry L. Dawes	Mass.	36	Giles W. Hotchkiss	N.Y.	79	James M. Marvin	N.Y.	24	Hiram Price	Iowa.	20	William Windom	Minn.
119	Henry C. Deming	Conn.	60	A.W. Hubbard	Iowa.	68	Archibald McAllister	Penn.	87	William Radford	N.Y.	111	Frederick E. Woodbridge	Vt.
46	Nathan F. Dixon	R.I.	6	John H. Hubbard	Conn.	44	John R. McBride	Oregon.	90	William H. Randall	Ky.	16	Henry C. Worthington	Nev.
						54	Joseph W. McClurg	Mo.	73	Alexander H. Rice	Mass.	93	George H. Yeaman	Ky.

3 Schuyler Colfax of Indiana Speaker

The Numerical Arrangement of this Key will be seen by following the "DOTTED LINE" which commences at the head of Speaker Colfax (No. 3) in the centre and UNCOILS OUTWARDLY till it reaches the head of Senator Doolittle (No. 159) at the top of the picture and to the left of Vice President Hamlin. The Senators are arranged in open order on the "MEDALLIONS" on the outside of the picture and the Representatives are arranged in close order around the Centre.

NOTES

1. "Speech at Cincinnati, Ohio," Sept. 17, 1859, in Roy P. Basler, ed., *The Collected Works of Abraham Lincoln*, 8 vols. (hereafter *Collected Works*) (New Brunswick, NJ: Rutgers University Press, 1953), 3:440.

2. "Protest in Illinois Legislature on Slavery," Mar. 3, 1837, in *Collected Works*, 1:75.

3. "Speech at Peoria, Illinois," Oct. 16, 1854, in *Collected Works*, 2:255.

4. Lincoln and white Americans believed that enslaved people would need time to adjust to the idea of freedom and the responsibilities that came with it. The enslaved thought otherwise. They knew they could take care of themselves if they received fair treatment.

5. Lincoln's ideas on emancipation are clearly articulated in his plan to abolish slavery in the District of Columbia. See "Remarks and Resolutions…Concerning Abolition of Slavery in the District of Columbia," Jan. 10, 1849, in *Collected Works*, 2:274–75. See also "Address on Colonization to a Deputation of Negroes," Aug. 14, 1862, in *Collected Works*, 5:372.

6. Quoted in National Archives News, https://www.archives.gov/news/topics/emancipation-proclamation.

7. See Jennifer Weber, *Copperheads: The Rise and Fall of Lincoln's Opposition in the North* (New York: Oxford University Press, 2006).

8. Lincoln to the Honorable James C. Conkling, Aug. 26, 1863, in *Collected Works*, 6:409.

9. Republican Party Platform, June 7, 1864, https://www.presidency.ucsb.edu/documents/republican-party-platform-1864.

10. See Michael Vorenberg, *Final Freedom: The Civil War, The Abolition of Slavery, and The Thirteenth Amendment* (Cambridge: Cambridge University Press, 2001).

THE DAVID M. RUBENSTEIN AMERICANA COLLECTION

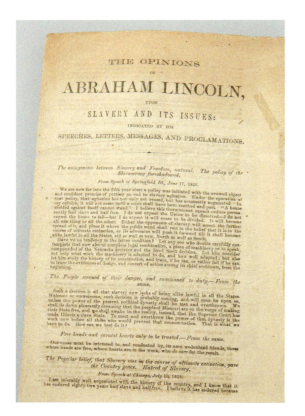

Abraham Lincoln, *Opinions…upon Slavery and Its Issues*
WASHINGTON: UNION CONGRESSIONAL COMMITTEE, 1864

Understanding Lincoln's opinions on slavery requires acknowledging that while he was against it from early in his career, his views on it evolved over time. Consider this rare pamphlet circulated for Lincoln's 1864 reelection by a Republican-aligned concern. It prints his admission in an 1858 speech in Chicago that "I have always hated slavery, I think, as much as any Abolitionist." It left out the statement he said right after: "But I have always been quiet about it [and] believed that…it was in course of ultimate extinction." Compare this to his 1863 Third Message to Congress, also printed here: "Of those who were slaves at the beginning of the rebellion, full 100,000 are [in] military service. No…violence…has marked the emancipation and arming the blacks."

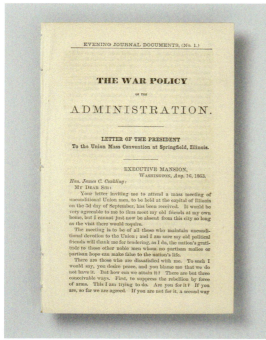

Abraham Lincoln, "War Policy of the Administration. Letter of the President to the Union Mass Convention at Springfield," *Evening Journal Documents*
ALBANY [NY]: ALBANY JOURNAL, 1863

Before, Lincoln wished only for slavery's containment; as president, he knew he must end it. Before, he waited for slavery's slow demise; as president, he instantly halted 240-plus years of it. Before, he doubted if former slaves could commingle in society; as president, he cheered armed Blacks fighting alongside whites. What changed? The Emancipation Proclamation shifted Lincoln's priority from "slavery" to the people who were enslaved. In this 1863 open letter, he doubled down on the proclamation: "There will be some black men who can remember that…they have helped mankind on to this great consummation; while I fear there will be some white ones unable to forget that, with malignant heart and deceitful speech, they have strove to hinder it."

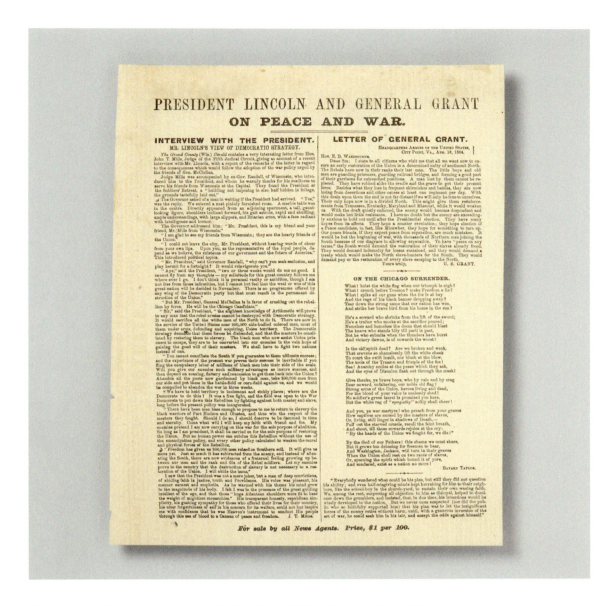

Abraham Lincoln and Joseph Trotter Mills, "Interview with the President," *President Lincoln and General Grant on Peace and War*

N.P.: N.P., [1864]

Lincoln found his antislavery voice in defending the Emancipation Proclamation. This 1864 reelection document has accuracy problems (it misprints the interviewer's name and publication source, and it misquotes the number of Black troops Lincoln said), but it shows that Lincoln saw emancipation as political currency: a vote for him was a vote for the Black fighters helping save the country. "There are… 200,000 able-bodied colored men… defending [Union] territory," he is quoted as saying. "The Democratic [Party] strategy demands that these forces be disbanded." He then adds: "Let my enemies prove… that the destruction of slavery is not necessary to a restoration of the Union." One could almost say Lincoln owed his reelection to former slaves.

LINCOLN THE ANTISLAVERY PRESIDENT · 1863 TO 1865

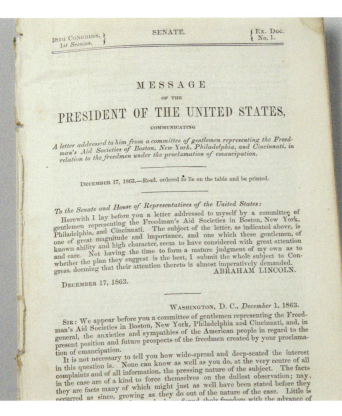

Abraham Lincoln, "Message of the President…Communicating a Letter [from] the Freedman's Aid Societies," *Senate Executive Documents*

WASHINGTON: GOVERNMENT PRINTING OFFICE, 1863

Lincoln's views on slavery changed because his views on African Americans changed. Previously, his expressions were legal defenses of the founding documents' guidance on slavery. But the end of slavery was not the beginning of rights being granted to Blacks. For the next step, Lincoln considered an idea from abolitionists. Seen here is a letter that Lincoln shared with Congress from the Freedman's Aid Society, an organization founded by Protestant churches to educate the recently freed. It asked for the creation of what became the Freedmen's Bureau, which after the war helped the formerly enslaved move (as the reprinted letter proposed) "from their old condition of forced labor to their new state of voluntary industry." This meant integration into society.

Abraham Lincoln, "Message from the President…at the Commencement of the Second Session of the Thirty-Eighth Congress," *Journal of the House of Representatives*

WASHINGTON: GOVERNMENT PRINTING OFFICE, 1864

While Lincoln's views on slavery are open to debate, the undeniable outcome of his presidency is that he ended it. A section in his Fourth Message to Congress urged amending the Constitution to abolish slavery. This linked Lincoln in the public record to the Thirteenth Amendment a full year before its official ratification in 1865. He asserted that such was the will of the people—and an inevitability once the next session of legislators was sworn in. On this point, Lincoln was aligned with the radical wing of the Republican Party. Earlier that year, a resolution to enshrine abolition in the Constitution passed in the Senate but failed in the House. Here he made clear his stance: "I shall not attempt to retract or modify the emancipation proclamation."

Abraham Lincoln, By the President of the United States of America: A Proclamation. [Proclamation of Amnesty and Reconstruction]

WASHINGTON: GOVERNMENT PRINTING OFFICE, 1863

In December 1863 Lincoln issued the Proclamation of Amnesty and Reconstruction. It cleverly employed the pardoning authority of the president (see Article II, Section 2 of the Constitution) to make the restoration of Southern property rights contingent on the swearing of an oath to comply with the Emancipation Proclamation. The intention was to make permanent the ending of slavery. This overture extended to any resident in states of rebellion except persons in high-ranking Confederate positions (officers, judges, etc.) and "all who have engaged [in] treating colored persons...otherwise than lawfully as prisoners of war." This added a humanizing poignancy to Lincoln's decree; it was a concession that emancipation could be dangerous to Blacks.

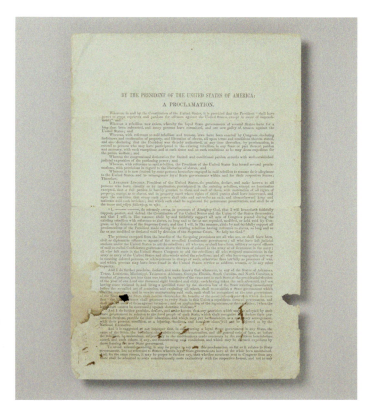

Abraham Lincoln, *Amnesty Proclamation and Third Annual Message*

WASHINGTON: N.P., 1863

The Proclamation of Amnesty and Reconstruction is so called for its semblance of forward thinking on the South after the war. Lincoln did not live to see Reconstruction, the era when the South, in its defeat, was politically transformed by the North for reintegration into the Union, and when African Americans gained constitutional protections relating to citizenship and voting. But this proclamation laid out how Lincoln thought reunification might happen in a postslavery America: if a tenth of the voters from rebelling states swore their allegiance to the Constitution and emancipation, then their state government, if it did the same, would be recognized by the Union. The proclamation also encouraged "any provision" that "provided for" "freed people."

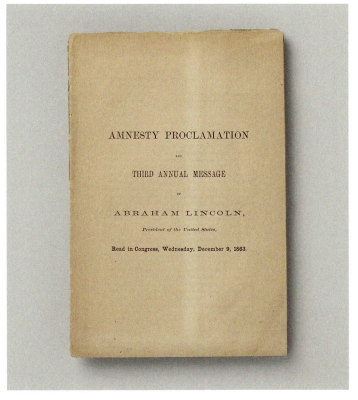

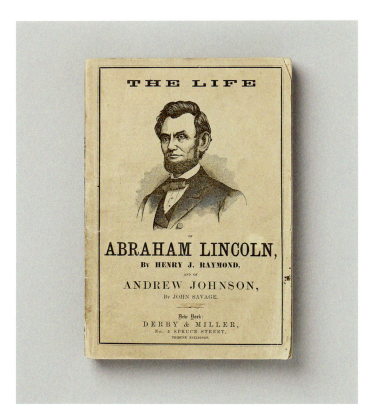

Henry J. Raymond and John Savage, *The Life of Abraham Lincoln... and of Andrew Johnson*

NEW YORK: DERBY & MILLER, 1864

Come 1864, Lincoln wished to be reelected but made no public statement about it. As in 1860, he outwardly entrusted the political apparatus to choose a nominee, although in confidence he involved himself in discussions about a new vice president, platform, and (temporary) name for the Republicans, the National Union Party. As in four years earlier, factional political alignments came at a cost to political parties. The fervid abolitionists of his coalition established the Radical Democracy Party. His main rivals, the Democrats, were split between war and peace camps, and ultimately chose a war candidate but a peace platform. The National Union Party, the distributor of this campaign biography, was formed to attract all nonaffiliated pro-Union voters to Lincoln.

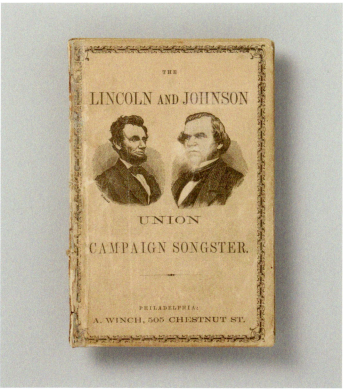

The Lincoln and Johnson Union Campaign Songster

PHILADELPHIA: WINCH, 1864

For the more inclusive National Union Party ticket, the Republicans nominated as vice president a War Democrat serving as Lincoln's military governor of Tennessee. Andrew Johnson was a slave-owning senator before the war. When Tennessee seceded, he was the only Southern member of the chamber not to resign, earning the enmity of Confederate leadership. As military governor, he was put in martial command of the western regions under Union army control. Although the Emancipation Proclamation did not apply to his state, he freed his slaves in 1863. His embrace of state-wide emancipation came in stages over two years and perhaps not as speedily as Lincoln would have wished. But eventually Johnson recruited 20,000 Black troops, both free and freed.

William M. Thayer, *The Character and Public Services of Abraham Lincoln*

BOSTON: DINSMOOR, 1864

"A class of true antislavery men have doubted Mr. Lincoln's fidelity to freedom. . . . How strange! Let them ponder the following facts." These words, printed in this reelection biography, tell us that being antislavery was no longer a liability, but instead a prerequisite to becoming president. The book lists Lincoln's bona fides: the alarm he engenders in Confederates, the Emancipation Proclamation, African American soldiers, and the abolishment of slavery in Washington. It adds, "The President was in advance of public opinion on the question of liberty." The party's platform named slavery as the cause of the Civil War and the Emancipation Proclamation's "employment as Union soldiers of men heretofore held in slavery" as the "salvation of the country."

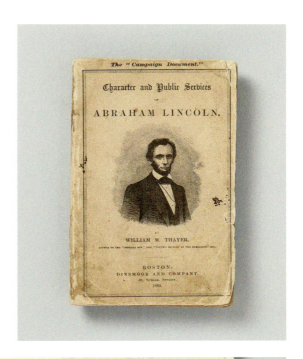

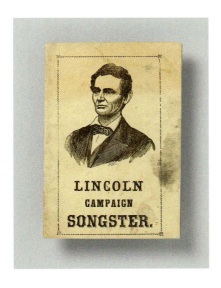

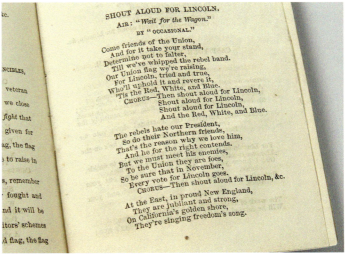

Lincoln Campaign Songster. For the Use of Clubs.

PHILADELPHIA: MASON & CO., 1864

This 1864 songster's pictorial wrapper strangely has a beardless Lincoln, although he began growing a beard four years earlier precisely to look more appealing to voters. The grooming suggestion famously was sent by a then eleven-year-old girl named Grace Bedell, from New York's southwestern corner, near Lake Erie. (The two met on his inaugural trip to Washington.) Unlike songsters from that political campaign, this edition is void of references to Lincoln's western extraction or his railsplitting skillfulness. The lyrics do praise "Honest Abe"—an image of him that lasted beyond his presidency. The first song tells us, "Honest Abraham is our leader . . . / He has borne four years of toil / He has braved defeat and danger, / Trying traitor's plans to foil."

Lincoln and Johnson, Republican Election Ticket, Connecticut, 1864

For the Union: Lincoln & Johnson, Republican Election Ticket, Michigan, 1864

Ohio Union Presidential Ticket, Republican Election Ticket, Ohio, 1864

Union Ticket, Republican Election Ticket, Illinois, 1864

Union Presidential Ticket, Republican Election Ticket, New Hampshire, 1864

Ohio Union Presidential Ticket, Republican Election Ticket, Ohio, 1864

Black Hawk County Union Ticket, Republican Election Ticket, Iowa, 1864

Republican Presidential Ticket, Republican Election Ticket, Ohio, 1864

Republican Union War Ticket, Republican Election Ticket, Wisconsin, 1864

Rally Round the Boys, Republican Election Ticket, California, 1864

Lincoln and Johnson, Republican Election Ticket, Connecticut, 1864

Union National Ticket, Republican Election Ticket, Vermont, 1864

The 1864 presidential campaign had uncertainties. It was the first wartime election in over fifty years, the last being James Madison's victory at the outset of the War of 1812. No incumbent had won reelection in over thirty years, the last being Andrew Jackson's lopsided win in 1832. West Virginia, Kansas, and Nevada were voting for the first time; eleven Confederate states were not voting; and the votes of Union-occupied Tennessee and Louisiana ended up not being counted.

Lincoln was anxious throughout most of 1864. As the war dragged on without Union strides, the Emancipation Proclamation looked either too extreme or too restrained to leaders on opposing sides of the issue. Fearing his cabinet would waver should he lose, he had them sign an unseen pledge to "co-operate with the President elect, as to save the Union between the election and the inauguration." On Election Day he admitted, "about this thing I am far from being certain."

After Election Day, Lincoln realized his fears were misplaced. He resoundingly won 212 out of 233 electoral votes (i.e., all but three states) and 55 percent of the popular vote. Pro-war and antislavery factions coalesced around him. Certainly, the good news from the military triumphs of Generals Grant, Sherman, and Sheridan elicited ballots of encouragement. And three-fourths of the votes cast by servicemen in the seven states allowing them to do so went to their commander in chief.

Shown here are a dozen ballots from 1864. We display these for what they prove: participation of a citizenry in elections. The Civil War did not suspend voting—nor has any war the United States has fought. Lincoln's words two days after his win sum up the accomplishment: "The election was a necessity. We cannot have free Government without elections. If the rebellion could force us to forego or postpone a national election it might fairly claim to have...conquered and ruined us."

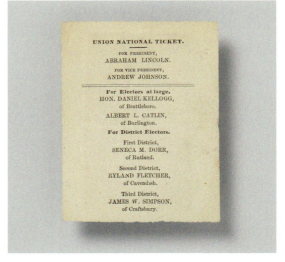

With Malice / Toward None / With Charity for All
NEW YORK: CURRIER & IVES [PRINTED LATER, CA. 1875]

The end of war was near when Lincoln gave his Second Inaugural Address. Far from being a jubilant speech, it was a deeply religious attempt to make sense of the preceding four years. His message: the war's enormous toll was necessary given slavery's enormous evil—both were foreordained by God's will. Quoting Jesus's words on judgment and sin in Matthew 18:7, Lincoln said, "Woe unto the world because of offenses, for it must needs be that offenses come. But woe to that man by whom the offense cometh." If slavery was the sin that God allowed but "now wills to remove," then "He gives to both North and South this terrible war as the woe due to those by whom the offense came." Lincoln reasoned that the war, as judgment for slavery, is a corrective: "If God wills that it continue until...every drop of blood drawn with the lash shall be paid by another drawn with the sword." Lincoln concluded with a twist: if judgment is thus reserved for God, then the imperative for Americans must be to forgive each other. It is the most quoted line from his speech: "With malice toward none, with charity for all, [let us] bind up the nation's wounds."

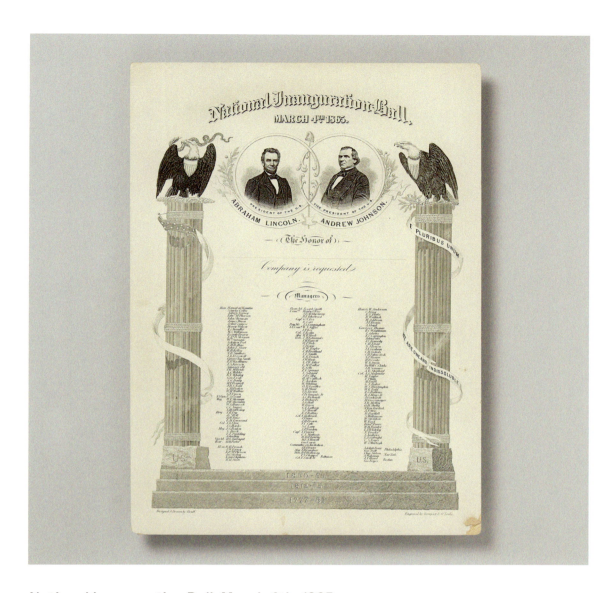

National Inauguration Ball. March 4th, 1865
WASHINGTON: N.P., 1865

The spectacle of Lincoln's Second Inaugural on March 4, 1865, was markedly different from that of his first. Whereas before the threat of war had subdued those gathered, now the prospect of victory made the spectators twice in number and outwardly triumphant. The inaugural procession along Pennsylvania Avenue, in addition to elected dignitaries, included over a mile of recently deployed infantry, cavalry, and artillery battalions, plus veterans, drum corps, and, for the first time in U.S. history, African American troops. The rainy weather of recent days had laden the streets with thick mud, but when Lincoln rose to give his speech on the east portico of the Capitol, the clouds parted in that instant and the sun shone on him. After taking his oath of office, Lincoln kissed the Bible on Isaiah 5:27, which, following a verse on God's wrath ("Therefore is the anger of the Lord kindled against his people"), promised hope: "None shall be weary nor stumble among them." Shown here is the invitation to the ball that evening, held in the Old Patent Office Building (now the Smithsonian Center for American Art and Portraiture).

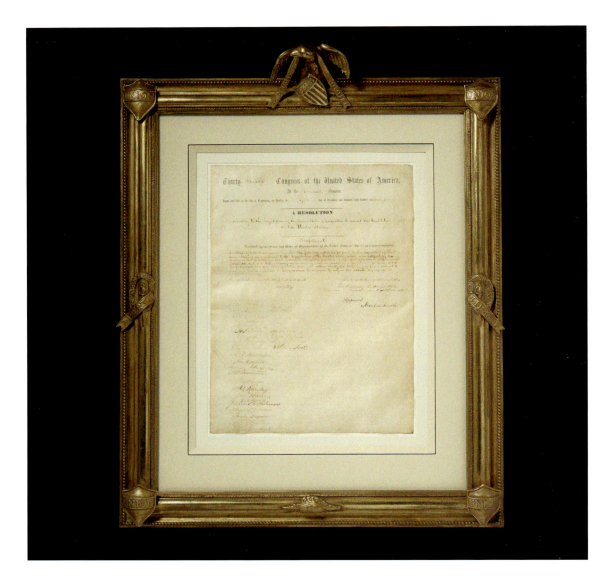

[Thirteenth Amendment], A Resolution Submitting to the Legislatures of the Several States a Proposition to Amend the Constitution of the United States. Signed by Abraham Lincoln, Hannibal Hamlin, and 36 Senators of the 38th Congress

WASHINGTON: VELLUM DOCUMENT ACCOMPLISHED IN MANUSCRIPT, 1865

Emancipation, or freeing slaves, was not the same as abolition, or ending slavery. This Lincoln knew from his deep knowledge of the Constitution. He knew that the freedom gains of the Civil War like the Emancipation Proclamation could be reversed by future administrations, and that a patchwork country of free and slave states forever risked conflict. The law of the land, however, did not give the executive branch (or legislature) the power to end slavery. Instead, it gave interpretable rights to both sides of the issue (e.g., proslavery: the three-fifths and fugitive slave clauses; antislavery: the slave-trade, search and seizure, and due process clauses, etc.). Indeed, Lincoln's liberating slaves as a military measure was in adherence to the war powers clause. Only by amending the Constitution—a process which hadn't happened in sixty years—could the nation's original ambiguities on slavery be fixed. Beginning in 1864, Lincoln and his political peers began the process that culminated in the Thirteenth Amendment. The copy shown here is a very rare souvenir issue signed by Lincoln when he signed the original.

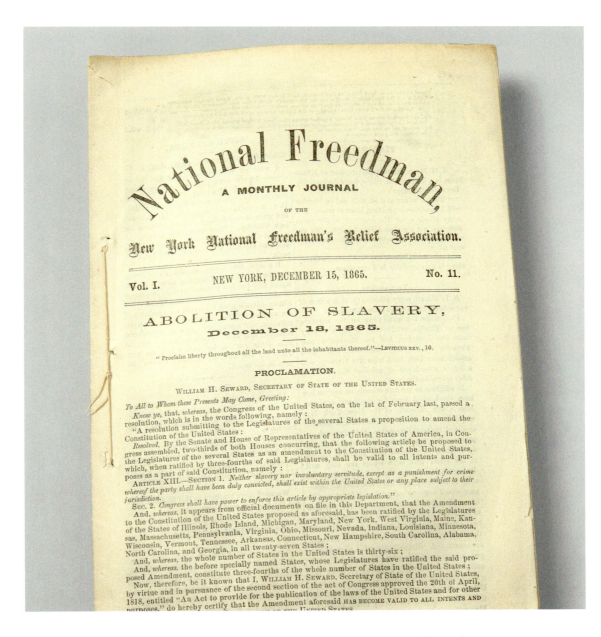

[Thirteenth Amendment], "Abolition of Slavery," *National Freedman*
NEW YORK: NATIONAL FREEDMAN'S RELIEF ASSOCIATION, 1865

The Thirteenth Amendment states, "Neither slavery nor involuntary servitude…shall exist within the United States, or any place subject to their jurisdiction." The path of this becoming law began in January 1864 with proposals in Congress that were reconciled in committee. On April 8 the Senate approved the amendment and sent it to the House of Representatives, where on June 15 it failed to get the necessary two-thirds votes in favor of it. In the summer and fall, the national elections consumed ministerial energies, but Lincoln made sure that his party's platform included a commitment to the amendment. After the election Lincoln's political cachet improved, and he used it to pressure members of the House who had less reason after the election to resist voting for the amendment. He and his allies' pressure campaign lasted through the winter and required them to make a multitude of pleas and promises to less biddable congressmen. On January 31, 1865, the House passed the measure and sent it to Lincoln to sign. But he would not live to see the Thirteenth Amendment ratified by three-fourths of the states.

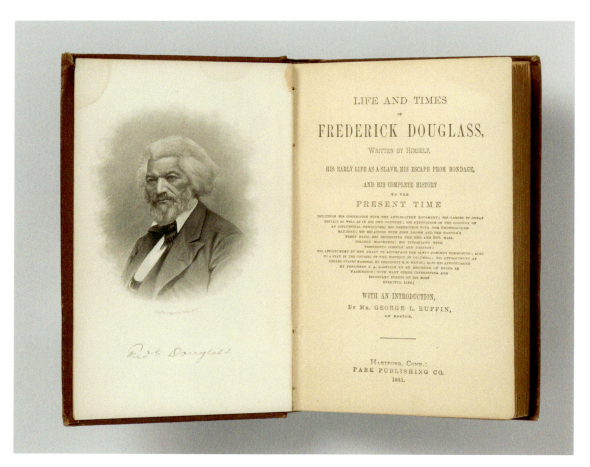

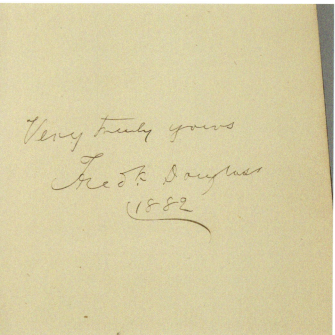

Frederick Douglass, *Life and Times of Frederick Douglass*

HARTFORD [CT]: HART, 1881

The great abolitionist writer and reformer Frederick Douglass met with Lincoln three times between 1863 and 1865, which he described in the 1881 printing of his memoirs shown here. Before the Emancipation Proclamation, Douglass had equally endorsed and scorned Republicans for their antislavery competence (Lincoln had "evaded his obvious duty" by not "calling the blacks to arms," he wrote in a newspaper). But after it, Douglass began recruiting African American soldiers, even enlisting his two sons in the valorous 54th Massachusetts Regiment. Their first meeting was at Douglass's request, to discuss deficiencies in Black servicemen's pay, protections, and promotions. Lincoln asked for their second meeting, to get Douglass's advice on spreading word of the proclamation to slaves—"devising some means of making them acquainted with it, and for bringing them into our lines." Their final meeting was at Lincoln's Second Inauguration. "Here comes my friend Douglass," Lincoln said as he saw him. Douglass in turn wrote of him: "Mr. Lincoln was not only a great President, but a GREAT MAN—too great to be small in anything."

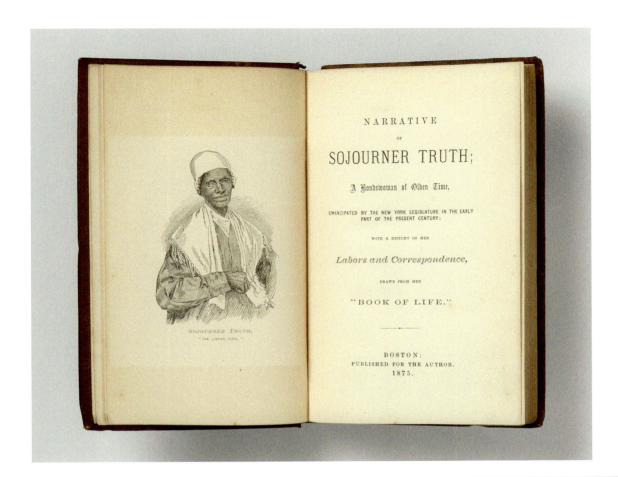

Sojourner Truth, *Narrative of Sojourner Truth*

BOSTON: PUBLISHED FOR THE AUTHOR, 1875

In 1850, Sojourner Truth's dictated biography, *The Narrative of Sojourner Truth: A Northern Slave*, which detailed her life's journey from slavery to freedom and religious conversion, made her a foremost abolitionist voice. A year later, at the Ohio Women's Rights Convention, she gave her "Ain't I a Woman" speech, so named for its refrain; it was reprinted in the 1860s and placed her and Black rights at the center of the women's suffrage movement. After the Emancipation Proclamation, she began actively recruiting African American troops (her grandson joined the 54th Massachusetts Regiment). She then moved to Washington and began volunteering at the Freedman's Hospital, caring for recently freed slaves. This third edition of her biography tells of meeting Lincoln in the White House. As he entered the reception area, filled with people of both races calling on him unannounced, Truth observed, "He showed as much kindness and consideration to the colored persons as to the whites." She added: "I never was treated by any one with more kindness and cordiality than were shown to me by that great and good man."

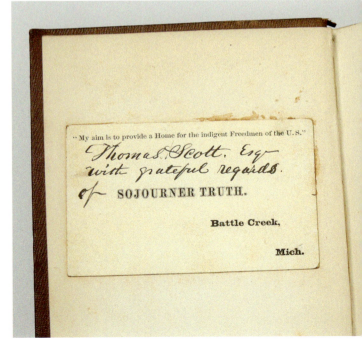

LINCOLN THE ANTISLAVERY PRESIDENT · 1863 TO 1865

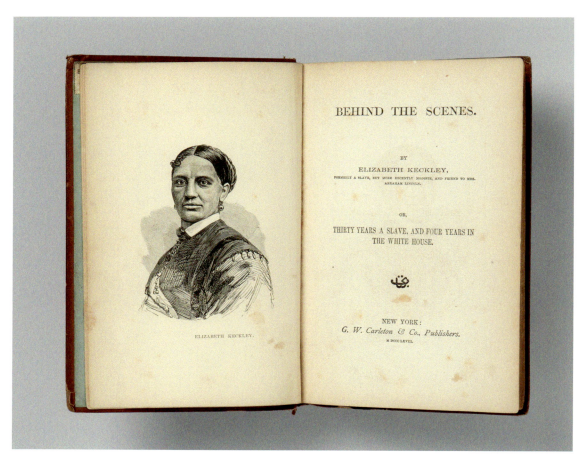

> President, as he stands there? He could be shot down from the crowd, and no one be able to tell who fired the shot."
>
> I do not know what put such an idea into my head, unless it was the sudden remembrance of the many warnings that Mr. Lincoln had received.
>
> The next day, I made mention to Mrs. Lincoln of the idea that had impressed me so strangely the night before, and she replied with a sigh:
>
> "Yes, yes, Mr. Lincoln's life is always exposed. Ah, no one knows what it is to live in constant dread of some fearful tragedy. The President has been warned so often, that I tremble for him on every public occasion. I have a presentiment that he will meet with a sudden and violent end. I pray God to protect my beloved husband from the hands of the assassin."

Elizabeth Keckley, *Behind the Scenes*
NEW YORK: CARLETON, 1868

Elizabeth Keckley was born a slave but bought her freedom through her work as a seamstress and the patronage of her clientele. She moved to Washington from St. Louis in 1860, and within a year, through recommendations, began making dresses for Lincoln's wife, Mary Todd Lincoln. The two women became close, first through the intimacy of tailoring, then in shared tragedy, as both women lost their sons within a year, Keckley's to the war and Mrs. Lincoln's to typhoid. As her reputation as the city's most fashionable dressmaker grew, so too did her friendship with Mrs. Lincoln, allowing her to witness the first family throughout the Civil War. She wrote about this and the enslaved period of her life in her memoirs, shown here. The book caused a scandal, as the press and her customers disapproved of Keckley printing private conversations between the president and his wife, as well as the confidential matters Mrs. Lincoln shared with her. From Keckley, we learn that "Mrs. Lincoln prided herself upon her ability to read character. She was shrewd and far-seeing." But in comparison, she "had no patience with the frank, confiding nature of the President."

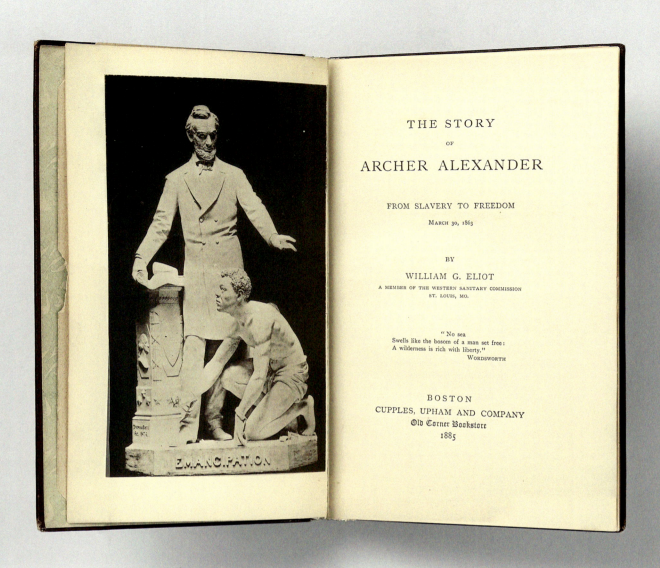

William G. Eliot, *The Story of Archer Alexander*
BOSTON: CUPPLES [ET AL.], 1885

Archer Alexander never met Abraham Lincoln, but he has been immortalized alongside the president in the Emancipation Memorial in Lincoln Park, one mile east of the U.S. Capitol. The bronze statue shows Alexander crouched on one knee, naked but for a loincloth, with broken shackles on both wrists, and one hand made into a fist. He stares forward as Lincoln stands above him with one hand out as if giving a blessing and the other hand atop the Emancipation Proclamation propped on a plinth. The statue is controversial today for its depiction of an African American in such a compromised position, wholly reliant on the merciful crusade of a saintlike president to give him freedom. In reality, Alexander escaped slavery on his own in 1863, from a state that did not benefit from the Emancipation Proclamation. He was forced to flee his home in Missouri after informing Union army agents about Confederate attack plans. In his escape, he met William Eliot, a minister who later wrote Alexander's posthumous biography. Eliot's photographs of Alexander were used to model the statue, unbeknownst to Alexander.

Lincoln the Target
1864 to 1865

BOOTH. SURRATT.

THE FATAL HOUR DRAWS NIGH. THE CONSPIRATORS ABOUT TO EXECUTE THEIR HELLISH DESIGNS.

"Now, By God, I Will Put Him Through"

EDWARD STEERS JR.

BEGINNING WITH HIS ELECTION in November 1860, and continuing through the night of April 14, 1865, eight plots were hatched to assassinate Abraham Lincoln.[1] These plots involved the use of poison, stabbing, shooting, and explosives. Only the final plot, carried out by John Wilkes Booth, succeeded. Ironically, Booth's original plan was not to assassinate the president but rather to capture him and turn him over to Confederate leaders as a hostage. A dead Lincoln had no value in Booth's plan to use him as a bargaining chip for the release of thousands of Confederate prisoners of war or for some other arrangement advantageous to the seceded states.

In 1864 Booth was twenty-six years old. A Maryland native, he was the son of an English actor who, upon emigrating, became the preeminent interpreter of Shakespeare in the United States (his brother, Edwin, became America's greatest Hamlet). Booth followed into the family business, and the years of the Civil War coincided with his emergence on the stage as a leading heartthrob—physically gifted, if a bit overly energetic. He never entered military service, touring theatrically instead, but he often made clear his allegiance to the South and his hatred of abolitionists, of which he counted Lincoln as one. These unconstrained statements got him in trouble in his northern and western travels, and with his family, who, like other Marylanders, were divided on the war.

Exactly when Booth first came up with the idea of abducting Lincoln is unknown, but he began to put it in motion in August 1864. Such an undertaking was not as remarkable as some scholars have claimed: between fall 1862 and fall 1864, there were at least three separate plots by members of the Confederacy to capture the president and take him to Richmond, Virginia, their capital.[2] Booth's seeming drift away from the acting profession, beginning in May 1864, suggests that by then he had committed himself to the plan. His first step that year was to recruit two boyhood friends, Samuel Bland Arnold and Michael O'Laughlen Jr., Confederate veterans from Baltimore, Maryland, to join his plot. They agreed.[3]

Alexander Gardner, *John Wilkes Booth* (Washington: Philp & Solomons, ca. 1865). Albumen print on carte de visite mount

Pages 210–11: Detail from *The Assassination of President Lincoln at Ford's Theatre* (New York: Currier & Ives, ca. 1865). Lithograph

Page 212: Detail from *Life, Trial and Extraordinary Adventures of John H. Surratt* (Philadelphia: Barclay, ca. 1867)

Having recruited two able-bodied ex-soldiers, Booth knew that a successful escape would have to go through southern Maryland. Because Maryland was a stronghold of Confederate sympathies, Booth needed the help of her people. But to gain this help, Booth went north to Montreal, Canada, rather than turn south. Montreal and Toronto were sanctuaries for major Confederate secret service cells. Heading one of the cells was a former southern Maryland merchant-turned-blockade-runner familiar to Booth, Patrick Charles Martin.

On October 16, 1864, Booth registered at St. Lawrence Hall, a since-demolished hotel in Montreal that served as the headquarters for several Confederate agents, including Martin. Martin was well connected with agents working throughout southern Maryland; meeting with Martin, Booth explained his plan and asked for help negotiating his way through the region with a captured Lincoln. Martin was more than helpful: when Booth left Montreal ten days later, he carried a substantial amount of money to facilitate his operation, along with a letter of introduction from Martin to Dr. Samuel Alexander Mudd.[4]

Mudd was a Southern sympathizer who aided agents servicing the Confederate line between Washington, DC, and Richmond, over which spies, important documents, and materiel flowed. He was a person who could make introductions to key parties whom Booth might recruit to his plan. In November Booth traveled to Charles County, Maryland, to meet with him. At a second meeting a month later, Mudd introduced Booth to John Surratt, a spy who had worked as a courier for Confederate secretary of state Judah P. Benjamin. Surratt agreed to join Booth and brought two more important people into Booth's conspiracy, George Atzerodt and Lewis Powell.[5] Atzerodt would ferry the capture party across the Potomac River while Powell provided the muscle. Within a month, Booth had convinced two other friends, David Herold and Edman Spangler, and, by association through her son, Mary Surratt, to join him.[6]

Time was running out for Booth. The Confederacy was losing the war, and if Booth were to capture Lincoln successfully, he needed to act soon. The opportunity came on March 17, 1865, when Booth learned that Lincoln planned to attend a special performance by the actors of Ford's Theatre for wounded soldiers at Campbell Hospital in northeast Washington. Here was the opportunity Booth was waiting for. He quickly sent word for his team to gather at a restaurant near the hospital. He told them to wait along the road on which Lincoln's carriage would return to the White House. On a given signal, the group would descend on the president's carriage and overtake it, disposing of the driver and other persons. With the president

CHAPTER TEN

secured, the group would dash across Benning's Bridge into Maryland, take the Confederate secret service line into the southern part of the state, and then cross the Potomac River into Virginia.[7] The plan was a good one and quite doable. Before any alarm could go out, the kidnappers would be in friendly territory and well on their way to Richmond.

Booth's plan failed when the president canceled his scheduled trip and stayed near the White House to present to the Indiana governor a Confederate battle flag captured by a regiment from that state. Sixteen days later, Richmond, the center of Confederate government, industry, and transportation, fell into Union hands. Booth now realized that his plot to grab Lincoln no longer had a strategic purpose. Even if his gang successfully kidnapped the president, where were they to go? Despite developments, Booth did not give up. He would later write in his pocket diary at the time of his escape, "Our cause being almost lost, something decisive & great must be done."[8] Clearly, he did not consider the struggle over; the words "almost lost" tell us that Booth thought there was still time to aid the Confederate cause.

On the evening of April 11, Lincoln appeared on the balcony of the White House to a cheering crowd. Two days earlier, Confederate general Robert E. Lee had finally surrendered his mighty Army of Northern Virginia, and Washington was aglow in victory. Perched in front of the crowd, Lincoln paused and waited for the cheering Americans to become silent. Standing amidst the audience on the White House lawn were two men who still believed there was hope for a failing Confederacy, John Wilkes Booth and Lewis Powell.

When Lincoln spoke, he explained his program for bringing the seceded states back into the Union. First among the eleven was Louisiana. It was an important state in Lincoln's plan for Reconstruction; slavery had been abolished by its 1864 constitution, but the state's postwar program stopped there. What about the now-freed slaves? What would their status be in the new Louisiana? Lincoln did not sidestep the question. "It [is] unsatisfactory to some that the elective franchise is not given to the colored man. I would myself prefer that it were now conferred on the very intelligent, and on those who served our cause as soldiers." Lincoln's bold and revolutionary statement fell hard on an enraged Booth. Did the president not have a single civilized bone in his body? Was it not enough to destroy the entire culture of Booth's beloved South? Now he wanted to give Blacks citizenship equal to white men. Never! Turning to Powell,

Booth and His Associates, 1865. Albumen print on card mount

LINCOLN THE TARGET · 1864 TO 1865

Ford's Theatre, Scene of the Assassination, 1865. Albumen print

Booth hissed through clenched teeth, "Now, by God, I will put him through. That will be the last speech he will ever make."[9]

Three days later, Booth stopped by Ford's Theatre to pick up his mail, where he learned from Harry C. Ford, the brother of the theater's manager, John T. Ford, that Lincoln, along with General Ulysses S. Grant, would attend the evening performance of "Our American Cousin," starring Laura Keene. "Now," he thought. "Now is the time to strike." Booth was able to reach three of his conspirators: Lewis Powell, David Herold, and George Atzerodt. Meeting in Powell's boardinghouse room, only a few blocks from Ford's Theatre, Booth laid out his plan. At approximately 10:00 that evening, Atzerodt would go to Vice President Andrew Johnson's room in the Kirkwood House hotel and kill him. At the same time, Powell would visit Secretary of State William H. Seward's house, where Seward was recovering from a serious carriage accident, and kill him too. Booth reserved the president for himself. The attacks would be coordinated.[10] After they accomplished their deeds, they would flee the city over the Navy Yard Bridge and rendezvous at Soper's Hill in Maryland. By killing all three men, Booth hoped to throw the federal government into a chaotic state, allowing the Confederacy a chance to regroup and bring its three remaining armies together to face Union forces in one last great battle.

Unrealistic? Perhaps. Even were the hoped-for success of a Confederate victory a pipe dream, at least the tyrant responsible for the South's defeat would be dead. Caesar must bleed for it. Shortly after 9:00 p.m., Booth rode his horse down Baptist Alley to the rear of the theater. Entering the stage door, he made his way using a series of maneuvers to an alleyway that led to the front of the theater. Arriving in the lobby, Booth slowly made his way up a set of stairs to the balcony seats. Across the mezzanine dress circle, to the far right of the auditorium, was the flag-draped presidential box and, within Booth's sights, the outermost door to access it.

As Booth crept across the rear aisle of the balcony, he was mindful of the play on the stage below. He knew every line, every beat, by heart. Reaching the steps in front of the box, Booth was confronted by the president's valet, Charles Forbes, seated in a chair outside the door. Lincoln's guard, John Parker, had left the theater and was drinking in a nearby tavern. After a brief discussion, Forbes allowed Booth to enter.[11] After all, Booth was a famous American actor, a matinee idol, who could have been asked by the president to visit. Once inside, closing the outer door, Booth jammed it by wedging a piece of wood between the door and the wall. He stood in the space between the outer and inner doors, waiting for the perfect moment.

The play reached Act 3, Scene 2, the part when the "American cousin," Asa Trenchard, played by the actor Harry Hawk, utters the punch line that always brings roaring laughter from the audience. It was the perfect moment for Booth to strike. Insulted by Mrs. Mountchessington for his lack of good manners, Trenchard replies, "Don't know the manners of good society, eh? Well, I guess I know enough to turn you inside out, old gal— you sockdologizing old man-trap." The audience roared as expected, just as a muffled boom and a small cloud of blue-gray smoke burst over the balustrade of the president's box. A woman's loud shriek pierced the theater. The president was shot in the back of the head. Booth then leaped twelve feet onto the stage and escaped. Lincoln would die in a boardinghouse the next morning. While the Union would survive, the country would never be the same again.

NOTES

1. Edward Steers Jr., *Lincoln's Assassination*, (Carbondale: Southern Illinois University, 2014), 6.

2. William A. Tidwell, James O. Hall, and David W. Gaddy, *Come Retribution* (Jackson: University Press of Mississippi,1988), 235–37.

3. Edward Steers Jr., *Blood on the Moon* (Lexington: University Press of Kentucky, 2001), 62.

4. Steers, *Blood on the Moon*, 71–72.

5. Tidwell et al., *Come Retribution*, 338–39.

6. Tidwell et al., *Come Retribution*, 341.

7. Steers, *Lincoln's Assassination*, 32–33.

8. Steers, *Lincoln's Assassination*, 35.

9. Steers, *Lincoln's Assassination*, 5.

10. Steers, *Blood on the Moon*, 112.

11. James L. Swanson, *Manhunt* (New York: Harper Collins, 2006), 38–39.

THE DAVID M. RUBENSTEIN AMERICANA COLLECTION

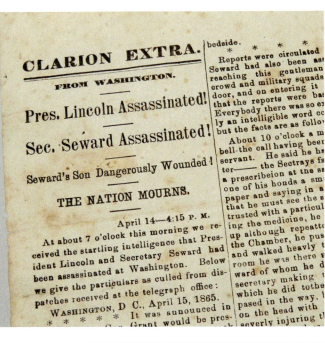

"From Washington. Pres. Lincoln Assassinated!" *Clarion Extra* (Princeton, IN)
APR. 15, 1865

Lincoln was shot in the back of the head at about 10:25 p.m. on April 14, 1865, while attending the theater. At that moment two other murders were supposed to take place, those of Vice President Andrew Johnson and Secretary of State William Seward. The three men had the highest-ranking positions in the administration responsible for the demise of the slave state secession. While each had an appointed assassin, Lincoln's was the only successful one. Seward's would-be killer managed to enter his home and stab him in the face and neck, but a metal brace Seward was wearing saved his life. The man chosen to attack Johnson backed out of the plan and spent the night getting drunk, although a loaded gun was found in his hotel room. The reasons for the targetings were a jumble of misguided and racist Confederate zealotry: to avenge the destruction of the South, to aid the rebel army by toppling the Union, and to prevent the possibility of Black voting or Black citizenship. Seen here is an example of the breaking news extras that spread across the country immediately after the shooting. This one wrongly reports that Seward died.

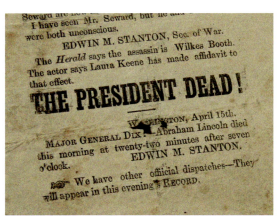

"Sad News! The President Assassinated!" [Newspaper Extra]
N.P.: N.P., 1865

Lincoln died at 7:22 a.m. on April 15, 1865, at fifty-six years of age. His killer was a well-known twenty-six-year-old actor, John Wilkes Booth, who, despite his success in the North as a leading man, held deep sympathies for the South. Booth and his collaborators originally planned to kidnap the president and ransom him in exchange for Confederate prisoners. The plan had less value the more that Confederate armies surrendered to or were defeated by Union forces. Booth was not in the play that Lincoln saw, but he knew the owner of Ford's Theatre; John Ford's brother Harry tipped off Booth on the morning of April 14 that Lincoln and General Grant should be there that night. Lincoln was undecided: he had had premonitions and dreams which, when learning of them, caused his bodyguard, who was off that night, to ask Lincoln to stay home. Lincoln went to save face after Grant changed his mind and took a trip with his wife. He tried to invite Secretary of War Edwin Stanton, who refused. Speaker of the House Schuyler Colfax also declined. Upon departing, Lincoln told Colfax, "I suppose it's time to go, though I would rather stay."

"The Nation's Calamity!" [Newspaper Extra]

N.P.: N.P., 1865

The truest words about the magnitude of Lincoln's death might be what appeared in this newspaper extra on the day he passed: *the nation's calamity*. Five days earlier the South's most fearsome force, the Army of Northern Virginia, capitulated. Two days earlier, on April 13, North Carolina's capital fell to General Sherman. That week the nation's capital expectantly observed the fourth anniversary of the Battle of Fort Sumter, which had started the war. The week began with a speech by Lincoln, in which he supported the idea of suffrage for Black men. The morning of his murder, he held a cabinet meeting and recommended not punishing rebel leadership and easing the South into self-governance after military rule. That day the loyalist government of Arkansas ratified the Thirteenth Amendment, the twenty-first out of twenty-seven states needed for it to pass, signaling hope that Southern reconciliation would be amicable. Lincoln's wife and members of his cabinet noted that he looked more at peace on April 14 than he had in years. The killing of the president happened at the exact moment when the country seemed to be turning a corner.

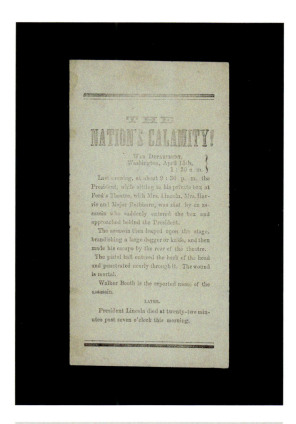

Abott A. Abott, *The Assassination and Death of Abraham Lincoln*

NEW YORK: AMERICAN NEWS, [1865]

At the theater Lincoln was seated in the presidential box at balcony level on the far right of the auditorium. The performance was *Our American Cousin*, a farcical, partly improvised comedy of manners wherein a Vermont bumpkin meets upper-crust English society. Booth entered the box after using his celebrity charm to coax the president's footman (the actual guard on duty had left the theater to drink at a nearby saloon). Booth barricaded the passageway door, then stood behind the president. During the third act, he shot his .44 caliber derringer pistol at point-blank range behind the president's left ear. Henry Rathbone, the army officer who, with his wife, had taken Grant's place in the box, grabbed Booth but was knifed deeply on his left arm. Booth, "waiving a long dagger in his right hand," as this first pamphlet printing of the incident tells us, yelled "'Sic semper tyrannis!' ["thus always to tyrants," the state motto of Virginia] and leaped...to the stage beneath." Mary Todd Lincoln began "uttering the most piteous cries." Lincoln was soon surrounded by three doctors from the audience, who all knew the prognosis was grim.

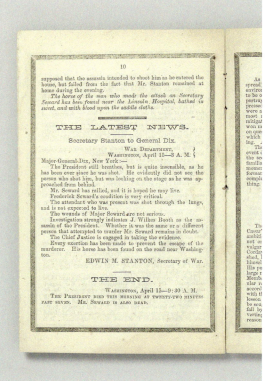

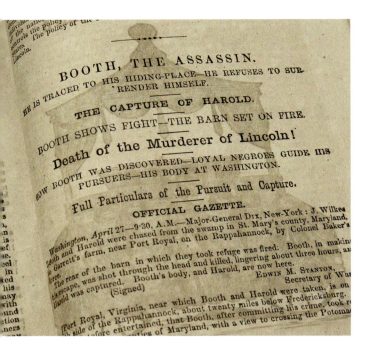

The Terrible Tragedy at Washington
PHILADELPHIA: BARCLAY, [1865]

The great unanswered question about the assassination was the size of the conspiracy. When Booth learned that the president would be at the theater on April 14, he rushed to find accomplices. That he only called on three obscures the fact that for months he had had access to networks of Confederate funding, intelligence, and collaborators. There is no evidence that his orders were given from the top levels of the rebel government. A likely scenario is that, like all terrorist cells, in the final operation, he acted without orders. Nevertheless, he was a Southern agent, and the expectation after Lincoln's death was that the North would punish the South collectively. As this early chronicle of the assassination noted, "One of the effects will be . . . to exasperate the North against the South, and to cause it to insist on much harder conditions, when the question of final reconciliation comes to be discussed, than it otherwise would have done. There were two parties in the North; one in favor of mild measures, . . . the other insisting on the hanging of Jefferson Davis [the Confederate president], and similar measures of extreme severity."

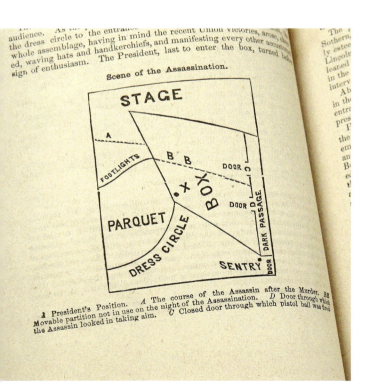

George Alfred Townsend, *The Life, Crime, and Capture of John Wilkes Booth*
NEW YORK: DICK & FITZGERALD, [1865]

The president sat slumped on his chair, barely breathing. News of that sad actuality spread from the theater to Washington's streets, to government leadership and the press, and to all corners of the country. Barely one step ahead of the news was the killer making his getaway by horse. Booth had talked his way across a guarded bridge and then stopped eleven miles beyond the Anacostia River in a Confederate-friendly Maryland township called Surrattsville. He was not alone; he was joined by David Herold, who had led Seward's attacker to the secretary's residence but fled in fear before he could aid the escape. That other man, Lewis Powell, a former Confederate fighter, was caught the morning after when he returned to his boardinghouse, a ten-minute walk from Ford's Theatre. The third accomplice, George Atzerodt, who had failed to attack Johnson, was caught on April 20 in Germantown, Maryland, in the opposite direction from Booth. As Booth made his way to Virginia, a $100,000 reward was posted for his capture, and the largest manhunt in the country's history, with thousands of federal troops, began.

Life, Trial and Extraordinary Adventures of John H. Surratt

PHILADELPHIA: BARCLAY, [CA. 1867]

The consequences of Lincoln's assassination consumed American printing presses from 1865 onward, as publishers reported on the succession of Andrew Johnson as president, the memorialization of Lincoln, the handling of Confederate surrenders (in North Carolina and Alabama), and the passing of unwavering Reconstruction laws. The most sensationalistic news was the capture, trials, and punishment of those linked to Booth's schemes. Most of the "conspirators," as they became known, were implicated in the original kidnapping plot. Shown on this spread are four well-preserved examples of the pamphlets that were produced (all with black borders on their covers, as seen here, to indicate mourning). The second in charge to abduct Lincoln was John Surratt, progeny of the Maryland town where Booth lay hiding. Before meeting Booth, Surratt had been the town's postmaster, allowing him to spy for the South. After the assassination Surratt fled to Canada, then England, then Rome, where he served in the volunteer papal army, was discovered, and then escaped to Egypt, where he was caught and brought home in 1866.

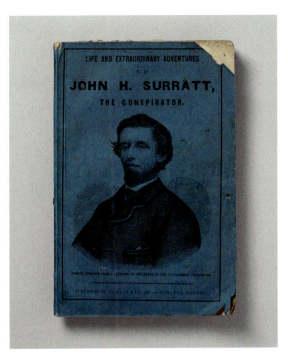

Trial of the Assassins and Conspirators for the Murder of Abraham Lincoln

PHILADELPHIA: BARCLAY, [1865]

Mary Surratt, John's mother, who owned the boardinghouse where the conspirators met and the tavern where Booth and Herold provisioned themselves in Maryland, was arrested on April 15. Michael O'Laughlen, Booth's childhood neighbor and friend, surrendered on April 17 for his connection to the abduction plot (his role in the killing was unsubstantiated). Edman Spangler, a stagehand at Ford's Theatre and a reliable friend of Booth's family, was arrested on April 17 for aiding his escape. Also on that day, Booth's former classmate and friend Samuel Arnold was arrested for his part in planning a failed March kidnapping. Booth and Herold fled for twelve days over Maryland's western coastal plain and into northern Virginia, contending with swamps, pine thickets, and two rivers, the Potomac and Rappahannock. They found respite southwest of Port Royal at a farm owned by a man named Richard Garrett. Within forty-eight hours, Union troops closed in after interrogating some rebel soldiers who earlier had escorted the two men. On April 26 Booth and Herold, hiding in a tobacco barn, were surrounded by the 16th New York Cavalry.

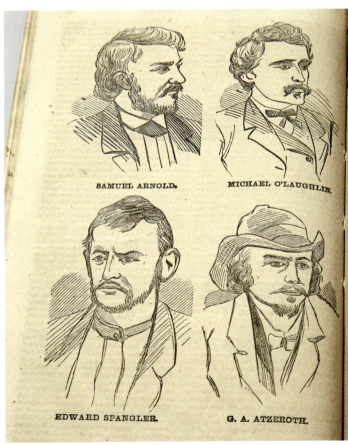

LINCOLN THE TARGET · 1864 TO 1865

"Execution of the Conspirators," *National Police Gazette* (New York, NY)

JULY 15, 1865

Many individuals presumed to be connected to Booth's plot were detained or interrogated; nine persons besides Booth were considered the main conspirators. Eight received sentences in 1865 by a military tribunal, which required only a majority vote of five out of nine judges, not a unanimous jury decision, for a guilty verdict. Their fates were as follows: David Herold, who escaped with Booth, was found guilty and hanged. Lewis Powell and George Atzerodt, the two non-Lincoln attackers, were also hanged. Mary Surratt, too, was found guilty, and attempts by clergy or members of the tribunal could not spare her life. A minister recalled that President Johnson, who did not pardon her, said she "kept the nest that hatched the egg." She was the first woman executed by the federal government. Michael O'Laughlen, Samuel Arnold, Edman Spangler, and Samuel Mudd, a doctor who had conspired with Booth earlier and aided his escape, were sentenced to hard labor in Florida. (O'Laughlen died in 1867; the rest Johnson pardoned in 1869.) John Surratt was tried in civil court in 1867. It resulted in a hung jury.

"Assassin of the President," *American Phrenological Journal* (New York, NY)

JUNE 1865

Between shooting the president and stopping in Maryland, Booth fractured his left leg from either a horse-riding accident or when jumping onto the stage from the presidential box when escaping the theater. A conspiring doctor, Samuel Mudd, set the bone. Booth and his accomplice Herold were aided across Maryland by a chain of Confederate sympathizers. One, a member of the South's secret service, took them to Virginia and gave them newspapers and food. Booth, reading of the reaction to his crime, the revilement of his character, and the price for his head, was incensed. He wrote in his diary: "Am looked upon as a common cutthroat... Yet I cannot see any wrong except in serving a degenerate people." In Virginia he and Herold were trapped in a barn by Union soldiers. Herold surrendered; Booth, hoping for a standoff, was shot in the back of the head, just as he had shot Lincoln. He died in agonizing pain several hours later. Booth became a constant subject of psychological study, such as in this journal of phrenology—a pseudoscience that claims the shape of one's skull determines one's personality.

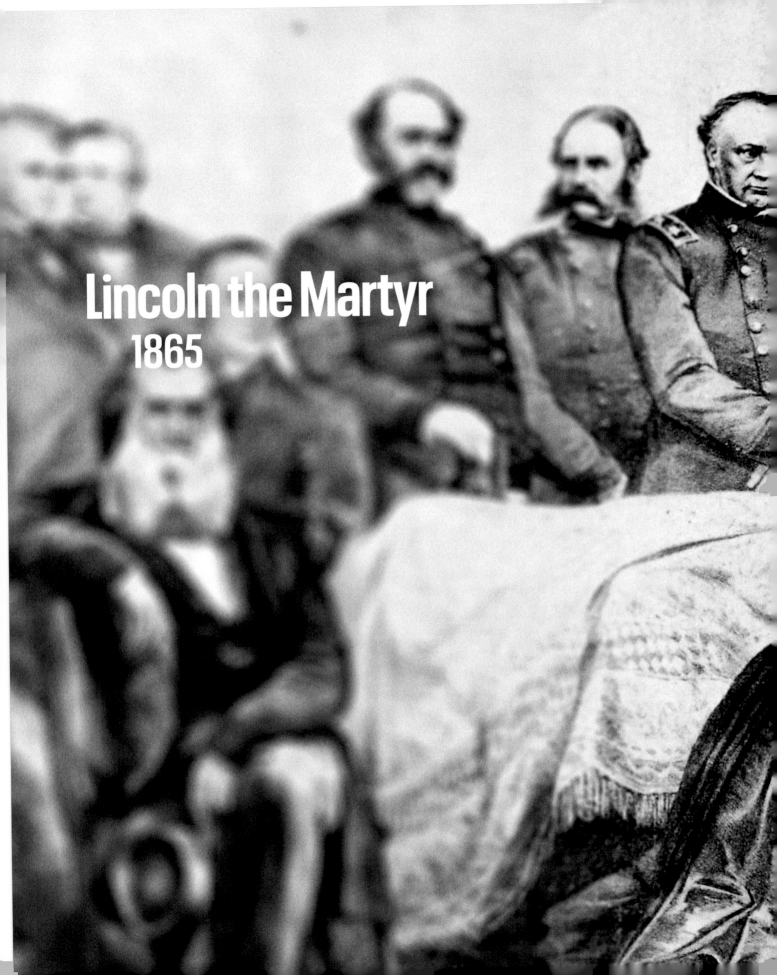

Lincoln the Martyr
1865

In Memoriam.

"Lincoln Died for We"

MARTHA HODES

"**WHAT A SHOCK!** like a thunder clap it came and no words could express enough of horror and grief at this unparalleled outrage." These words, recorded in the diary of a New England woman, capture the emotions of so many Americans as they learned of their nation's first presidential assassination: first shock, then sorrow, then anger.[1]

On the night of Friday, April 14, 1865, when John Wilkes Booth, an out-of-work actor and Confederate sympathizer, shot President Abraham Lincoln at Ford's Theatre in Washington, DC, word spread across the nation, from telegraph wires to newspaper headlines, as sharing the tidings became the first act of mourning. Knocking on doors and calling into windows: uttering the news aloud was a way to make real what felt so unreal. Magnifying the shock was the timing of the murder, barely a week following word of Union victory in the Eastern Theater of the Civil War. On the same day one mourner wrote, "the sun rose upon a nation jubilant with victory" and set "upon one plunged in deepest sorrow."[2]

Astonished. Astounded. Startled. Stupefied. A calamity. A catastrophe. It felt like a "dreadful dream," and it was "too terrible to believe." For the soldiers of the all-Black 54th Massachusetts Regiment, the news was "too overwhelming, too lamentable, too distressing" to comprehend. Mourning drapery instantly shrouded cities, towns, and villages. In daytime Washington, DC, the streets showed only "the blackness of darkness"; in Savannah the homes of even the most impoverished African Americans displayed "a bit of black suspended upon door or window."[3]

From the first moment, sorrow mixed with shock. Mourners heralded President Lincoln as far more than a statesman. "Brothers mourn! sisters weep!" exclaimed the *The Anglo-African*, a New York newsweekly, "for our best friend has passed away." A freedwoman in North Carolina felt as if both her father and mother had died at the same time, and in Chicago a white mourner mused that "almost every family circle seems to be broken." As Black soldiers in camp in Pennsylvania listened to a spontaneous sermon, many wept freely, while on city streets white men were "sobbing

President, Abraham Lincoln: Voices from the Pulpit of New York and Brooklyn. Oration by Hon. Geo. Bancroft, Oration at the Burial, by Bishop Simpson (New York: Tibbals and Whiting, 1865), 170 ("Intense"); *Fourteenth Annual Report of the Rochester Ladies' Anti-Slavery Society* (Rochester, NY, 1865), 6 ("trees").

5. Francis Lieber to Henry W. Halleck, New York, Apr. 15, 1865, box 28, Lieber Papers, Huntington Library, San Marino, CA ("Slavery!"); Charles H. Mallory diary, Apr. 15, 1865, Mallory Family Collection, G. W. Blunt White Library, Mystic Seaport, Mystic, CT ("agent"); Anna M. Ferris diary, Apr. 15, 1865, Ferris Family Papers, Friends Historical Library, Swarthmore College, Swarthmore, PA ("hate").

6. Ferris diary, Apr. 16, 1865 ("incredible"); J. H. Elliot to Robert Anderson, Brattleboro, VT, Apr. 25, 1865, Anderson Papers, Manuscript Division, Library of Congress, Washington ("cloud").

7. Laura Towne to unknown, Saint Helena Island, SC, Apr. 29, 1865, in *Letters and Diary of Laura M. Towne: Written from the Sea Islands of South Carolina, 1862–1884*, ed. Rupert Sargent Holland (1912; reprint, New York: Negro Universities Press, 1969), 162 ("died for we"); Robert H. Williams to David and Carrie Thurber, City Point, VA, Apr. 29, 1865, Goff-Williams Papers, Huntington Library, San Marino, CA ("no equal").

8. *The Assassination of Abraham Lincoln, Late President of the United States of America . . . Expressions of Condolence and Sympathy Inspired by These Events* (Washington: Government Printing Office, 1867), 75 (Creoles), 736 (Polish); B. F. Morris, *Memorial Record of the Nation's Tribute to Abraham Lincoln* (Washington: W. H. and O. H. Morrison, 1865), 254 ("horror").

9. William Calder diary, Apr. 24, 1865, Calder Family Papers, Southern Historical Collection, University of North Carolina, Chapel Hill ("Pity"); Emma F. LeConte diary, Apr. 20 and "Friday" [Apr. 21], 1865, reel 22, Southern Historical Collection, University of North Carolina, Chapel Hill, American Women's Diaries: Southern Women, Readex Newsbank, microform ("Hurrah"); Thomas Jackson, #3920, vol. 133, M273, roll 142, RG125, National Archives and Records Administration, Washington ("laughter"); Frederick Bodmer, file MM1997, RG153, National Archives and Records Administration, Washington ("cheering," "cap"); Patrick O'Donnell, file OO1191, RG153, National Archives and Records Administration, Washington ("joviality"); Henry Peters, file OO719, RG153, National Archives and Records Administration, Washington ("for the Negro").

10. Rose Pickard to Angeline Flagg, Alexandria, VA, Apr. 24, 1865, Pickard Papers, Manuscript Division, Library of Congress, Washington.

11. Phineas D. Gurley, "Funeral Address," in Morris, *Memorial Record*, 85–91; Harry Gibbons to Samuel Bancroft Jr., Washington, DC, Apr. 19, 1865, Bird-Bancroft Collection, Delaware Historical Society, Wilmington.

12. "The Day of the Obsequies," *San Francisco Elevator*, Apr. 21, 1865, #4812, Black Abolitionist Papers, ProQuest; Zoe J. Campbell diary, Apr. 22, 1865, ser. E, reel 5, Louisiana State University Libraries, Southern Women and Their Families in the Nineteenth Century: Papers and Diaries, University Publications of America, microform (translation from French by the author); William H. Richards to "Anna," Camp Lowell, VA, Apr. 20, 1865, Brown Family Papers, Manuscripts and Special Collections, New York State Library, Albany.

13. Ferris diary, Apr. 22, 1865; "Funeral Oration by Bishop Simpson," in Morris, *Memorial Record*, 230, 236.

14. "Cornelia" to parent(s), New York, Apr. 17–19, 1865, Lincoln Miscellaneous Manuscripts, Patricia D. Klingenstein Library, New-York Historical Society, New York ("postcards"); Margaret B. Howell diary, May 9, 1865, Historical Society of Pennsylvania, Philadelphia ("custom"); Anna Cabot Lowell diary, May 5, 15, 13, 1865, Massachusetts Historical Society, Boston ("memorial books").

IN MEMORY
OF
ABRAHAM LINCOLN,

PRESIDENT OF THE UNITED STATES

Born February 12th, 1809.

Departed this Life April 15th 1865.

"YET SPEAKETH."

"For thou art Freedom's now, and Fame's —
One of the few — the immortal names —
That were not born to die."

"With malice toward none, with charity for all."

March 4th 1865.   *Second Inaugural.*

REQUIESCAT IN PACE!

HIS WORKS DO FOLLOW HIM.

His Works Do Follow Him [Abraham Lincoln Mourning Card]
N.P.: N.P., [1865]

Various Authors, Sixty Printed Eulogies of Abraham Lincoln
VARIOUS CITIES: VARIOUS PUBLISHERS, CA. 1865

The sixty pamphlets shown on pages 240–41 provide a broad publishing constellation of the response to Lincoln's death. They are eulogies of the president from different cities and towns, each spoken soon after the assassination but printed for posterity given the enormity of the tragedy. They tell us how people coped: by finding meaning in scripture, seeking clerical wisdom, and gaining strength in religious assembly. They tell us that at a time when mass media was in its infancy, the most trusted conveyor of information was the pulpit. As such, these eulogies are local in character, unique even to one congregation down the street from another. They arrive from every corner of the North: New York, Chicago, Cincinnati, Boston, etc. The eulogy as a rhetorical form still exists today—funereal words of remembrance and praise for citizens and celebrities alike. Today's style has its antecedents in the nineteenth century, in the Golden Age of American Oratory, when the truest test of leadership was the ability to convince others with words. The task before these eulogizers was unenviable, for the subject of their words was the country's finest orator.

Afterword: Lincoln the Subject
1866 to the Present

sugge
ceptio
is rea
pose
istic –
dram
comn
of co
the c
Linco
ideali
obtru
ized
in tre
we se
typic
thoug
and t
true
more
cance
dame
as a
plant

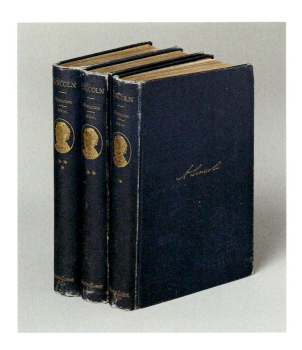

William Herndon and Jesse Weik, *Herndon's Lincoln: The True Story of a Great Life* (Chicago: Belford, 1889)

Pages 244–45: Detail from John G. Nicolay and John Hay, "Abraham Lincoln: A History," *Century Illustrated Monthly Magazine* (New York), Nov. 1887 to Apr. 1888

Page 246: Detail from William Herndon and Jesse Weik, *Herndon's Lincoln: The True Story of a Great Life* (Chicago: Belford, 1889)

publication. The outcome was the massive, ten-volume *Abraham Lincoln: A History* (1890), which emphasized Lincoln's virtues as a wartime president. Ann Rutledge is dismissed in eight lines, and Lincoln's premarital jitters are included without mention of when his engagement with Mary Todd was temporarily suspended. Hay and Nicolay attribute Lincoln's lifelong melancholy to malarial fever he caught in the western woods.

The muckraking journalist Ida M. Tarbell wrote on Lincoln in two articles for *McClure's Magazine*, which she reworked and published as the two-volume *Life of Abraham Lincoln* (1900). The American frontier of Lincoln's boyhood, which previous biographers had described as harsh and deleterious, becomes, in Tarbell's handling, a nurturing environment where Lincoln honed values and skills that would later carry him to the presidency. Tarbell, who perpetuates the Ann Rutledge story, details Lincoln's life through the 1850s but less so his role as head of state.

In *Abraham Lincoln* (1916), the British politician and author Lord Charnwood (Godfrey Rathbone Benson) places the president on an American and international continuum. Charnwood devotes an initial chapter of his book to reviewing American history, from the American Revolution through the Missouri Compromise to territorial expansion and the slavery crisis. Having set the historical stage, Charnwood follows the arc of Lincoln's life, pointing out his subject's flaws as well as virtues. He reviews Lincoln's role as a war strategist, necessitated by the responsibilities of being commander in chief. Taking a large perspective, Charnwood discusses Lincoln's contributions to global democracy.

An even larger perspective came in Carl Sandburg's massive Lincoln biography, comprising *The Prairie Years* (two volumes, 1926) and *The War Years* (four volumes, 1939). Appropriately, for an author who also wrote expansive poetry in the tradition of Walt Whitman, Sandburg's 2,500-page opus portrays a multitude of people, settings, and events that captured Lincoln in his time. Devoid of footnotes or other scholarly apparatus, Sandburg's lively, fluid biography won over general readers and earned the Pulitzer Prize. Later generations, however, found the biography impressionistic, sentimental, and at times inaccurate.

In contrast to Sandburg's anecdotal biography is Albert J. Beveridge's four-volume *Abraham Lincoln: 1809–1858* (1928), replete with footnotes that fill in information lacking from the main text. Beveridge's Lincoln is a canny Illinois lawyer and Whig-turned-Republican politician, whose public life mirrors that of the nation. Beveridge keeps alive the Ann Rutledge story, which was forcefully questioned by James G. and Ruth Painter

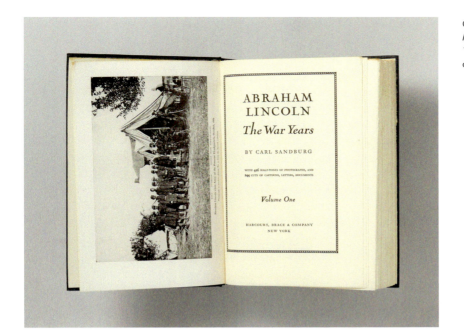

Carl Sandburg, *Abraham Lincoln: The War Years* (New York: Harcourt, 1939)

Randall in the 1940s, setting the stage for Benjamin P. Thomas's *Abraham Lincoln: A Biography* (1952), which minimizes the lost romance theme and portrays Mary Todd Lincoln more positively than do previous biographies. Thomas's one-volume work was greeted as a refreshingly concise yet comprehensive life that emphasized Lincoln's dual devotion to the Union and extirpating slavery, accentuated by his skills as a military strategist.

The onset of the civil rights movement brought new attention to Lincoln's racial views. No biographer had ever seriously disputed Lincoln's devotion to ending slavery, but a nagging question from the start was: What did he envisage for African Americans once they were emancipated? Between 1854 and 1863, Lincoln had sometimes recommended the voluntary relocation of freed Blacks to a foreign place—what was called colonization. Moreover, in his 1858 debates with the white supremacist senator Stephen A. Douglas, Lincoln made a few statements on race that are jarring to modern ears. Stephen B. Oates addressed the racial issue in his 1977 biography *With Malice toward None*, showing that Lincoln seemingly used conservative presumptions as rhetorical prows to open the way for advanced positions on emancipation and African American suffrage. Variations of this interpretation are offered by several Lincoln scholars, including LaWanda Cox, Gabor S. Boritt, and Mark E. Neely Jr.

Small wonder, given the increasing recognition of the complexity of Lincoln's racial views, that Gore Vidal's *Lincoln: A Novel* stirred controversy when it appeared in 1984. In the novel, which yielded a made-for-TV film, Vidal brings to life people surrounding Lincoln—journalists, reformers, generals, politicians, and others—to cast light on the president's beliefs. Vidal's novel received glowing reviews for its entertaining style and piquant human portraits. Some historians, however, attacked the novel

John Nicolay and John Hay, "Abraham Lincoln: A History," *The Century Illustrated Monthly Magazine* (New York), Nov. 1886 to Apr. 1890

for its depiction of Lincoln's colonization policy, supposedly based on his anti-integrationist prejudices, as sadly distant from the progressiveness of radicals around him. In a letter exchange in the *New York Review of Books*, Vidal was taken to task by the historians Harold Holzer, Richard N. Current, and C. Vann Woodward, who separately charged Vidal with oversimplification, distortion, and creating "a potpourri of his own inventions and bits and pieces he has picked up from other authors—bits and pieces mostly long discredited" (Current). The historians pointed out that Lincoln was not as hidebound on race as Vidal suggested. Vidal fought back but finally brought attention to his book's subtitle: *A Novel*.

In light of Vidal's shakiness on facts, it is surprising that his book was approved by the seasoned Lincoln scholar David Herbert Donald, whom Vidal thanked "for his patient reading—and correction—of the manuscript." Donald portrays a more solid figure in his 1995 biography *Lincoln*. Relying mainly on Lincoln's words, Donald aimed to recapture the president's point of view. The result is a straightforward life that takes at face value Lincoln's expressions about colonization and African Americans without placing them in their contexts. Donald's Lincoln is a passive figure, controlled by events, swept into greatness by inexorable forces because of his unyielding devotion to the Union and his innate fairness.

The next major biography, Michael Burlingame's two-volume, 2,024-page *Abraham Lincoln: A Life* (2008), notes that Lincoln's early race-baiting, reflective of the prevailing views of his era, gave way to his later egalitarianism. Burlingame traces Lincoln's hatred of slavery to his childhood, when his father virtually enslaved him, hiring him out to do menial jobs. In Burlingame's telling, the barely literate Thomas Lincoln was an overbearing rube against whom Lincoln rebelled by becoming a lawyer and antislavery politician. Burlingame revives Herndon's view of Mary as a termagant who made married life hellish for her husband.

Ronald C. White Jr.'s *A. Lincoln: A Biography* (2009) presents a more positive version of the marriage (though not as affirmative as Catherine Clinton does in her 2009 biography *Mrs. Lincoln: A Life*, where the Lincolns appear as a companionate couple devoted to each other). Like Burlingame, White sees Lincoln as strongly influenced by outside events but also emphasizes the president's strong will and constructive energy. White's Lincoln became increasingly religious; while never a church member, Lincoln moved from the skeptical deism of his early Illinois years to a chastened acceptance of God and the Bible in response to the deaths of his two sons and the tragedy of the Civil War. The religious theme is also prominent in the British scholar Richard J. Carwardine's 2006 biography, *Lincoln: A Life of Purpose and Power*, which argues persuasively that Lincoln drew from a variety of faiths to arrive at an ecumenical religion. Carwardine's Lincoln, far from being passive, found strength and agency from his innate ambition, ability to adapt to public opinion, and skills in party politics.

Valuable biographical information has come in focused studies of Lincoln's life. In-depth accounts of Lincoln's coming of age appear in Douglas Wilson's *Honor's Voice: The Transformation of Abraham Lincoln* (1998)

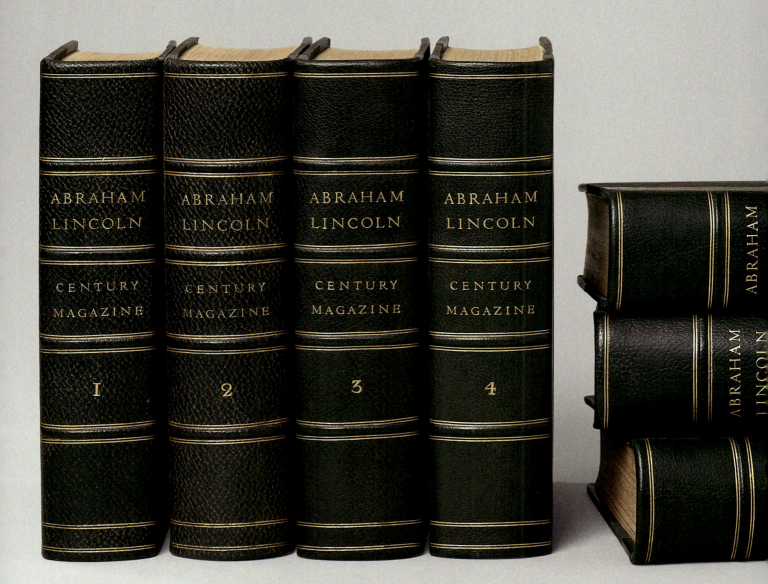

and Kenneth J. Winkle's *The Young Eagle: The Rise of Abraham Lincoln* (2001). Notable theme- or period-specific works include Garry Wills's *Lincoln at Gettysburg* (1992), Jay Winik's *April 1865* (2001), Gabor Borrit's *The Gettysburg Gospel* (2006), Joshua Wolf Shenk's *Lincoln's Melancholy* (2005), Allen C. Guelzo's *Lincoln and Douglas: The Debates That Defined America* (2008), Eric Foner's *The Fiery Trial: Abraham Lincoln and American Slavery* (2010), Martha Hodes's *Mourning Lincoln* (2015), Ted Widmer's *Lincoln on the Verge: Thirteen Days to Washington* (2020), and Harold Holzer's many works, including *Lincoln at Cooper Union* (2004), *Lincoln President-Elect: Abraham Lincoln and the Great Secession Winter 1860–1861* (2008), and *Lincoln and the Power of the Press* (2014).

The politically shrewd Lincoln, a strong presence in Lincoln biographies ever since James G. Randall's four-volume *Lincoln the President* (1945–55), becomes the main subject of Doris Kearns Goodwin's *Team of Rivals* and Sidney Blumenthal's *The Political Life of Abraham Lincoln*. Although not a cradle-to-grave biography, Goodwin's book (2005) vividly captures Lincoln's life as candidate and head of state. As her title indicates, she emphasizes Lincoln's mastery in assembling politicians around him who had formerly competed against each other and him. Blumenthal, a former senior advisor of Bill and Hillary Clinton, has published three volumes of a projected five-volume political life of Lincoln: *A Self-Made Man* (2016), *Wrestling with His Angel* (2017), and *All the Powers of Earth* (2019). Blumenthal probes Lincoln's political contexts, locally in Illinois and nationally in the competition for the presidency, demonstrating that the sectional turmoil of the Civil War era yielded the politically balanced, principled Lincoln, fully prepared by the party wars to guide the nation through actual war.

The contextual approach of Goodwin and Blumenthal is expanded in biographies by David S. Reynolds and Jon Meacham, who work from the premise that the person and the milieu—the inner Lincoln and his outside influences—merged to shape his greatness. Reynolds, in *Abe: Abraham Lincoln in His Times* (2020), shows that Lincoln, far from distant to his time, was thoroughly immersed in it. Lincoln redefined democracy precisely because he experienced culture in all its dimensions—high and low, sacred and profane, conservative and radical, sentimental and subversive. He loved both smutty jokes and the King James Bible; he enjoyed sappy popular songs but could recite complex passages from Shakespeare; he was a hero to wild street roughs known as the "b'hoys" as well as to the age's most sophisticated poet, Walt Whitman. A consummate politician, Lincoln adapted to his political environment by airing traditional positions when needed. Yet he was ultimately an egalitarian who became personally close to African Americans, including the militant activist Martin Delany, the feminist Sojourner Truth, and the abolitionist Frederick Douglass, all of whom testified to his lack of racial prejudice.

For Jon Meacham, Lincoln's openness to exterior influences pertained especially to ones that nurtured his conscience. In his 2022 biography *Then There Was Light*, Meacham, whose previous books include one on religion in American government, traces a Lincoln whose meditation on the Bible mingled with a consideration of rationalist "freethought," scientific theories of evolution, and Emersonian Transcendentalism to yield an exceptionally broad philosophy that combined fatalism and free will. In Meacham's reading, Lincoln believed that larger forces, physical and spiritual, provided a rich, nebulous background for pragmatic, ethical action. Meacham's Lincoln, imperfect and sometimes inconsistent, possesses a steady moral compass that drives him to preserve the Union and open the way for human rights.

Pages 260–61: A representation of recent biographies of Abraham Lincoln pulled from our reference bookshelf but restricted to titles printed in the twenty-first century and excluding works written by contributors to this catalogue

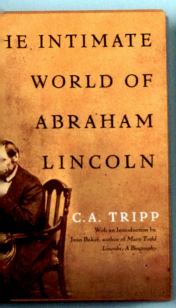
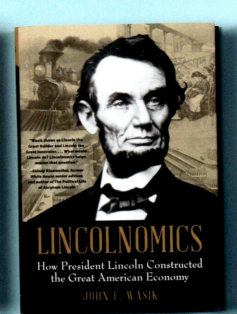
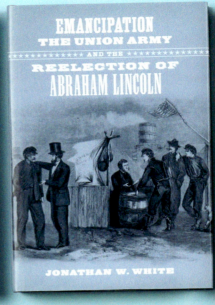

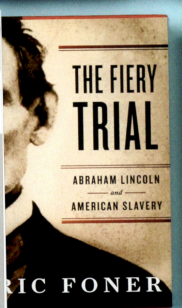
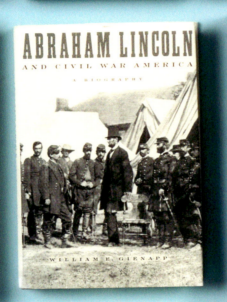
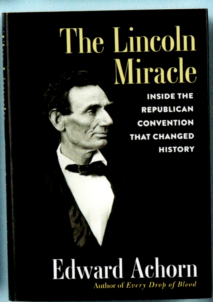

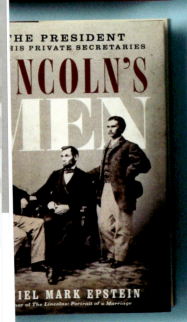
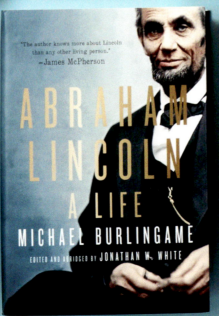
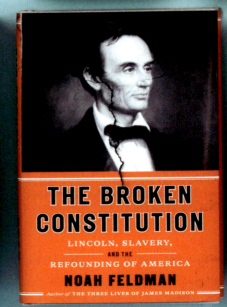

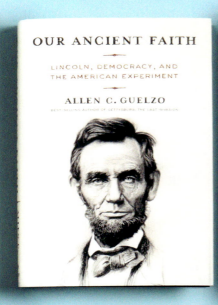
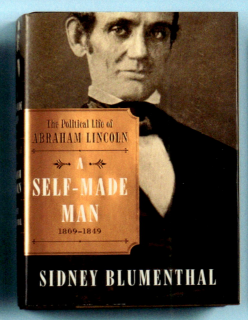
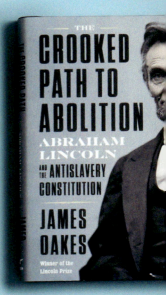

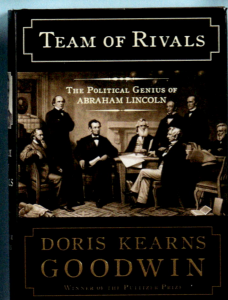
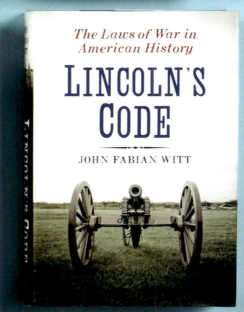

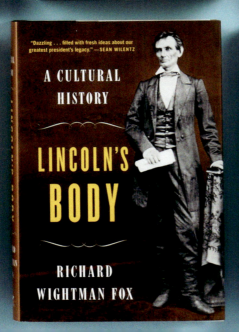
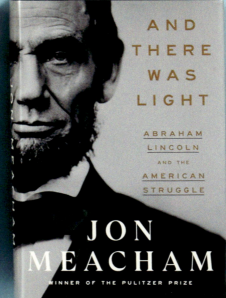
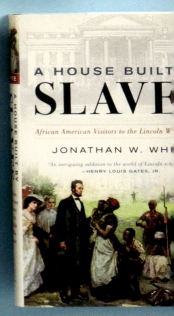

THE FATHER, AND THE SAVIOR OF OUR COUNTRY.

Entered according to Act of Congress, in the year 1865, by Jas. F. Bodtker, in the Clerk's Office of the District Court of the United States for the District of Wisconsin.

MADISON. - - WISCONSIN.

Acknowledgments

THE OCCASION FOR *Abraham Lincoln: His Life in Print* is the eponymous fall 2024 exhibition at The Grolier Club in New York City. Credit goes to the club for the freedom they gave the David M. Rubenstein Americana Collection to present to the public the books and ephemera shown in this catalogue. It was in a 2022 meeting with Michael T. Ryan, chair of The Grolier Club's Committee on Public Exhibitions during the making of this catalogue, that we decided an election year would be the ideal time to present Lincoln's life rendered in print. The club's commitment to offering free book exhibitions makes it an indispensable destination on the cultural circuit. Thank you to The Grolier Club and to Michael for the freedom to present Lincoln rigorously.

The Grolier Club's publications team, led by Marie Oedel, was particularly helpful in providing us guidance throughout the making of *Abraham Lincoln: His Life in Print*. Ann Donahue, a staff member there, was a continual resource for us as we assembled the parts. Even during the writing of these acknowledgments, Marie and Ann are lending their eyes to the production and their energies to help get this catalogue printed on time. Special thanks also must go to The Grolier Club's exhibitions team, headed by Shira Buchsbaum, for their expertise in making the show come together. Shira and now Oscar Salguero, newly hired by the club, are two of the brightest young stars in the rare book and printed arts cosmos, and we all profit from their talents.

This catalogue would not have happened without Donna Wingate. She shone the light that led the way to the book's completion. She held the book's parts together in the critical stages of production. Thanks must go to her and to Gina Broze, whose leadership of Marquand Books and confidence in her team elevated *Abraham Lincoln: His Life in Print* to the level of other books in the company's repertoire. Perhaps our luckiest break was working with Marquand Books' Ryan Polich, whose masterful design of this book truly elevated all of its parts. The whole Marquand Books team deserves praise, particularly Melissa Duffes for her editorial oversight. We

NATIONAL LINCOLN MONUMENT

SPRINGFIELD, 1869. ILLINOIS.

THIS CERTIFIES THAT

has contributed Fifty Cents to the erection of a Monument in memory of Abraham Lincoln our martyred President.

Springfield, Ill. 1869.

J. H. Beveridge
TREASURER

LARKIN G. MEAD, SCULPTOR.   WESTERN BANK NOTE & ENG. CO., CHICAGO.

Contributors

ROBERT BRAY trained at the University of Chicago before becoming a professor of American literature specializing in the nineteenth century. As an adopted citizen of Illinois, he inescapably became interested in Abraham Lincoln. His fascination led to research in and classroom teaching about Lincoln's life, seen less through the glass of political history and more finely through that of personality and literature. In 2010 he published *Reading with Lincoln*, an attempt through close reading—of what Lincoln himself was known to have read—to get at both the man and the political artist.

JOSHUA CLAYBOURN is an attorney and historian who edited the books *Abe's Youth: Shaping the Future President* (Indiana University Press, 2019) and *Abraham Lincoln's Wilderness Years* (Indiana University Press, 2022). He serves on the boards of both the Abraham Lincoln Association and the Abraham Lincoln Institute.

JONATHAN EARLE is dean of the LSU Ogden Honors College and a professor in the LSU Department of History. A native of suburban Washington, DC, Dr. Earle is a specialist in the history of the antebellum United States. Educated at Columbia (BA) and Princeton (MA, PhD) universities, he is the author of numerous books and articles, including *Jacksonian Antislavery and the Politics of Free Soil* (UNC Press, 2004), winner of the Society of Historians of the Early American Republic's 2005 Broussard prize and co-winner of the Byron Caldwell Smith Book Prize; *John Brown's Raid: A Brief History with Documents* (Bedford/St. Martin's Press, 2008); *The Routledge Atlas of African American History* (Routledge, 2000), and co-author of *Major Problems in the Early American Republic* (Cengage, 2007). In 2013 the University Press of Kansas published his edited collection *Bleeding Kansas, Bleeding Missouri: The Long Civil War on the Border*, which was named a Notable Book by the Kansas State Library. Dr. Earle is currently working on a book on the election of 1860 for the Pivotal Moments in U.S. History Series published by Oxford University Press.

DAVID S. REYNOLDS is a distinguished professor at the Graduate Center of the City University of New York. His book *Abe: Abraham Lincoln in His Times* (Penguin Press, 2020) is winner of the Lincoln Prize and the Abraham Lincoln Book Prize, one of the *Wall Street Journal*'s Top 10 Books of the Year, and the basis for the Apple TV+ docuseries *Lincoln's Dilemma*. Reynolds is the author or editor of sixteen books, including *Walt Whitman's America* (Knopf, 1995), winner of the Bancroft Prize and the Ambassador Book Award; *John Brown, Abolitionist* (Knopf, 2005), winner of the Gustavus Myers Outstanding Book Prize; *Mightier Than the Sword: Uncle Tom's Cabin and the Battle for America* (W. W. Norton, 2011); *Waking Giant: America in the Age of Jackson* (Harper, 2008); and *Beneath the American Renaissance* (Knopf, 1988), winner of the Christian Gauss Award. He regularly reviews for the *New York Review of Books*, the *Wall Street Journal*, and the *New York Times Book Review*. Reynolds earned a BA at Amherst College and a PhD at the University of California at Berkeley.

EDWARD STEERS JR. had a prominent career as a scientist before he retired and began writing full time. Steers received his AB degree in microbiology in 1959 and his PhD in molecular biology in 1963 from the University of Pennsylvania in Philadelphia and joined the staff of the National Institutes of Health (1963–94). Upon his retirement in 1994, Steers began writing in the field of history and is regarded as the leading authority on the assassination of Abraham Lincoln. He has authored numerous publications, articles, and eight books on Lincoln's death, including *Blood on the Moon* (University Press of Kentucky, 2001), *The Lincoln Assassination Conspirators* (Louisiana State University Press, 2009), *His Name Is Still Mudd* (Thomas Publications, 1997), and *The Lincoln Assassination Encyclopedia* (Harper Perennial, 2010).

TED WIDMER is a distinguished lecturer at Macaulay Honors College (CUNY). In addition to his teaching, he writes about American history for *The New York Times*, *The New Yorker*, and *The Washington Post*, among other publications. He has taught for or directed research centers at Harvard University, Brown University, Washington College, and the Library of Congress. He was a foreign policy speechwriter and senior adviser to President Clinton, served in the State Department during the Obama administration, and was a senior adviser to Secretary of State Hillary Clinton. His most recent book is *Lincoln on the Verge: Thirteen Days to Washington* (Simon & Schuster, 2020).

Image Credits

Unless otherwise noted, all photography by Vincent Dilio, courtesy of David M. Rubenstein

Library of Congress (loc.gov): pp. 6, 10, 36, 40, 54, 58–59, 77–78, 93, 95–96, 116, 118, 138, 140–41, 154, 157–58, 160, 184–85, 189, 214–16, 230, 232

New York Public Library Digital Collections (digitalcollections.nypl.org): pp. 56, 92, 142, 156

House Divided: The Civil War Research Engine at Dickinson College (hd.housedivided.dickinson.edu): p. 79

The District of Columbia Compensated Emancipation Act Celebrations (janehistory390.omeka.net): p. 119